Communications
in Computer and Information Science 1790

Rationale

The CCIS series is devoted to the publication of proceedings of computer science conferences. Its aim is to efficiently disseminate original research results in informatics in printed and electronic form. While the focus is on publication of peer-reviewed full papers presenting mature work, inclusion of reviewed short papers reporting on work in progress is welcome, too. Besides globally relevant meetings with internationally representative program committees guaranteeing a strict peer-reviewing and paper selection process, conferences run by societies or of high regional or national relevance are also considered for publication.

Topics

The topical scope of CCIS spans the entire spectrum of informatics ranging from foundational topics in the theory of computing to information and communications science and technology and a broad variety of interdisciplinary application fields.

Information for Volume Editors and Authors

Publication in CCIS is free of charge. No royalties are paid, however, we offer registered conference participants temporary free access to the online version of the conference proceedings on SpringerLink (http://link.springer.com) by means of an http referrer from the conference website and/or a number of complimentary printed copies, as specified in the official acceptance email of the event.

CCIS proceedings can be published in time for distribution at conferences or as post-proceedings, and delivered in the form of printed books and/or electronically as USBs and/or e-content licenses for accessing proceedings at SpringerLink. Furthermore, CCIS proceedings are included in the CCIS electronic book series hosted in the SpringerLink digital library at http://link.springer.com/bookseries/7899. Conferences publishing in CCIS are allowed to use Online Conference Service (OCS) for managing the whole proceedings lifecycle (from submission and reviewing to preparing for publication) free of charge.

Publication process

The language of publication is exclusively English. Authors publishing in CCIS have to sign the Springer CCIS copyright transfer form, however, they are free to use their material published in CCIS for substantially changed, more elaborate subsequent publications elsewhere. For the preparation of the camera-ready papers/files, authors have to strictly adhere to the Springer CCIS Authors' Instructions and are strongly encouraged to use the CCIS LaTeX style files or templates.

Abstracting/Indexing

CCIS is abstracted/indexed in DBLP, Google Scholar, EI-Compendex, Mathematical Reviews, SCImago, Scopus. CCIS volumes are also submitted for the inclusion in ISI Proceedings.

How to start

To start the evaluation of your proposal for inclusion in the CCIS series, please send an e-mail to ccis@springer.com.

Todor Tagarev · Nikolai Stoianov
Editors

Digital Transformation, Cyber Security and Resilience

Second International Conference, DIGILIENCE 2020
Varna, Bulgaria, September 30 – October 2, 2020
Revised Selected Papers

 Springer

Editors
Todor Tagarev 🄳
Institute of Information and Communication
Technologies
Sofia, Bulgaria

Nikolai Stoianov 🄳
Bulgarian Defence Institute
Sofia, Bulgaria

ISSN 1865-0929   ISSN 1865-0937 (electronic)
Communications in Computer and Information Science
ISBN 978-3-031-44439-5   ISBN 978-3-031-44440-1 (eBook)
https://doi.org/10.1007/978-3-031-44440-1

This Springer imprint is published by the registered company Springer Nature Switzerland AG
The registered company address is: Gewerbestrasse 11, 6330 Cham, Switzerland

Paper in this product is recyclable.

Preface

The rapid development and integration of information and communication technologies influence the ways in which people work, fight, study, organize their political representation, communicate, and relax. The process of digitalization transforms our lives but also brings new threats and ways to promote security and safety. To reflect on the new opportunities and challenges and present novel solutions, a group of academics and practitioners decided in 2019 to launch the series of international scientific conferences under the title "Digital Transformation, Cyber Security and Resilience", or DIGILIENCE for short. The proceedings of the first conference were published by Springer Nature in volume 84 of the series "Studies in Big Data" [1].

This volume includes selected papers from the second DIGILIENCE conference, hosted during Sept. 30 – Oct. 2, 2020 by the Bulgarian Naval Academy, Varna, Bulgaria. 119 submissions went through a single-blind review process, with three reviews per paper. The conference program included fifty-eight accepted and six invited papers, along with plenary discussions. It was structured in the following themes:

- ICT Governance and Management for Digital Transformation
- Human Systems Integration Approach to Cybersecurity
- Education and Training for Cyber Resilience
- Novel Conceptual Approaches and Solutions
- Cyber Situational Awareness and Information Exchange
- Security Implications and Solutions for IoT Systems
- Protecting Critical Infrastructures from Cyberattacks
- Big Data and Artificial Intelligence for Cybersecurity
- Secure Communication and Information Protection
- Advanced ICT Security Solutions

Due to the COVID-19 pandemic, the conference was conducted in a mixed format with approximately 50 participants physically present at the Bulgarian Naval Academy, and the remainder participating online. Eighteen of them were Ph.D. students or young researchers. In total, the participants represented 13 different countries, the NATO Communications and Information Agency and the European Defence Agency.

The Steering Committee of the conference invited the authors of selected papers to contribute to this volume. The final product, presented here, includes 17 papers organized in six sections:

- Cyber Situational Awareness, Information Sharing and Collaboration
- Protecting Critical Infrastructures and Essential Services from Cyberattacks
- Big Data and Artificial Intelligence for Cybersecurity
- Advanced ICT Security Solutions
- Education and Training for Cyber Resilience
- ICT Governance and Management for Digital Transformation

We continue to work towards turning the DIGILIENCE conference series into a valuable platform for exchanging and strengthening cybersecurity knowledge and contributing to the resiliency of our societies in the process of digital transformation.

February 2023   Todor Tagarev
                                                                 Nikolai Stoianov

Reference

1. Tagarev, T., Atanassov, K., Kharchenko, V., Kasprzyk, J. (eds.): Digital Transformation, Cyber Security and Resilience of Modern Societies, in Studies in Big Data, vol. 84. Springer Nature, Cham (2021).

Organization

Steering Committee Chairs

Todor Tagarev	Institute of ICT, Bulgarian Academy of Sciences, Bulgaria
Nikolai Stoianov	Bulgarian Defense Institute, Bulgaria

Steering Committee

Natalia Derbentseva	Defence Research and Development Canada, Canada
Andrzej Dziech	AGH University of Science and Technology, Poland
Vyacheslav Kharchenko	National Aerospace University KhAI, Ukraine
Alexander Kott	Army Research Laboratory, USA
Peter Lenk	NATO Communications and Information Agency, Belgium
Boyan Mednikarov	Nikola Vaptsarov Naval Academy, Bulgaria
Wim Mees	Royal Military Academy, Belgium
Dimitrina Polimirova	National Laboratory of Computer Virology, Bulgaria
Velizar Shalamanov	Institute of ICT, Bulgarian Academy of Sciences, Bulgaria
George Sharkov	European Software Institute - Eastern Europe, Bulgaria
Stefanos Vrochidis	Centre of Research and Technology Hellas, Greece
Yantsislav Yanakiev	Bulgarian Defense Institute, Bulgaria
Volodymyr Zaslavskyi	Taras Shevchenko National University of Kyiv, Ukraine

Program Committee Chairs

Boyan Mednikarov	Nikola Vaptsarov Naval Academy, Bulgaria
Nikolai Stoianov	Bulgarian Defense Institute, Bulgaria
Marcin Niemec	AGH University of Science and Technology, Poland
Yuliyan Tsonev	Nikola Vaptsarov Naval Academy, Bulgaria

Technical Program Committee

Kirsi Aaltola	VTT Technical Research Centre of Finland, Finland
Kiril Aleksiev	Bulgarian Academy of Sciences, Bulgaria
Rumen Andreev	Bulgarian Academy of Sciences, Bulgaria
Kiril Avramov	University of Texas at Austin, USA
Stoyan Avramov	Bulgarian Academy of Sciences, Bulgaria
Nikolaos Bardis	Hellenic Military Academy, Greece
Nazife Baykal	Middle East Technical University, Turkey
Madahar Bhopinder	Defence Science and Technology Laboratory, UK
Mitko Bogdanoski	Military Academy "General Mihailo Apostolski", North Macedonia
Maya Bozhilova	Bulgarian Defense Institute, Bulgaria
Eugene Brezhnev	Kharkiv Aviation Institute, Ukraine
Alan Brill	Texas A&M University School of Law, USA
Oleg Chertov	National Technical University of Ukraine, Ukraine
Michael Cooke	Maynooth University, Ireland
Stefan-Antonio Dan-Suteu	Carol I National Defense University, Romania
Natalia Derbentseva	Defence Research and Development Canada, Canada
Mariya Dorosh	Chernihiv National University of Technology, Ukraine
Andrzej Dziech	AGH University of Science and Technology, Poland
Avram Eskenazi	Bulgarian Academy of Sciences, Bulgaria
Herman Fesenko	Kharkiv Aviation Institute, Ukraine
Bruce Forrester	Defence Research and Development Canada, Canada
Luis Angel Galindo	Telefonica, Spain
Trayan Georgiev	NATO, Bulgaria
Venelin Georgiev	New Bulgarian University, Bulgaria
Gudmund Grov	Norwegian Defence Research Establishment, Norway
Anne Holohan	Trinity College Dublin, Ireland
Ruslan Hryschuk	Zhytomyrs'kyy Viys'kovyy Instytut Imeni S. P. Korol'ova, Ukraine
Oleg Illiashenko	Kharkiv Aviation Institute, Ukraine
Rosen Iliev	Bulgarian Defense Institute, Bulgaria
Vasilis Katos	Bournemouth University, UK
Volodymyr Kazymyr	Chernihiv National University of Technology, Ukraine

Jan M. Kelner	Military University of Technology, Poland
Mikko Kiviharju	Finnish Defence Forces, Finland
Maryna Kolisnyk	Kharkiv Aviation Institute, Ukraine
Alexander Kott	United States Army Research Laboratory, USA
Marcin Kowalski	Military University of Technology, Poland
Andreas Kriechbaum-Zabini	Austrian Institute of Technology, Austria
Dmitry Lande	National Academy of Sciences of Ukraine, Ukraine
Andon Lazarov	Nikola Vaptsarov Naval Academy, Bulgaria
Hervé Le Guyader	École Nationale Supérieure de Cognitique, France
Peter Lenk	NATO Communications and Information Agency, Belgium
Tomáš Lieskovan	European Defence Agency, Belgium
Salvador Llopis Sanchez	European Defence Agency, Belgium
Vitalii Lytvynov	Chernihiv National University of Technology, Ukraine
Petr Machník	Technical University of Ostrava, Czech Republic
Anastas Madzharov	Bulgarian Academy of Sciences, Bulgaria
Vlasimil Maly	University of Defence, Czech Republic
Federico Mancini	Norwegian Defence Research Establishment (FFI), Norway
Vasiliki Mantzana	Center for Security Studies, Greece
Julie Marble	Johns Hopkins University, USA
Sylvie Martel	NATO Communications and Information Agency, Belgium
Jean-Paul Massart	NATO Communications and Information Agency, Belgium
Wojciech Mazurczyk	Warsaw University of Technology, Poland
Dennis McCallam	Northrop Grumman, USA
John McLean	US Naval Research Lab, USA
Wim Mees	Royal Military Academy, Belgium
Matteo Merialdo	RHEA Group, Belgium
Pantelis Michalis	Center for Security Studies, Greece
Michael Meier	Fraunhofer Institute for Communication, Information Processing and Ergonomics FKIE, Germany
Zlatogor Minchev	Bulgarian Academy of Sciences, Bulgaria
Ira S. Moskowitz	US Naval Research Lab, USA
Dimitris Myttias	Center for Security Studies, Greece
Atanas Nachev	University of Library Studies and Information Technologies, Bulgaria
Frederica Nelson	United States Army Research Laboratory, USA
Pałka Norbert	Military University of Technology, Poland

Contents

Advanced ICT Security Solutions

Education and Training for Cyber Resilience

ICT Governance and Management for Digital Transformation

Cyber Situational Awareness, Information Sharing and Collaboration

Digital Modernisation in Defence: Communications and Information Systems Challenges

Salvador Llopis Sánchez[1]([✉]), Bernardo Martinez Reif[2], Isabel Iglesias Pallín[2],
Álvaro Díaz del Mazo[2], and Guillermo González[2]

[1] European Defence Agency, Brussels, Belgium
info@eda.europa.eu
[2] Ingeniería de Sistemas Para la Defensa, ISDEFE, Madrid, Spain
general@isdefe.es

Abstract. A digital modernisation of the European Armed Forces requires the setting up of a structured and scalable process to ensure mission readiness. Modern implementations of fielded systems coexist with legacy systems. A plethora of platforms, nodes and information sources integrate a hyper connected battlefield. This article analyses the challenges in seeking harmonized solutions in the field of communications and information systems and especially at the tactical edge which is one of the most demanding areas when it comes to ensure availability and interoperability. Emerging technologies such as Artificial Intelligence, Internet of Things and others are at the core of this modernisation.

Keywords: digitalisation · legacy systems · tactical communications and information systems · command and control · information advantage

1 Introduction

Signals doctrine is taught in military academies. One of the immutable principles learned throughout history is that the most effective communication mean is the "direct conversation between commanders". This article aims to analyse the novelties introduced by a drastic digital modernisation in Defence without losing sight of enduring principles that have shaped the way of working of signals corps.

Digital modernisation is a fact in our society, digital services are gradually permeating every area of our lives. Almost without realizing it, sectors like communication, finance, manufacturing, commerce, or entertainment are becoming more digital and more connected. Few years ago, we tuned in to our favourite radio station instead of installing an application in a smartphone to hear our favourite songs stored in our own list of preferences. We do not need to reserve the last film in the closest video club - one year after its premiere in the cinema - and return the video tape 24 h later. Now, we have got several media platforms e.g. internet video on demand in our own living room, and the last premiere can be watched by pressing no more than four buttons of

© The Author(s), under exclusive license to Springer Nature Switzerland AG 2024
T. Tagarev and N. Stoianov (Eds.): DIGILIENCE 2020, CCIS 1790, pp. 3–11, 2024.
https://doi.org/10.1007/978-3-031-44440-1_1

a TV remote control. There are several examples of how things were done before and how they are done now, for instance: instant messaging or social networking [4]. The coronavirus disease pandemic is accelerating our preparedness for a digitalised world. Society requires services that provide ubiquity, simplicity, efficiency, reliability, security and speed. These features force a design on digital technologies to ensure a quick accessibility, a pervasive connectivity and a certain degree of automation and resilience.

Defence cannot be left behind in this unstoppable process on digital modernisation. Combatants in operations, whether these be at sea, land or air, expect to use similar digital advantages like in the civil world. The special characteristics of the context of the work carried out by the armed forces put additional challenges and issues to build a digital ecosystem adapted to missions: information must preserve its confidentiality, integrity and availability under any circumstances, special equipment is required to withstand harsh weather conditions and to be deployed, or an ad hoc connectivity is required in places where a permanent telecommunications infrastructure does not exist. This leads the military to be more precise in defining specific requirements and verify their compliance prior to fielding products or solutions. A set of needs has to be defined in terms of requirements by analysing typical scenarios. Systems engineering will assure a methodological approach to identify and validate these user requirements.

In the battlefield, a combatant needs to have a clear situational awareness including a threat assessment, the location of the enemy forces, the details of the terrain orography, the supply points, etc. [5]. Information regarding the mission is key to accomplishing its tasks. The information flows follow a multiple path of transmissions and receptions of orders between tactical units and higher command echelons supported by a wide area network.

Information supplied to the combatant has to be useful in order to take decisions in a few seconds. In many occasions, there is no chance to analyse the overwhelming amount of information available. This could lead to a situation of information overload and the inability to discern what information is more important. Research activities are to be pursued to achieve innovative human-system interfaces to present this information to the combatant as a useful knowledge that would permit to choose an option among several alternatives.

Ensuring freedom of access to cyberspace is paramount. One of the resulting tasks is to protect systems and networks including mission-critical data against cyber-attacks. A whole bunch of disruptive technologies 'are here to stay'. Technologies like Big Data to facilitate a quick analysis of huge quantities of data, Internet of Things (IoT), sensors (used as sources of information) and Artificial Intelligence (AI) to assist decision-makers are enablers at tactical level with future applications yet to be tested. The "ease of use" should be a design criterion that recalls the simplicity when someone wants to select a film in his living room just by pressing four buttons in the TV remote control. The underlying issues (related to the connectivity and data transfer) could be considered only a subject of interest for technicians. This reasoning could be seen as a further look into the future technological environment although the main purpose addressed in this paper is to analyse the "digitalisation" - a phenomenon involving the digital ecosystem and the system engineering practice as two pillars with specific goals on supporting decision making and creating knowledge respectively (Fig. 1).

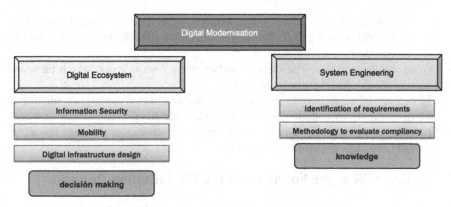

Fig. 1. Digital modernisation in the information domain.

2 Consequences of the Rapid Pace of Technological Development

Immediate consequences can be summed up as the unprecedented network interconnectivity, the need of real-time information to feed faster decision cycles and the abundance of raw data (data which has not been subject to processing). Demands on data processing have increased in terms of the volume of data to be processed and the velocity expected for this data processing.

The digital landscape is predominantly a data-rich one characterized by the known five V's of Big Data that define any kind of problem to be solved: Volume, Velocity, Variability, Veracity and Value. These attributes are referred to the amount of data that is produced, the speed of which data is generated, the various sources of origin and its diverse formats, its trust as a reliable information and its worth to gain insights. In the battlefield, the military needs to achieve a clear situational awareness. A common operational picture assists to interpret on a geographical information system different information layers (facilities, weather, bridges, forces, etc.) and threats (terrain, signal coverage, etc.).

To be able to support the above-mentioned services, systems and networks configurations must be flexible, even adapting themselves to the worst conditions that may arise and, if necessary, be self-reconfigured according with the mission needs. Technologies such as software defined network (SDN) and related network function virtualization (NFV) could facilitate to obtain the best performance of the network resources. Some of the main difficulties in the implementation of SDN in tactical networks reside in the high mobility of heterogeneous end-nodes, a limited bandwidth coupled with low data rates wireless links, the adoption of cyber security measures and the importance of attain interoperability [2]. SDN will be discussed in more detail in the last section.

In a nutshell, the following list describe some CIS challenges to be tackled when keeping pace with a rapid digital modernisation:

– The management of *obsolescence*. Fast-moving technologies are being introduced in operations while legacy systems are still in use.

- *Limited radio spectrum.* There is a need to increase the spectrum capacity to accommodate new demands e.g. IoT. It is key to maximize the effective use of available radio frequencies.
- *Digital market pressure.* The market establishes its own rules on which pace and direction should the investments be going.
- The menace of *cyber-attacks.* It emphasises the need for a cyberspace situational awareness capability complemented with incident handling.
- Cross the *'valley of death'.* Despite a risk mitigation strategy, technology initiatives may fail to become acquisition programmes.

3   Tactical CIS at the Forefront of the Digitalisation Process

Tactical Communications and Information Systems (CIS) address the military telecommunications and services enabling small units, teams or individual combatants to accomplish a mission. They could be seen as the "last frontier" in a hierarchical telecommunications structure which is often referred as the *tactical edge.*

The tactical environment could be seen as a suitable experimentation laboratory except for the fact that failures are not allowed. Newly fielded equipment passes a rigorous testing prior to be deployed. Flexibility and adaptability are two characteristics to achieve in the tactical field in order to take advantage of the resources available at any time.

In addition, it is necessary to add and synthesize information in the most proper way to present it at higher levels: the operational and the strategic command levels. Interoperability across different domains of warfare, the physical ones, land, air and sea but also space and cyberspace, is a driving factor. Information must flow among domains and, each new bit of information must be complementary to the information available in order to be relevant for command and control (C2) functions. A C2 system would automatically discard any redundant information. Interoperability is a must for coalition forces and comprises computational semantics (linguistics) as a sub-field. Due the development of ontologies as a mean to represent the knowledge, coalition systems of different nature with distinct computer languages can understand each other and cooperate.

Tactical CIS and information security issues in the digital realm pose many challenges to overcome. On one hand, CIS must be able to operate securely in a fast-developing digital environment and ensure mission readiness. On the other hand, they need to permanently ensure the freedom of access to cyberspace, which is not only a cross-cutting domain, but also a domain in itself in which cyber threats affecting the mission are numerous.

In a world providing more and more digital services every day, cyber threats increasingly evolve. Therefore, cyber protection of assets as well as capabilities to enhance the detection of cyber-attacks will be the focus. Security by design on digital components followed by a pro-active security engineering would facilitate the transition to a cyber resilient CIS. Cyber defence is even more necessary not only to protect systems but also to anticipate or prevent the occurrence of cyber-attacks. Cyber threat intelligence-based solutions analyse attack vectors used to exploit vulnerabilities and propose risk mitigation measures.

Military assets will need to include evolving powerful computing capabilities in order to resist to new forms of cyber-attacks expected with the advent of future quantum computing and quantum communication technologies. In multinational coalition environments, a *"digital trust"* is probably the most difficult aspect to ensure when users join, group or leave a network infrastructure in a dynamic fashion. Tactical CIS are characterized by an extensive use of radio links capable of being integrated into computer networks and vice versa.

With the paradigm of everything connected in the battlefield, a definition of end-nodes (based on their remote locations away from the core of a centralised network) would necessarily apply equally to platforms and sensors. The proliferation of unmanned aerial, ground and underwater vehicles (UXVs) resourced with sensors and enabled by AI-algorithms put a stronger emphasis on human-machine teaming [3] notably at the tactical level. The collaboration with these robots operating in isolation or in groups (swarm) reaches another level of complexity in the management of the digital communications infrastructure. Priority setting, quality of service and dynamic network segmentation features assisted by intelligent software agents could enhance the properties of a potential saturated mission network. Intelligent agents are digital artifacts (pieces of software code) that can monitor the network autonomously.

Lightweight solutions of AI algorithms would reduce the necessary computational power and energy to perform mathematical calculations. If these algorithms are widespread into platforms, they could add functionalities like survivability of naval ships, aircrafts or underwater systems in the event of disrupted or interrupted communications [6].

Talking about deployable networks and in particular at the tactical edge, there is an increasing trend to explore novel applications such as a "combat cloud" to alleviate network bandwidth demands and processing power constraints. A tactical network connected to the cloud may bring new advances by speeding up information exchanges and reducing the equipment to be deployed. It offers advances on storage, accessibility and data analytics to name only a few.

The impact is expected in areas such as information management, decision making and situation awareness. The rationalization of CIS resources would consist in a reorganization of assets available for a mission in view of obtaining an operational efficiency. Legacy systems live together with modern implementations. As soon as the novel systems achieve a full operating capability, obsolete equipment could be replaced in an orchestrated manner. Notwithstanding the arguments in favour of maintaining an operational capacity (reserve) of analogue systems when analysing the risks linked with a full implementation of digital technologies [1].

4 Information Superiority as the Ultimate Aim

Without any intention of defining the term "Information Superiority", a first reflection refers back to the two pillars mentioned in preceding sections - decision and knowledge - and their intertwined nature to produce an "information advantage" for mission commanders.

For the next years, the digital modernisation trend is expected to accelerate producing an impact on military operations and capabilities. New communication technologies and the development of new analytical methods (that follows the scientific method and derives general principles supported by mathematical tools) will increase the ability to understand the information around us.

Today's conflicts are characterized by an ever-increasing complexity demanding the management of huge and heterogeneous volumes of information and simultaneously, requesting shorter reaction times. This will require strengthening the capabilities related to data science and its rapid transformation into valuable information to support commanders' decisions which are aimed to properly coordinate various forces at different levels in joint operations.

Closely related to this requirement is the need to have a tactical CIS with a higher degree of interoperability. The complexity of future conflicts and the variety of forces that participate in operations necessitate the ability to inter-operate at different levels of command and even cross-domain. To ensure this, a robust management, a protection and free of access to the electromagnetic spectrum and cyber domain is necessary. The proliferation of sensors, from satellites to micro-drones, will generate a vast quantity of data which needs to be effectively communicated, shared and processed. Information management capabilities should be improved to support large amounts of information coming from heterogeneous sources. A higher degree on interoperability consists of developing a semantic interoperability, which, in addition to the meaning of the concepts agreed in a military ontology, establishes mechanisms for classifying information or inferring knowledge.

AI embedded into in-field systems will play a fundamental role in achieving the so-called information advantage. AI requires high-quality (unbiased) training data sets to develop new algorithms and applications. Current trends advocate for an actionable and interpretable AI instead of an explainable AI in an attempt to incorporate quantifications of the user confidence in AI recommendations [7]. AI can even train itself by using generative adversarial networks (GAN) techniques.

Machine learning is a promising computational technique capable of processing large volumes of information and carrying out a prediction of possible future actions and events based on experience. Cognitive computing can be seen as an integration of algorithms and methods from various fields such as AI, machine learning, processing natural language (PNL) jointly with a representation of knowledge to improve human performance. It is capable of learning and understanding natural language, as well as reason, and even interact more naturally with humans than traditional programmable systems. Cognitive computing systems can complement human work notably in: better evidence-based decision-making, and discovery of insights/patterns hidden in large amounts of data.

AI is expected to provide the means to increase the operational efficiency, to reduce costs, to improve situational awareness at strategic, operational and tactical levels and above all, to lead to a decision superiority.

Additionally, the use of AI on sensors to pre-process information and provide adaptive use of frequencies and bandwidth will impact military communications. The concept of distributed sensors will be significantly enabled by the growth of the fifth-generation technology standard for broadband cellular networks (5G) and the IoT. The unprecedented pervasive connectivity at the battlefield will permit distributed sensors to establish remote communication links with a command post.

Secure communications and data storage are essential in military operations. Databases are the traditional means to store and maintain structured data used as a technical assistance for instance on logistics. Distributed ledger technologies, like blockchain are being explored to provide additional features regarding the integrity of tactical communications and data storage [14].

Systems engineering is another discipline in which the digital modernisation will be focused on. Traditional life cycle of products -comprising from inception to disposal - are conceived for a long lifetime duration in service. Engineers and developers of the new digital age can no longer follow strictly previous approaches. Needs are evolving more and more rapidly. Therefore, the use of agile methodologies is being increasingly adopted to keep pace with rapid technological progress. These methodologies, such as Scrum, are characterized by the development of frequent prototypes presented to the end user including proofs of concept and modular designs that advance in parallel towards the final product. All this happens taking into account future scenarios of use introducing a modular adaptability in the engineering design.

5 Technologies and Hyperconnectivity

Deployable communications in areas of operations need to overcome difficulties in terms of power, latency or jitter. This is due to the fact that the environmental conditions are adverse in most cases, and communication devices are not generally prepared to support these limiting conditions. These factors are considered to improve the interconnectivity of systems and provide a better communication channel to combatants and thus enabling a free movement of forces throughout the battlefield while remaining continuously interconnected [8, 11].

In operations, satellite communications are extensively used. Latency times are reduced to provide a robust and reliable communication within the satellite coverage area. Radio, wireless links and other CIS assets complement the communications means available for deployable tactical networks. The use of these networks poses some challenges in terms of cybersecurity, limited bandwidth, limited data storage and low data rate wireless links, which are expected to be improved by the use of cognitive networks/software defined radio (SDR) [9, 13] and SDN [10] among others. Both technologies complement each other. No distinction is made when the information flows between radio and network segments. SDR enables a spectrum optimization, finding free frequency bands on which to transmit or receive information.

SDR main features are flexibility, high performance with high data transmission rates, easy to integrate combat radios (CNR) and easy to manage. However, there are some drawbacks that need to be addressed like the high cost of configuration and deployment of SDR-based systems. These drawbacks could be enhanced with SDN, which is based on the separation of the control layer and the application layer. This technique offers greater flexibility, agility and efficiency, as well as reducing the necessary hardware. The use of SDR and SDN will facilitate a greater mobility and interoperability making use of the existing infrastructure e.g. federated mission networks. This network architecture avoids the existence of a single point of failure [12].

6 Conclusions

The digital modernisation is affecting particularly systems, networks and tactical communications. Digital modernisation is part of the digital transformation addressing specific objectives on materiel and interoperability issues.

This modernisation must be accompanied by new technologies which are expected to be introduced rapidly in defence. Tactical CIS are at the heart of this modernisation since they are key to connect the network boundaries. New technologies and trends in communications have emerged in the last years, which allow the communications to improve their distance ranges, and their robustness.

Communications are the basis of cooperation, and cooperation is essential to accelerate the pace of adaptation. Civilian investments could shed some light on potential dual-use of technologies like the 5G in the military context.

The transition to new technologies must be smoothed, allowing legacy solutions to coexist with new developments. The change has to be progressive and the technology has to be adapted according with the operational needs. To accompany this modernisation, some enabling technologies for the tactical CIS such as AI, IoT and edge computing will guide an evolution of the operating procedures. It cannot be excluded future advances in laser communications, quantum communications and new generation information exchange gateways. The use and application of these technologies within Tactical CIS will ensure an "information advantage" with greater situational awareness.

Disclaimer
The contents reported in the paper reflect the opinion of the authors and do not necessarily reflect the opinions of the respective agency/institutions. It does not represent the opinions or policies of the European Defence Agency or the European Union and is designed to provide an independent position.

References

1. Fiott, D.: Digitalising Defence, Protecting Europe in the Age of Quantum Computing and the Cloud, Brief 4, Institute of Security Studies (2020)
2. https://ec.europa.eu/research/participants/data/ref/other_eu_prog/edidp/wp-call/edidp_call-texts-2019_en.pdf. Accessed 22 Oct 2020
3. https://eda.europa.eu/webzine/issue16/cover-story/cyber-resilience-a-prerequisite-for-aut onomous-systems-and-vice-versa/. Accessed 22 Oct 2020
4. Gómez Ruedas, J.: The digital transformation of the Ministry of Defense. http://www. ieee.es/Galerias/fichero/docs_marco/2015/DIEEEM28-2015_Transformacion_Digital_MIN ISDEF_JesusG.Ruedas.pdf. Accessed 22 Oct 2020
5. Jiménez Martín, J.L.: Tecnologías aplicadas al Mando y Control. Sistemas C4ISR. http://www.upm.es/sfs/Rectorado/Gabinete%20del%20Rector/Agenda/2010/2010-11/Actapanel TecnologiasaplicadasalMandoyControl.SistemasC4ISRelato_C4ISR.pdf. Accessed 22 Oct 2020

6. Husain, A.: Three coming shifts in AI, Forbes (2020). https://www.forbes.com/sites/amirhu sain/2020/09/25/three-coming-shifts-in-ai/#45ca1121d2d4. Accessed 22 Oct 2020
7. Linkov, I., Galaitsi, S., Trump, B.D., Keisler, J.M., Kott, A.: Cybertrust: From Explainable to Actionable and Interpretable Artificial Intelligence. Computer **53**(9), 91–96 (2020). https://doi.org/10.1109/MC.2020.2993623
8. Gansler, J.S., Lucyshyn, W., Rigilano, J.: The Joint Tactical Radio System: Lessons Learned and the Way Forward, Center for Public Policy and Private Enterprise (2012). https://apps.dtic.mil/dtic/tr/fulltext/u2/a623331.pdf. Accessed 22 Oct 2020
9. Saarelainen, T.: Towards Tactical Military Software Defined Radio (2014). https://www.res earchgate.net/publication/275152720_Towards_Tactical_Military_Software_Defined_Rad io_SDR. Accessed 22 Oct 2020
10. Soresen, E.: SDN Used for Policy Enforcement in a Federated Military Network. Norwegian University of Science and Technology (2014). Accessed 22 Oct 2020
11. Marrone, A., Nones, M., Ungaro, A.R.: Technological Innovation and Defence: The Forza NEC Program in the Euro-Atlantic Framework, Instituto Affari Internazionali (2016). http://www.iai.it/sites/default/files/iairp_23.pdf. Accessed 22 Oct 2020
12. Rose, L., Massin, R., Vijayandran, L., Debbah, M., Martret, C.J.L.: CORASMA program on cognitive radio for tactical networks: high fidelity simulator and first results on dynamic frequency allocation. MILCOM 2013 - 2013 IEEE Military Communications Conference, San Diego, CA, pp. 360–368 (2013). https://doi.org/10.1109/MILCOM.2013.69
13. Military & Aerospace electronics (2004). https://www.militaryaerospace.com/computers/art icle/16710419/softwaredefined-radio-and-jtrs. Accessed 22 Oct 2020
14. https://www.eda.europa.eu/webzine/issue14/cover-story/blockchain-technology-in-defence. Accessed 22 Oct 2020

Distributed Ledger-Based Trustful Information Exchange on the Tactical Level

Daniel Ota[1]([✉]) and Okan Topçu[2]

[1] Fraunhofer FKIE, Wachtberg, Germany
daniel.ota@fkie.fraunhofer.de
[2] Middle East Technical University, Kalkanli, Turkey
otopcu@metu.edu.tr

Abstract. Fast, secure, and tamper-proof information sharing between NATO units on a need-to-know basis is crucial. Data quality and integrity are core needs but also resilience to failures and manipulations. The core idea of this paper is to use dis-tributed ledger technology to allow for a secure information exchange between Command and Control Information Systems of different NATO nations and non-NATO stakeholders such as non-NATO nations or mission observers. Moreover, the distributed ledger supports available NATO standards and formats for da-ta exchange and storage.

Keywords: Blockchain · Distributed Ledger · Information Exchange · Tactical Level · Coalition Operations

1 Introduction

Battle management majorly involves command and control (C2) processes and functions such as setting the objectives and intent, determining roles, responsibilities, and relationships, and commanding forces as well as monitoring and assessing the situation. The basis of command and control relies on exchanging (submitting) battle orders that conform to the (operation) plans to the subordinate commanders for a specific mission and receiving reports (e.g. battlefield information) that support the control function. From the perspective of a C2 system, information exchange and data sharing become the main focus. In case of NATO, where nations have different Command and Control Information Systems (C2IS), interoperability becomes a crucial factor in order to process information shared among the systems. Even when we have full interoperability between systems, we still need fast, secure, and temper-proof information sharing on a need-to-know basis. Data quality and integrity are at the core of these solutions but also their resilience to failures and manipulations. In case of coalition operations, these needs are crucial. As reported in [1] "[…] managing and operating in a Military Coalition is really, really hard". Based on that we claim that trustful information exchange in a coalition operation is a real challenge.

In this paper, we try to frame how we can employ some disruptive technologies such as Blockchain Technology (BCT), which is a well-known way of a distributed ledger

T. Tagarev and N. Stoianov (Eds.): DIGILIENCE 2020, CCIS 1790, pp. 12–22, 2024.
https://doi.org/10.1007/978-3-031-44440-1_2

(DL) to address the trustful information exchange in coalition operations on a tactical level. In this regard, the core idea of this paper is to use distributed ledger technology (DLT) to allow a secure information exchange between C2ISs of different NATO nations and non-NATO stakeholders such as non-NATO nations or mission observers, e.g. non-governmental organizations (NGOs). Moreover, the DL should support data exchange and storage based on available NATO standards and formats like the Multilateral Interoperability Program (MIP) Information Model or the Battle Management Language (BML).

The paper is organized as follows: first, we present the use case of trustful information exchange in a coalition scenario in Sect. 2. This is followed by an explanation, which properties of DLT address the needs of this use case in Sect. 3 and a justification why DLT is an adequate solution in Sect. 4. Section 5 discusses design decisions that have to be taken for the realization and that have to be well-balanced. Then, a hypothetical case study is provided in Sect. 6 to demonstrate the proposed framework. Finally, conclusions and future work conclude the paper.

2 Use Case Description

NATO nations undertake more and more missions in multilateral coalitions and interoperability between all partners is a key issue [2]. Often the coalitions do not consist of NATO nations only, but also involve partner or host nations. Additionally, the coalition is often supported by non-military local partners or accompanied by non-governmental organizations. All these stakeholders have the need to communicate based on a joint information exchange infrastructure as depicted in Fig. 1 in order to always have an up-to-date and consistent operational picture. The core idea is to use distributed ledger technology to allow information sharing between C2ISs of different NATO nations as well as non-NATO stakeholders.

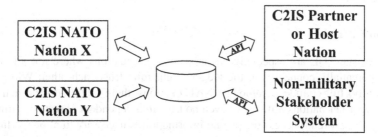

Fig. 1. Information Exchange between Mission Stakeholders in a Coalition Operation

However, the different stakeholders might have different information needs as well as access rights to information. E.g. these differ between the NATO core nations and other partners. Having full access to the DL, NATO nations can write new and receive all information stored in a traditional way, e.g. by using NATO standards such as MIP and BML via national gateways. Other partner or host nations may not support these standards. Therefore, information might be exchanged via an Application Programming

Interface (API) granting full read access but maybe allowing only limited write access. For example, it can be necessary that information originating from host nations is first checked and confirmed by a NATO nation before being added to the distributed ledger. For more trusted partner nations such as Partnership for Peace (PfP) nations, direct write access might be granted. NGOs in contrast might not be able to write information to the mission ledger at all. However, they can receive limited information via an API and monitor the mission progress. Since the DL is an append-only data storage, meaning that information is only added but cannot be deleted, the DL can also function as a war log which allows after-mission audits.

3   Exploitable DL Characteristics

This section underpins how a distributed ledger can support the information exchange of the use case presented.

Distributed ledgers such as Blockchain are tamper-evident and tamper-resistant data storages that are implemented in a distributed fashion and usually work without a central authority deciding, which information is stored in the ledger [3, 4]. They enable a community of users to record transactions – in our case information exchange elements during a coalition mission – in a shared ledger under the constraint that transactions cannot be changed once approved and published. These transactions are added under consensus determined amongst community members expressing the common view of the actual situation.

Distributed ledgers can be permissioned or permissionless. In a permissionless DL infrastructure, anyone can read and write to the ledger without authorization. Permissioned DL limit participation to specific people or organizations and allow finer-grained read and write controls.

Distributed Ledgers support the use case introduced in Sect. 2 with respect to the following properties.

3.1   Limited Trust

Tamper-resistant DL are especially advantageous in situations where not all entities that are potentially connected to the ledger might fully trust each other. While there is (hopefully) full confidence amongst NATO nations, there might be weaker trust in local/host/partner nations military or even no trust in independent observers. However, granting (at least read) access to specific information is necessary to allow partners to perform supporting tasks.

3.2   No Mediator or Central Decision Point

There is no central data source in a DL environment. Information might be created and distributed by all DL entities. This happens in form of "new transactions", which are submitted and pooled to be stored in the DL afterwards. In our use case, however, only NATO peers might be allowed to decide on (i.e. vote for) new transactions which are actually stored in the DL.

3.3 Data Integrity

Once stored in the DL, information is "immutable" since only new information can be added. This allows to have a consolidated view of which information was available to mission stakeholders at which point in time. This supports especially the war log functionality and facilitates later after-action reviews and audits.

3.4 Encryption

Information can be stored encrypted in the DL to enable a secure transmission between military units. Mission observers might only see encrypted information during the mission. However, the actual content might be disclosed for investigations of incidents. Being part of the DL during the mission allows observers to ensure that no information is tampered.

4 Distributed Ledger Justification

Many decentralized use cases for distributed ledgers have already existing (de-) centralized solutions – and they work! As for many hyped research topics, new technologies such as Blockchain are applied to existing problems even though these problems have more suitable and less complex solutions. For this reason, research has been undertaken that analyzed when DLT-based solutions are appropriate [5, 7].

Figure 2 presents a flowchart giving indications that a Blockchain-based solution supports our selected use case. However, it should be noted that the questions in Fig. 2 are no hard requirements but provide hints on whether a DL is actually needed.

The flow starts at the top right. Following the bold and uppercase printed answers and a permissioned Blockchain approach is justified as follows:

1. For our use case, we need more than a traditional database. We want to share C2 data with other peers on the battlefield and store them in a distributed, immutable (append-only) and tamper-proofed data structure.
2. Multiple military units engaged in the mission want to contribute to the common operational picture and want to share C2 data. Observers such as NGOs may be read-only participants.
3. We have a situation of partial trust. NATO units probably trust each other. This might be different for PfP and host nations. However, especially in the case of an incident, every participant wants to be sure that information stored in the DL is unchanged.
4. For the same reasons, participants would not trust a third party.
5. The C2 data shall be kept private with permissioned write and read access. C2 data of NATO missions shall not be publicly available.

In case of NATO-only missions, one might argue that all participants trust each other (cf. Point 3.). Then, the flow changes with respect to the underlined subgraph in Fig. 2. The new question would be raised if a redundant data storage is necessary. This is of course true and this triggers a return to the old flow.

16   D. Ota and O. Topçu

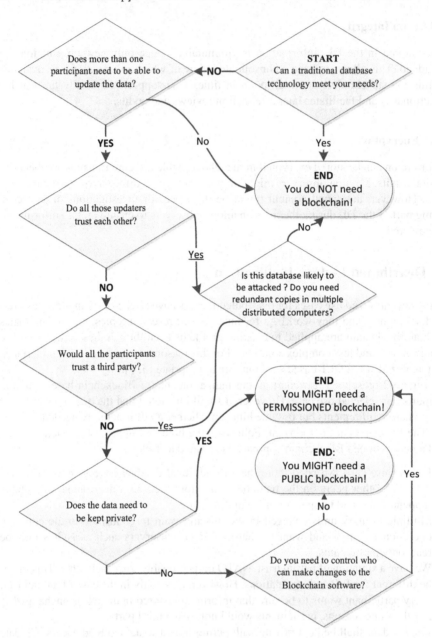

Fig. 2. Does a DLT-based solution support our use case needs? (adapted from [5])

5   Distributed Ledger Parametrization

After giving a rationale why a distributed ledger-based solution supports the presented use case, a parametrization for an implementation needs to be derived. However, the actual parametrization is dependent on the needs of the specific coalition operation.

5.1   Permissioned Distributed Ledger

As indicated by the flowchart in Sect. 4, the DL infrastructure should create a closed environment for sharing and storing data between different mission stakeholders that is completely inaccessible to those that do not participate in the military mission. This means that data is encrypted and only accessible to those having the proper decryption keys.

Similarly, read and write access to the DL must be determined. Core entities such as NATO units should always have full access to the DL while stakeholders that only observe the course of a mission, e.g. NGOs, have only rights for reading the C2 data. For other stakeholders such as PfP or host nations, access might differ for each (type of) mission.

5.2   Consensus Models

The consensus model chosen for a DL implementation determines which ledger entity is allowed to publish the next block of transactions. A proper model is highly relevant if not all publishers trust each other. In multinational missions with a limited number of trusted publishers, the participants should not need to spend a significant amount of resources on "mining" the next block like in untrusted Blockchains like Bitcoin. This calls for a different consensus mechanism, e.g., round robin- or vote-based consensus instead of proof-of-work [3, 6].

5.3   Need-to-Know Principle

Usually, information in military missions is exchanged on a need-to-know basis. In case of distributed ledgers, all stakeholders with write access can publish their data in the ledger, which then can be read by all participants. Therefore, it must be defined how the need-to-know principle can be enforced.

One option to ensure that only relevant participants can read particular C2 information is encrypting it with a group key that is shared between the military participants. This hinders for example NGOs to understand messages in real-time but enables them to gather encrypted C2 data during the mission and decrypt and analyze it in the case of an incident when the key is disclosed afterwards.

A second option is that only the cryptographic hash of the actual information is published in the ledger and the C2 information is stored elsewhere. Blocks stored in the DL can be seen as events with reference to C2 data (called an event ledger), while the referred C2 data is stored at other places, for example on a distributed file system or another distributed ledger, which is only accessible by the respective military participants. In the case of an incident, the distributed hash values together with the actual C2 data disclosed afterwards would also allow to validate the state of information exchange during the mission.

5.4 Distributed Ledger Lifetime

The scale of a particular ledger infrastructure and endurance of data stored in the ledger are to be defined. The lifetime of the ledger infrastructure might be limited to a particular military mission only, implying that its scope has known boundaries in time and place. (Not long) after completion of a military operation, the DL infrastructure might be deleted and data archived. The supposed lifetime has implications on other parameters as discussed for the need-to-know principle.

5.5 Network Fragmentation

Traditional Blockchains – as the name implies – rely on a concatenation of cryptograph-ically linked blocks where each block has exactly one predecessor and one successor. This causes problems if the underlying communication network is (at least temporary) fragmented. If the DL entities are split into two segments, a fork of the Blockchain is created. That leads to the situation that the blocks created in one branch are discarded when the fragmentation is resolved (cf. Fig. 3 left side). This a serious problem and its occurrence highly is probable on the tactical level since entities are weakly connected and tactical networks are volatile in nature.

To overcome this problem, a DL realization based on a Directed Acyclic Graph (DAG) might be chosen. A DAG allows that coinciding transactions are confirmed in different branches of the distributed ledger as long as they do not contradict each other.

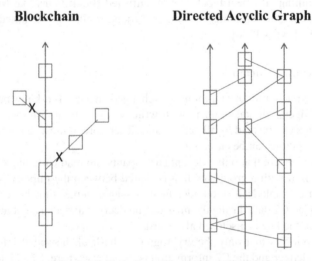

Fig. 3. Blockchain vs. Directed Acyclic Graph

Having a fragmented network is uncritical for our use case, since C2 data-publishing entities are located only in one and are writing only in one of the network fragments.

This means that C2 events that are confirmed in one network fragment can be approved in the other network fragments later when network fragments are merged (cf. Fig. 3 right side).

5.6 Data Distribution

In order to exchange the actual C2 data in form of transactions, an efficient peer-to-peer (P2P) transmission protocol needs to be chosen for the DL synchronization. Traditional Blockchain implementations rely on a strong and reliable, often internet-based, communication infrastructure with implications such as a high bandwidth and a small latency available. On the tactical level, the network has sparse connectivity and link connectivity is dynamically changing as spatial and temporal parameters change. Therefore, a P2P protocol is needed that is tuned with respect to entity discovery, entity synchronization, and data exchange overheads.

5.7 Integration into Existing NATO Infrastructure

A distributed ledger solution has to be integrated into existing NATO mission networks. NATO defines profiles to achieve interoperability for Federated Mission Networking (FMN). The FMN profiles have to be considered with regard to implications on the deployment of distributed ledger technology. This might have impact on afore-mentioned parameters, for instance, if information exchange across different security domains needs to be realized.

6 Case Study

This section provides an example for how a traditional information exchange infrastructure might be adapted to a DL-based one.

Figure 4 depicts how information is typically exchanged nowadays between two NATO nations. Since all nations use roughly the same infrastructure, it is described for NATO Nation A in detail only. For simplicity, the infrastructure is limited to a C2IS and a gateway. Further components such as networks or radios are neglected.

The national C2IS maintains the Common Operational Picture (COP) and displays it to the user. It maintains the identities of the different stakeholders on the battlefield, which are needed for verifying senders and receivers of messages, for example. The C2IS stores the order of battle (ORBAT) that defines the hierarchical subordination of units. Further, it keeps a local database containing all relevant information such as exchanged messages, received requests and reports.

In order to exchange information with other units, standardized information exchange elements are used. For battle space objects (BSO) Multilateral Interoperability Program (MIP) [8] messages are used on the higher echelons or APP-11 Message Text Format (MTF) [9] messages are used for plans and orders. Similarly, on the tactical level, Joint Dismounted Soldier System (JDSS) [10], NATO Friendly Force Information (NFFI) [11], or Battle Management Language (BML) [12] messages would be used to transmit information.

20   D. Ota and O. Topçu

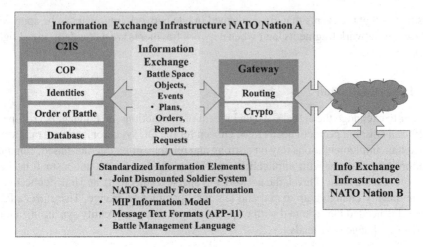

Fig. 4. Classical Information Exchange Infrastructure

All messages are passed from the national C2IS to some kind of gateway which encrypts the data and forwards it based on the available routing information to the C2IS of other nations represented by the cloud and behind.

Figure 5 shows the traditional model after adaptation in order to incorporate the DL approach for the use case discussed in Sect. 2.

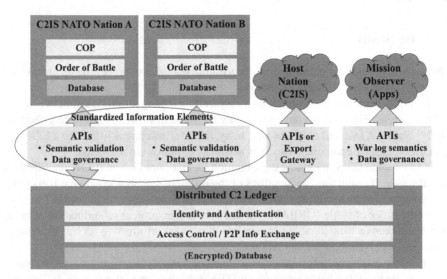

Fig. 5. Information Exchange Infrastructure based on a Distributed C2 Ledger

As before, COP and ORBAT stay at the C2 level within national C2IS.

The exchanged messages, received requests and reports are no longer stored only locally since the C2IS also passes this information to the distributed ledger. The DL is also responsible for the identity management, access control, and information transmission.

Further, the exchanged data is still processed and stored in the same standardized way (e.g. as MIP or BML messages), but the dissemination is now done by API calls to the DL, which also allows to validate the messages syntactically and semantically.

As discussed earlier, host nations have read access to the DL and can also propose new transactions. Approving/voting for including these transactions to the DL might however be restricted to NATO nation peers. For accessing the ledger, the host might use the same API as NATO nations in case the C2IS supports the NATO standards. As an alternative, a gateway can be provided to export relevant data to the host nation's C2 system. Of course, exports and ledger access via gateways might also be a solution for the integration of NATO legacy systems.

As depicted on the right of Fig. 5, further mission stakeholders such as NGOs or observers can access the DL via specific APIs. This war log API might provide them with encrypted transactions transmitted in real-time during the mission, which however are only disclosed in case of incidents or in case of other investigation needs.

7 Conclusions

This paper introduced a use case for distributing information in a coalition scenario based on a DLT approach. It discussed the benefits of using DLTs and justified why it is an adequate technical solution. For providing a direction for future realizations, DL parameters to be determined were identified, followed by a discussion of a possible adaptation of existing NATO infrastructure.

The discussed ideas represent first results from ongoing research in NATO IST-ET-110. The paper illustrates a first use case for the usage of BCT/DLT in a NATO context. Besides this, further use cases for secure supply chain management and for a decentralized identity management are under investigation.

Acknowledgments. This paper is based on preliminary results of the Exploratory Team NATO IST-ET-110 "Blockchain Technology for Coalition Operations". The authors would like to thank the team for all the stimulating and fruitful conversations.

The views and conclusions contained in this paper are those of the authors and should not be interpreted as necessarily representing the official policies or endorsements, either expressed or implied, of any affiliated organization or government.

References

1. McInnis, J.K.: Lessons in coalition warfare: past, present and implications for the future. International Politics Rev. **1**, 78–90 (2013)
2. Derleth, J.: Enhancing Interoperability – The Foundation for Effective NATO Operations. Romanian Military Thinking 2 (2015)
3. Yage, D., Mell, P., Roby, N., Scarfone K.: Blockchain Technology Overview (2018)

4. Narayanan, A., et al.: Bitcoin and Cryptocurrency Technologies: A Comprehensive Introduction. Princeton University Press (2016)
5. Peck, M.E.: Blockchain world - Do you need a blockchain? this chart will tell you if the technology can solve your problem. IEEE Spectr. **54**(10), 38–60 (2017)
6. Wüst, K., Gervais, A.: Do you need a blockchain?. 2018 Crypto Valley Conference on Blockchain Technology (CVCBT). IEEE (2018)
7. Nguyen, G., Kyungbaek, K.: A survey about consensus algorithms used in blockchain. J. Information Processing Syst. **14**(1) (2018)
8. Gerz, M., Bau, N.: MIP information model 4.0: semantic interoperability in multinational missions. In: 21st International Command and Control Research and Technology Symposium (ICCRTS) (2016)
9. NATO Message Catalogue – APP-11(D). North Atlantic Treaty Organization (2015)
10. NATO - STANAG 4677. Dismounted Soldier Systems Standards and Protocols for Command, Control, Communications and Computers (C4) Interoperability (DSS C4 Interoperability) (2014)
11. NATO - STANAG 5527. Friendly Force Tracking Systems (FFTS) Interoperability (2017)
12. Schade, U., Hieb, M.R.: Battle management language: a grammar for specifying reports. IEEE Spring Simulation Interoperability Workshop (2007)

An Empirical Evaluation of Cyber Threat Intelligence Sharing in the ECHO Early Warning System

Ioannis Chalkias[1], Cagatay Yucel[1], Dimitrios Mallis[1], Jyri Rajamaki[2(✉)], Fabrizio De Vecchis[3], Peter Hagstrom[3], and Vasilis Katos[1]

[1] Bournemouth University, Fern Barrow, Poole, Dorset BH12 5BB, UK
{ichalkias,cyucel,dmallis,vkatos}@bournemouth.ac.uk
[2] Laurea University of Applied Sciences, Espoo, Finland
jyri.rajamaki@laurea.fi
[3] RHEA Group, Avenue Einstein 8, 1300 Wavre, Belgium
{f.devecchis,p.hagstrom}@rheagroup.com

Abstract. This paper reports on the information sharing practices of cyber competency centres representing different sectors and constituencies. The cyber competency centres participated in the form of CSIRTs employed the ECHO Early Warning System. Through a structured tabletop exercise, over 10 CSIRTS were engaged and a number of features were captured and monitored. A key research question was to determine the factors that can potentially hinder or amplify Cyber Threat Intelligence information sharing. The exercise imitated real attack scenarios using state-of-the-art tactics techniques and procedures as observed by real-world APT groups and daily incidents. The findings revealed differences in terms of timeliness, response time and handling tickets with different Traffic Light Protocol classifications, duration of handling a ticket and intention to disclose.

Keywords: cybersecurity tabletop exercise · extra-constituency information sharing

1 Introduction

As attacks become frequent and with high impact, an Early Warning System (EWS) for Cyber Threat Intelligence (CTI) aims at serving as a security operations support tool enabling the members of the network to coordinate and share information in near real-time in order to develop and maintain efficient incident handling capabilities. At the same time EWS, stakeholders must retain their fully independent management of cyber-sensitive intelligence and related data management.

The design and development of the proposed EWS followed the main concepts and practices of information sharing and trust models from the cyber domain. The requirements elicitation and analysis process included the requirements for information sharing

A preliminary version of this paper appeared in DIGILIENCE 2020 [17].

T. Tagarev and N. Stoianov (Eds.): DIGILIENCE 2020, CCIS 1790, pp. 23–40, 2024.
https://doi.org/10.1007/978-3-031-44440-1_3

within and between partners across organisational boundaries as derived from a multi-sector analysis. This paper reports on the empirical evaluation of the proposed EWS which was conducted through a table-top exercise (TTX). To the best of our knowledge, the literature currently lacks publicly available datasets capturing the communication dynamics and exchange between different CSIRTS, across different sectors. In this work we attempt to create such a dataset and use it in order to evaluate both an information sharing system (namely the Early Warning System of the ECHO pilot project) as well as the team and communication dynamics within and among the participating CSIRTS.

The rest of the paper is structured as follows. In Sect. 2 we outline how tabletop exercises provide the means to evaluate CTI sharing approaches. Section 3 outlines the particular features of ECHO's Early Warning System (EWS). In Sects. 4 and 5 the empirical analysis and evaluation through TTX exercise are presented. Section 6 summarises the findings and presents areas for future research.

2   CTI Sharing and Tabletop Exercises

The literature review indicates that there is no pervasive or widely agreed upon definition of "cyber security information sharing". As such, the structures of the information sharing models can be sector-specific and created in different environments. There is a need for a common early warning solution. The fight against hybrid threats means not only preventing cyber attacks, but also identifying, tracing and prosecuting a criminal/criminal group [19]. This means an even deeper integration of government systems in the future as the term "warning" includes also preventive functions.

Relevant information from the site of a major hybrid incident should be directly shared with the national CERTS and follow a coordinated response. Combining pieces of information to ensure the correct and reliable information to be shared is deemed to be significant in establishing cyber capacity. The shared information should be in a form that is unambiguous and accessible to the involved parties. In the future cyber defence operations are expected to be more integrated and automated according to local capabilities, authorities and mission needs [15]. A shared common operational picture means that real-time communication link from the local level to nation and EU level exist. A common cyber situational awareness is needed for both operating Cyber Physical Systems (CPS), and for emergency and crisis management [4]. There should be the connection between cyber situational awareness and emergency management [13].

Moreover, it is important to take into account how national Cyber Security Centres cooperate with other organisations within critical infrastructure on a national level. The states departments of the United States work closely together in the fight against cyber security threats. The organisations of public administration of the Member States in European Union cooperate on a formal basis as set out in the NIS directive [1] and the Cyber Security Act [2].

It could be argued that cooperation outside the EU borders can be hindered by the fundamental differences of administrative functions between European Union and the other country/coalition. However, as Ilves et al. [12] mentioned, there are no crucial barriers to increase collaboration concerning early warning solutions between US, NATO and EU. US's Cyber security sharing act and Europe's directive on Network and Information Security (NIS) have similar goals. In addition to this, EU and NATO signed a technical arrangement in 2016 to increase information sharing between the NATO Computer Incident Response Capability and EU Computer Emergency Response Team [10]. Public safety actors like European law enforcement agencies need common shared situational picture for the cross-boarding tasks in a way that operational cooperation will be based on reliable platform [7].

As part of cyber crisis management, Tabletop Exercises (TTXs) for cyber security were established around the early 2000s to provide the response-plan developers with insights about the efficiency and the effectiveness of the proposed action plan in case of a malicious cyber incident. In [20], the authors discuss in detail the very first government/multi-sector joint event known as the "Dark Screen" that took place in San Antonio, Texas. The aim was to assess the preparedness and the abilities of the districts of San Antonio and Bexar against cyber terrorist threats. Dark Screen was a TTX separated into 3 stages, each of them with different objectives; these included the successful interconnection among the participating organisations, penetration and incident response testing, and information sharing observation. Moreover, examples of sector based tabletop exercises are presented in the same document, where the respective sectors make up national critical infrastructures. In all cases, information sharing among the various sectors and the related organisations has been repeatedly identified as a critical and necessary measure towards cyber resilience enhancement.

A TTX must be designed by experienced facilitators and includes one or more realistic, but fictional, scenarios tailored to the participants of the exercise; these scenarios include cyber attack simulations with well-defined objectives that aim at exploiting loopholes in systems, response plans, behaviours, but also highlight the importance of individual roles and responsibilities, and timely decision-making activities, such as attack mitigation and information sharing, against potential cyber threats [14]. Upon the completion of each TTX an "after-action" report is deemed necessary in order to describe if the original goals were met, the overall experience of the participants, the lessons learned and the associated proposed solutions. Such an example is given by the EU Agency for cyber security (ENISA) [5] who recently conducted a TTX in an attempt to assess and evaluate the EU's crisis plans and mitigation mechanisms in case of malevolent cyber incidents related to the EU elections. Similarly, the U.S. Department of Homeland Security (DHS) Cybersecurity and Infrastructure Security Agency (CISA) designed the Elections Cyber Tabletop Exercise Package (ECTEP) Situation Manual (SitMan), based on the TTX format, as part of a strategic initiative to strengthen the cyber training capability of stakeholders [6].

As EWS and CTI play a supportive role on security operations [16], the approach of conducting tabletop exercises has been chosen for the evaluations of EWS, throughout its development.

3   Early Warning System Features and Requirements

At the kernel of information sharing lies the intelligence data item (IDI). In the context of ECHO, an intelligence data item is defined as any piece of data that potentially contains actionable information relating to cyber security [8]. Appreciating the enormous value of information and its potential, an information sharing framework is required in order to appropriately manage the life-cycle of the corresponding data items, from their generation, processing, dissemination all the way to their destruction. This approach is expected to facilitate the creation of a community of a large pool of stakeholders who will engage in joint intelligence activities and reliably share information and collaborate in handling security incidents in an effective and timely manner. As such, establishing and ensuring trust is a key factor for the successful adoption of the EWS [18].

3.1 Characteristics of Intelligence Data Items

At a first level of discrimination, IDIs can be structured, semi-structured or unstructured. Typically unstructured data refer to primary sources of information that are normally processed by automated or human means for extracting the necessary information. This process would generate structured IDIs that would allow automated processing. It should be noted though that there can be primary sources ingested into the EWS that are structured (e.g. log files).

IDIs can also be distinguished as reference information or operational information. Reference information refers to the IDIs that contribute in achieving situational awareness, allowing the beneficiary to make informed judgements on the cyber risks of the organisation. Operational information relates to those IDIs that support the actual decision making, handling incidents and so forth.

The IDIs should be accompanied with metadata that will contextualise the contained information but also enable the EWS to implement and enforce authorisation and access control mechanisms. Common identifiers and enumerations should be used whenever possible.

Table 1 presents an initial list of the categories of information and their expressions as IDIs. IDIs that potentially contain Personal Information will need to also meet the privacy requirements. These categories were further expanded and refined following the requirements elicitation and specification.

Information Sharing Model Assumptions

Against all the above, the proposed ECHO information sharing model is based on the following assumptions or premises:

- There will be a clear and concise governance model for the intelligence data items, where each item will be described by a comprehensive list of contextual information (metadata) to allow fine-grained decision making on the management and handling of the data.
- There will be a clear process for on-boarding and off-boarding of participating organisations.
- It is expected that it would be easier for organisations being in the same sector or having similar goals and purpose to form easier clusters for sharing threat intelligence information, as they are more likely to have established and mature exchange arrangements; therefore they are more likely to reach consensus. On the contrary, organisations that operate in orthogonal industries (i.e. where their respective industries have virtually nothing in common) is expected that would be less forthcoming in sharing information.

Table 1. Intelligence data items

Information category	IDI	structured/ unstructured	reference/ operational	Personal Information
Technical threat indicator	IOC (email, IP address, file hash, mutex, domain)	S	R	
Intrusion attempt	Threat Actor	S	O	X
	IOC (atomic, composite, behavioural)	S	O	
Security alert	Ticket	Semi	O	
	Readiness level	S	R/O	
Vulnerability information	CVE	S	R/O	
	CVSS	S	R/O	
	Threat identification	Semi	O	
	Geopolitical	U	R	
	Exploitability	S	R	
Vulnerability report	Vulnerability scanning report	S	R	
Incident report	Report	U	O	?
TTP	ATT&CK	S	R/O	
	STIX object	S	R/O	
Remediation actions	Operating procedure	U	O	
	Playbook	U	O	
Asset	CPE to describe system platforms	S	R/O	
	CCE (common configuration enumeration)	S	R/O	
Discussion	Discussion item	U	R/O	?
Blog post	Reference	U	R/O	
Poll	Poll item	U	R/O	
Raw data	Log-file	S	O	
	Netflow	S	O	X
	Packet capture	Semi	O	X
	RAM image dump	Semi	O	X
	Malware sample	Semi	O	?
	VM Image	U	O	X
	File	U	R/O	X
	Email	U	R/O	

- Stakeholders and participants are expected to join predefined and ad-hoc groups.
- Trust will be delivered through technical, organisational and human means.
- Due to the nature and diversity of sectors, in order for information sharing to provide a meaningful and accurate services, the scope of the data items should be extended to encompass Cyber Physical Systems; indicatively, this can consider the practices found in the Maritime Sector where there is a clear distinction between cyber (e.g. IT networks) and Physical (e.g. Operational Technology networks) highlighting the existence and inter-dependencies between the physical and cyber plane.
- Translation and normalisation services will allow the standardisation of intelligence data items. The underlying taxonomies and schemas should cater for the verticals by including optional fields.
- Existing standards for information processing and sharing will be adopted wherever possible.

3.2 Information Sharing Architecture

Information sharing is highly dependent upon and influenced by the regulatory frameworks as well as the cultural norms both within a sector and the organization itself. In academia for example, barriers to sharing are expected to be lower than the other sectors, due to the culture of freedom of academic expression and an academic citizen mentality of peer review and dissemination of research output. On the other hand, in critical infrastructure type of sectors such as Energy, or in banking [3], information sharing is more intensely regulated, and this also is reflected in the respective organisational cultures. This creates a tessellation of regulatory frameworks and cultural antecedents on the following levels:

- Intra-Organisational, influenced by specific internal policies and procedures.
- Intra-Sector, imposed by the respective sector.
- National-governmental, governed by the respective strategic decisions on a national level.
- Transnational, through the international agreements, treaties and EU legislation and directives, in the case of the organisation operating within the EU. This may include frameworks for information sharing with Law Enforcement entities.

The above are also complemented by horizontal legislation such as the GDPR that cuts across all sectors. Provided that:

- The jurisdictional and operational environment of the proposed system relates to the EU initiative on establishing a network of competency centres, and
- the EWS is intended to support information sharing among and between a multitude of sectors such as Healthcare, Energy and Maritime,

A modified hybrid model architecture is recommended as this appears to best fit the requirements following the cross-case analysis. In essence, the hybrid approach will allow to maintain a basic form of hierarchy, and at the same time it will allow the connection of different hubs, forming a higher peer to peer level. This is also in accordance to how CERTs operate and share information, which is done on a peer to peer basis but also within their level of operation (e.g. national, organisational, etc.). Allowing some degree of centralisation will also enable centralised decision making and support the emergence of Coordination Centres. A hub could represent a variety of communities, such as a specific sector, an interest group or a national point. It is recommended that each hub will refer to organisations of common characteristics, goals or sector, simplifying its management, internal governance and deployment complexity.

This would be inline with the EWS architecture supporting tenants allowing also seamless integration through the sharing API capability that will connect EWS instances.

From a governance perspective, the immediate consequence of this would be to have trust realms, two tiers of cross organisational boundaries, as shown in Fig. 1.

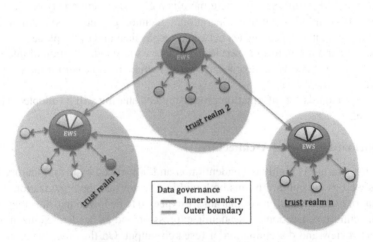

Fig. 1. Information sharing architecture

In this example, three trust realms are presented. Each realm can correspond to any type of organisational cluster, e.g. realm 1 could be academic CERTs, realm 2 national cyber security competency centres and realms 3 maritime sector. Every trust realm can have more than one EWS instances, for scalability and resilience purposes. The governance model could refer to policies and security certification requirements for deploying an EWS instance.

The first step for an organisation or individual joining the EWS ecosystem is to complete the on-boarding process. Upon successful application, the organisation is allocated a tenant slice. This will host all information provided by the participating organisation. Organisation boundaries can be crossed within a given trust realm and these are specified through the inner boundary data governance. It is expected that these will be the first to be formed, upon the emergence of the EWS.

Inter-realm information sharing is controlled by the outer boundary data governance models. These are expected to be more complex and diverse and will require a longer maturity period. It should be noted that not all trust realms will necessarily connect to each other; such configurations imply that some realms will emerge to be more authoritative and trustworthy than others, but should also indicate that transitive trust should not be guaranteed or offered.

IDIs containing personal information will be go through anonymization and redaction layers prior to leaving a tenant's area. For structured IDIs, automated processes would seamlessly and efficiently implement the underlying privacy policy. Information classification schemes will be enforced at the organisational boundaries (coarse grained access control) as well as internally (fine grained).

As the organisation participation and connectivity between the hubs increase, the value of the network is expected also to increase, in accordance to Metcalfe's Law. However, as this increase is very likely to result to generation of large volumes of data, the perceived usefulness is expected to decrease. In order to compensate for this, information sharing should not only be limited by access control criteria, but additional contextual features to enable effective filtering of non-relevant information (noise). A representative feature for this task is asset information. For example, by using the Common Platform Enumeration (CPE) convention, an organisation can describe their assets in a standardised way. By doing this it would be possible to quickly filter out attacks and vulnerabilities that are not applicable to a particular organisation's attack surface.

3.3 Features of the Information Sharing System

A modular approach for the EWS is considered. The core EWS should be comprised of a ticketing system supporting distributed workflow among a number of different partners and organisations. The EWS should allow the enrichment and contextualisation of the introduced and ingress information [11]. As such, a standard description and an expandable information taxonomy should be considered.

An initial list of features of the perspective EWS is presented below:

– **A suitable confidentiality model, such as the traffic light protocol.** All intelligence items will need to be assigned with a designation to ensure that the sensitive information is shared with the appropriate audience. The Traffic Light Protocol (TLP) is recommended because it is less formal, does not really require NDAs, etc., it is more of a "gentlemen's agreement" and allows a faster communication of incident data. TLP will of course run in conjunction with the standard system's access control mechanisms, such as RBAC. For the EWS system in particular and upon a joint decision, FIRST's TLP definition is adopted to support future interoperability and standardisation with all pilots. Moreover, the confidentiality model – due to the nature of the EWS – should include introduction of information by protecting source attribution (Chatham House rule), in order to facilitate the submission of any information that can be vital when handling security incidents. A direct consequence of this is the consideration of the reliability of the data, defined further below.

- **An access control scheme, capable of making fine-grained access control decisions.** The audience accessing intelligence items shall be controlled through access classifiers such as organisations, groups, and roles.
- **Support of multiple taxonomies and standards for intelligence sharing.** This will allow the hosting of organisations belonging in different sectors.
- **Capabilities for a structured sharing of intelligence data e.g. use of Structured Threat Information eXpression (STIX).**
- **The system should facilitate the exchange of intelligence between CERTS/CSIRTS and LEAs.** Terminologies used in the two communities are sometimes different. ENISA recommends using the 'Common Taxonomy for Law Enforcement and The National Network of CSIRTs' [7].
- **Common data and document formats support.** Use of common formats e.g. Word, PDF, and CSV facilitate intelligence sharing where the use of specialised formats is not an option.
- **Capability to evaluate the reliability of the source of an intelligence data item.** All information sources should be assessed for reliability based on a technical assessment of their capability, or in the case of human intelligence source, their history.
- **Assessment of the credibility of an intelligence data item based on likelihood and levels of corroboration by other sources.** An EWS allowing a quick turnaround and fast decision making requires that the ingress information is trusted. The system should have mechanisms to assess the credibility of the information and include fake news protection mechanisms.
- **A shared workflow management system for incident handling.** This is one of the main purposes and core functionalities of the EWS, allowing also to monitor the effectiveness and efficiency of the system.
- **Trust-boosting security technologies.** Supporting the creation of closed communities and encrypted peer to peer communication.
- **Data redaction capabilities, for privacy compliance.** The system will need to redact personal information for data items marked to contain PI when exporting them to other EWS instances based on a privacy protection policy. For structured data, this can be done automatically. For unstructured data, this can be done semi-automatically, but may require human inspection and approval.
- **Attribution capabilities, identification of the origins of the source of information.** For traceability, disseminated information shall contain appropriate origin describing meta-data.

- **Anonymous sharing of information.** Despite the attribution requirements, it is advised that the system would still allow anonymous information, however, these items will need to be clearly marked as anonymous and is expected to have an impact on the reliability of the information.
- **Customisable exchange of intelligence data.** Customisation may be in accordance with internal (originating organisation) or external requirements.
- **Predefined criteria for data dissemination.** This relates to both the originator of the information (e.g. the criteria a set in accordance with audience, trust realms etc.) and the consumer of the information (e.g. data versions and revisions, severity, etc.)
- **Data normalisation.** The system shall normalise all ingress data under a common format, or data model. This will enable compatibility, interoperability and other functions (correlation).
- **A flexible data model.** Expansion of the data model is a prerequisite to allow EWS to grow across different domains and verticals. The system can allow custom creation of tags and the enrichment of existing IDIs. This could be automatic or manual. For example, an IDI may be enriched by external information from OSINT activities.
- **Correlation capabilities.** At a minimum level, the system should automatically link newly imported IDIs with existing IDIs.
- **Data items curation.** The system shall curate and de-duplicate IDIs imported from different sources and datasets. This is for ensuring that the integrity and accuracy of analytics is offered.
- **Advanced data analytics.** Situational awareness will be considerably supported from data analytics techniques (e.g. clustering and classification). This could include production of trends over time related data to support predictive analytics.
- **Visual analytics.** The system should provide visual analytics through a dynamic, interactive UI.
- **Pivoting capabilities.** In order to support the analytics processes and allow complex correlations and analytics, the system should offer pivoting capabilities over data.
- **Data exporting formats.** The system shall support exporting of data in different formats e.g. STIX, OpenIOC, CSV, Yara, sigma, etc.
- **Filtering capabilities.** The system should support filtering of information across a number of parameters and features. This also includes both whitelisting, blacklisting, to filter out benign activity and to pin down suspicious/malicious events.
- **Triaging.** The system should provide a high level overview of the data so that the analyst can quickly get a "gist" of what they contain. For example, for numerical data, the basic statistical information should be presented.
- **Alerting and communication.** This feature is required to improve the response times to incidents. This involves capabilities to match asset configuration with vulnerability information (for example describing assets as CPE and pairing with CVE and CVSS items) and sending a message to a designated contact point if a criticality level of an event exceeds some threshold. For example, this can be done if an asset described through a configuration is detected to be vulnerable to an exploit with a CVSS score.
- **Intelligence report generation.** The information shared should be available to the stakeholders in an appropriate format and level of detail.

4 Tabletop Exercise Approach

The tabletop exercise (TTX) was conducted as part of the evaluation of the development of the EWS platform. During the TTX the developers were given the chance not only to evaluate the technical features of the platform but also to test the assumptions mentioned above and ECHO's information-sharing architecture. It can be segmented in three stages: preparation, exercise conduct and post-analysis. The preparation of the exercise was based on the evaluation objectives, set from the ECHO consortium. For this TTX the defined objectives were the following:

- Assess the information-sharing policies of the EWS
- Evaluate the development of the EWS
- Detect and identify bugs and possible improvement
- Cyber attribution of the attacks

The next step of the preparation stage was to align the background of the exercise with current events or a major event that increases the alert status of a CSIRT or requires different incident management. In the case of the TTX, a mixture of the current Pandemic and a fictional EU-elections was used. An event like the EU-elections (and the extended period that is affected by it) can be exploited by the perpetrators of the cyber realm and this fact would create an environment that the participants would be prompted to optimise the information-sharing decisions and also attribute the incidents appropriately. To complete the backstory of the exercise, a scenario was created, according to which members of the consortium were the developers of an e-voting application that would allow the European citizens to vote electronically; requesting from the remaining members to contribute to the development by taking part in the evaluation and testing of the tool.

In the process of creating a coordinated framework that would coordinate the efforts of the participants, TTX also adopted the basic principles of the "Blueprint for Coordinated response to large scale cross border cyber security incidents and crises" [9]. Following the guidelines for increased technical and situational awareness, two entities were created and added to the platform with the purpose of providing appropriate information to the participants.

The remainder of the preparation process was focused on the preparation of the incidents that were developed under selected taxonomies and stages as follows.

The first taxonomy reflected on the identity of the receiver of the incident:

- Incidents addressed from the whole consortium
- Inter-sector incidents
- Sector-specific incidents
- Organisation-specific incidents
- The second taxonomy reflected on the content of the incidents
- EU-Elections focused content
- Covid-19 focused content
- Miscellaneous content

The incidents would involve the use of commonly known malware, recently released vulnerabilities, fake news dissemination and alerts for unauthorised activities. The actions were related and attributed, mostly, to APT-28, other APT groups and other criminal actors. The intentions behind the choice of criminal actors were aiming to highlight that fact that cyber perpetrators could take advantage of a period when the attention is focused to a major event and target other areas that would appear of a lesser priority at that time.

The second stage of TTX, the exercise conduct, lasted three hours during which the participants were exposed to the incidents designed and delivered by the organisers. The participating teams were equally shared between two instance servers. The incidents were delivered in three waves with alternating volumes of information flow that would simulate a notion of realistic flow of incidents that are reported to a CSIRT.

Along with the injections, the teams were receiving hourlies, from two entities run by the organisers, as described in the preparation stage. The hourlies were delivered in three sets and offered the teams the opportunity to increase their awareness in the following topics:

- Voting applications
- E-voting
- APT groups
- APT-28
- Newly exposed vulnerabilities

The development of the scenarios of the injects aimed to trigger the exchange of CTI between the members of the EWS constituencies; the interaction, for each wave, between the teams and the related incident are displayed in Fig. 2.

During the three hours of the exercise the participants processed the information they received from the incoming reports and hourlies and proceeded on exchanging tickets internally and externally. After the conclusion of the exercise, the participants completed an online questionnaire focusing on the following aspects

- Profiling of the participants
- Information-sharing decisions
- Bug reporting
- Technical aspects of the tickets
- Evaluation of the exercise

The outcome of the questionnaire combined with the analysis of the log files of the instance servers are discussed in the following section.

5 Analysis

The two sources of the primary data used for the analysis were the logs of the EWS system and the questionnaire provided to the team members at the end of the exercise. The analysis includes merging these two sources to produce results for the exercise. The analysis is composed of three parts: i) the activity of the exercises including the sharing activities of the teams and constituencies; ii) the analysis on team dynamics which includes the following features: the number of team members, experience of team members and the correlation of those with the alive time of the tickets and the distribution of tickets; and iii) the characteristics retrieved from the nature of the tickets such as the assigned TLP levels and their distribution in general.

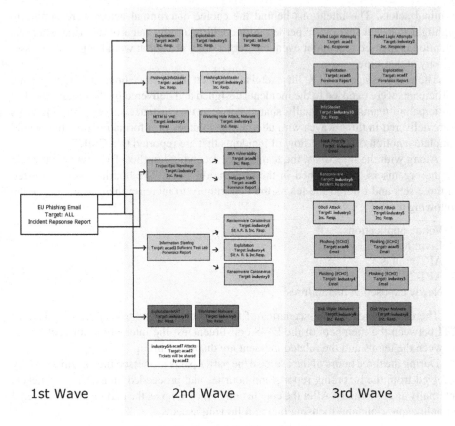

Fig. 2. Staging and timeline of the TTX

5.1 Exercise Activity Analysis

As explained in the description of the exercise, the teams are separated into logical constituencies defined by the election scenario. These constituencies consist of sectors of Defense, (European) Elections, IT and Healthcare. In addition to these 4 sectors, an ECCC constituency which represents member states from EU and a MEDIAROOM constituency were defined to distribute information to all of the audience from the participants. The MEDIAROOM constituency was created and utilised to share hourlies publicly by the organisers of the exercise.

Above all of these logical constituencies, the teams are coming from the industry or academia, therefore research and private sector constituencies were also utilised to create distribution channels between universities and private sector representatives respectively.

As can be seen from the Fig. 3, Elections Constituency which is the main theme of the scenario retrieves the most tickets during the exercise. Since the theme also includes European Elections process, the second high attraction constituency is the ECCC. The third one is the MEDIAROOM since this constituency is utilised for the distribution of the hourlies as aforementioned in the previous chapters.

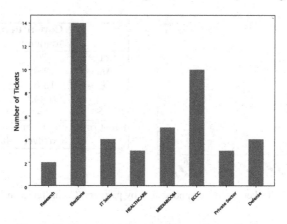

Fig. 3. Number of tickets shared by each constituency

The number of tickets shared by each organisation is given in Fig. 4. All the tickets are separated into two colours - internal (orange) and external (blue). As you can see from the figure, there are some organisations that didn't share any internal or external tickets. The organisation acad2 was included in the organisation committee, acad4 had technical issues and therefore they couldn't share any tickets.

On the day of the exercise, as explained above, incidents that are related to the elections theme of the scenario and incidents crafted for specific partner targets were released. It was seen that the majority of the partners shared these incidents via tickets after discussing them using the internal tickets while partners industry2, acad5 and industry5 only shared tickets internally.

As it can be seen from Fig. 4, the highest number of tickets are shared by the team acad3 although they received approximately the same amount of injects with all the partners. After the inspection of logs, this has been explained by the workflow decided by the team acad3. acad3 had decided to create several templates and workflows regarding the incident management; for each incident there are several tickets created for all the subtasks of the incident response. Therefore, most of the tickets were shared internally between these sub-teams of the incident response team of acad3 and after the closure of the event, a ticket is decided to be shared or not. To this end, we defined the metric extrovert to measure the percentage of tickets our unit of enquiry (team/constituency category) that were shared externally:

$$extrovert = \frac{\#externally\_shared\_tickets}{total\_tickets} \qquad (1)$$

Following an analysis on a sample of 70 tickets, the academic constituency was (significantly) faster in closing the tickets than the industrial partners. In terms of making the tickets externally, there were no significant differences.

Figure 5 is an example analysis of the ticket alive time and also shows the breakdown the steps a ticket is going through the incident response workflow. Orange markers show the ticket operation such as assigning to a specific handler or updating the status of a

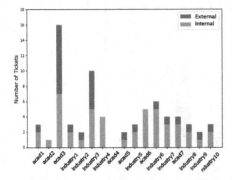

	Constituency category	
	Academic	Industry
tickets	30	40
$\bar{x}_{time}$	13.08	31.60
S_{time}	15.60	29.41
$\bar{x}_e$	0.543	0.612
S_e	0.41	0.40
t-test[prob]	mean time -3.397[0.0011]	
	extrovert -0.700[0.4862]NS	

Fig. 4. Tickets produced and shared by partners (Color figure online)

ticket. Green and blue markers represent attaching a document and referencing a resource to a ticket on the system respectively. Red markers show that a comment is added.

5.2 Team Analysis and Characteristics

Figure 6 shows the results of a regression on the number of team members against the produced number of tickets. We observe that the relationship between these two is exponential, showing that the larger the team size, the exponentially more the number of tickets are produced. However, there was no significant relation in the average lifetime of a ticket and the number of team members (p = 0.778).

5.3 Ticket Analysis

All the tickets that are created and shared within the system has a TLP level as described in Sect. 4. White tickets are for the general audience and can be considered open source while the red level being the disclosed information only distributed to the respondent of the incident. As can be seen in Fig. 7, the average alive time increases monotonically following the increase of confidentiality with a high correlation coefficient of $r = 0.9463$. This could be attributed to the nature of the cyber security incidents as the white and green level tickets are considered as public or generally publishable information and do not necessarily need an action while amber and red tickets are more organisation specific and need more time to analyse, plan and resolve. The pairwise comparisons between partners on their TLP assignments is also shown. While in many instances the sample size may not be considered large enough, the particular comparison of acad3 and industry3 which is significant is noteworthy, as these two partners have the highest number of tickets.

Figure 8 shows the results of a hierarchical clustering using Ward's method on the alive times (as shown with the example partner in Fig. 5) across all partners. Setting the cutoff at 4, we observe three clusters. Interestingly, while there are two small clusters with pure academic or industry members, the bigger cluster (in red) displays itself some visible segmentation between academia and industry, suggesting that these two constituency categories have emergent and esoteric behaviours and dynamics.

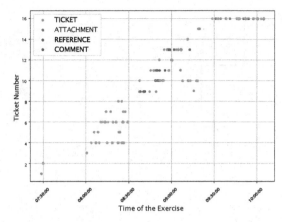

Fig. 5. Example life time of a ticket from the constituency acad3 (Color figure online)

Model Info			Model Fit	
Observations: 17			F(1,15)=52.65, p=0.000	
Dependent variable: ltickets			R^2 = 0.778	
Type: OLS			Adj. R^2 = 0.763	
Coefficients				
	coef.	std. error	t	p
intercept	0.6174	0.120	5.140	0.000
members	0.2656	0.037	7.256	0.000

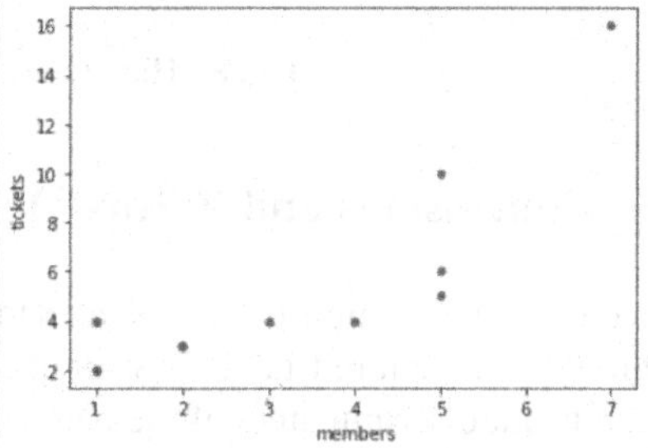

Fig. 6. Regression results (members˜log(tickets))

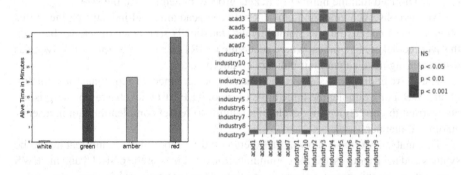

Fig. 7. TLP time and pairwise comparisons (Color figure online)

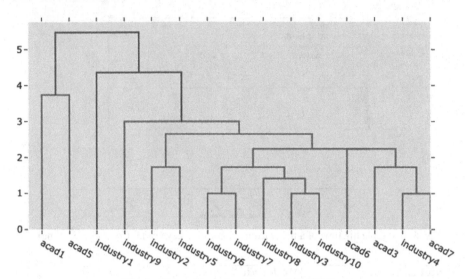

Fig. 8. Hierarchical clustering on ticket lifetime

6 Conclusions and Future Directions

In this paper we empirically evaluated the deployment of ECHO's Early Warning System through a structured tabletop exercise. We observed that the key features that were significant discriminators of the behaviours of the various constituencies were the TLP level and the size of the respective team. Specifically, the higher the confidentiality the ticket was deemed, the more time it took to resolve it. With regards to the size of the team, we noticed that the number of tickets grow exponentially to the size.

We also observed emerging clusters between academic and industry partners; this observation can be partially explained by the statistically significant difference between the average ticket alive times, where academic CSIRTs seems to be more than twice as fast in closing tickets than their industry counterparts.

The above findings can support and guide the development of additional functionality of an EWS. For example, the large alive times of TLP:RED tickets are non surprising, but warrant the investment in developing plugins to redact confidential data in a semi-automated manner.

The analysis exercise showed that there could be more metrics and features to be synthesized in order to assess the communication dynamics of the CSIRTS and the EWS system itself. In this paper we introduced the metric extrovert which shows the degree of a CSIRT sharing their tickets with their peers; however with the current dataset there were no significant differences observed with the average alive time.

For future work, a more expanded dataset would allow the application and exploration of this domain through more advanced algorithms.

Acknowledgement. This work has received funding from the European Union's Horizon 2020 research and innovation program under the grant agreement no 830943 (ECHO).

References

1. Directive (EU) 2016/1148 of the European Parliament and of the Council of 6 July 2016: Concerning measures for a high common level of security of network and information systems across the union. OJ **L 194**, 1–301 (2016)
2. Regulation (EU) 2019/881 of the European Parliament and of the Council of 17 April 2019 on ENISA (The European Union Agency for Cybersecurity) and on information and communications technology cybersecurity certification and repealing regulation (EU) no 526/2013 (cybersecurity act). OJ **L 151**, 15–69 (2019)
3. Bianchi, G., Dargahi, T., Caponi, A., Conti, M.: Intelligent conditional collaborative private data sharing. Futur. Gener. Comput. Syst. **96**, 1–10 (2019). https://doi.org/10.1016/j.future.2019.01.001
4. Burger, E.W., Goodman, M.D., Kampanakis, P., Zhu, K.A.: Taxonomy model for cyber threat intelligence information exchange technologies. In: Proceedings of the 2014 ACM Workshop on Information Sharing and Collaborative Security, WISCS 2014, pp. 51–60. Association for Computing Machinery, New York, NY, USA (2014). https://doi.org/10.1145/2663876.2663883
5. Cybersecurity and Infrastructure Security Agency: Elections Cyber Table-Top Exercise Package (2020)
6. ENISA: EUELEX 19 After Action Report, May 2019
7. ENISA, Europol/EC3: Common Taxonomy for Law Enforcement and The National Network of CSIRTs, p. 16 (2017). https://www.europol.europa.eu/sites/default/files/documents/commontaxonomyforlawenforcementandcsirtsv1.3.pdf
8. ENISA, C., Polska/Nask, C.: Actionable Information for Security Incident Response, November 2014
9. European Commission: Blueprint for Coordinated Response to Large Scale cross-border Cybersecurity Incidents and Crises (2017)
10. European Council: EU Cyber Defence Policy Framework. Technical report, Brussels, November 2018. https://www.consilium.europa.eu/media/37024/st14413-en18.pdf
11. Faiella, M., Gonzalez-Granadillo, G.: Enriching Threat Intelligence Platforms Capabilities (2016)
12. Ilves, L., Evans, T., Cilluffo, F., Nadeau, A.: European Union and NATO global cybersecurity challenges: a way forward. PRISM **6**(2), 126–141 (2016)
13. Kaufmann, H., Hutter, R., Skopik, F., Mantere, M.: A structural design for a pan-European early warning system for critical infrastructures. Elektrotechnik und Informationstechnik **132**(2), 117–121 (2015). https://doi.org/10.1007/s00502-015-0286-5
14. Kick, J.: Cyber exercise playbook. Cyber Exerc. Playbook **7013**(November), 1–40 (2014)
15. Li, V.G., et al.: Reading the tea leaves: a comparative analysis of threat intelligence, pp. 851–868 (2019)
16. Mavroeidis, V., Bromander, S.: Cyber threat intelligence model: An evaluation of taxonomies, sharing standards, and ontologies within cyber threat intelligence. In: Proceedings - 2017 European Intelligence and Security Informatics Conference, EISIC 2017, pp. 91–98, January 2017. https://doi.org/10.1109/EISIC.2017.20
17. Rajamaki, J., Katos, V.: Information sharing models for early warning systems of cybersecurity intelligence. Inf. Secur. Int. J. **46**(2), 198–214 (2020)
18. Schaberreiter, T., et al.: A quantitative evaluation of trust in the quality of cyber threat intelligence sources. In: ACM International Conference Proceeding Series (2019). https://doi.org/10.1145/3339252.3342112

19. Wang, K., Du, M., Sun, Y., Vinel, A., Zhang, Y.: Attack detection and distributed forensics in machine-to-machine networks. IEEE Network **30**(6), 49–55 (2016). https://doi.org/10.1109/MNET.2016.1600113NM
20. White, G.B., Dietrich, G., Goles, T.: Cyber security exercises: testing an organization's ability to prevent, detect, and respond to cyber security events. Proc. Hawaii Int. Conf. Syst. Sci. **37**(C), 2635–2644 (2004). https://doi.org/10.1109/hicss.2004.1265411

Approaching Cyber Situational Awareness Through Digital Services Availability Monitoring and Threat Intelligence: The MonSys Platform Experience

George Sharkov[1,2]([✉]) [iD] and Christina Todorova[1,2] [iD]

[1] European Software Institute – Center Eastern Europe, Sofia, Bulgaria
{gesha,tina}@esicenter.bg
[2] Cybersecurity Laboratory at Sofia Tech Park, Sofia, Bulgaria

Abstract. The security community has long identified cyber situational awareness as a critical component of effective cyber defense on a national, sectoral, and international scale. Additionally, in recent years, and particularly as the online operations of many sectors of daily life have become increasingly interdependent, the need to safeguard individual services to protect entire economic sectors has become increasingly apparent. Intrusion detection and prevention systems (IDS/IPS) are widely recognized as a critical component of an organization's cyber resilience and situational awareness skills, as they are an excellent tool for preventing and detecting malicious activity directed at business operations. The extensive majority of scientific and commercial advances in the field, however, remain widely focused on the development of complex solutions for large enterprises or specific infrastructures, rendering them inaccessible to small and medium-sized enterprises (SMEs), academic institutions, and non-profit organizations that are unable to afford, administer, manage, or even consider employing IDS/IPS in their organizational frame of reference.

This article is a revised and extended version of the "MonSys: A Scalable Platform for Monitoring Digital Services Availability, Threat Intelligence, and Cyber Resilience Situational Awareness" article, published in Information & Security: An International Journal vol. 46, 2020, and proposes an approach to making monitoring systems more widely accessible and shares the lessons learned, and the key findings from the pilot implementation of a platform, specifically designed to address those needs – MonSys. MonSys is a flexible, robust, and scalable monitoring platform, implemented as a cloud-based service and an on-premise solution, which is specifically designed at addressing the need for ensuring digital service availability. It includes customized and standard service integrity and availability checks. Furthermore, this contribution will present some achievements, findings, and ongoing efforts concerning the planned integration of this platform, with the Early Warning System of the ECHO project, while ensuring long-term data storage, custom tests, and alerts, behavior analysis, and information sharing with very little limitations, while preserving excellent scalability with thousands of ad-hoc tests for online services and devices, such as IoT and IIoT.

Keywords: Cybersecurity · Resilience · Early Warning · Situational Awareness

T. Tagarev and N. Stoianov (Eds.): DIGILIENCE 2020, CCIS 1790, pp. 41–60, 2024.
https://doi.org/10.1007/978-3-031-44440-1_4

1 A High-Level Overview of the Cybersecurity Context

Secure data sharing and exchange over the web has proven to be increasingly important for maintaining a standard quality of life nowadays, as well as on the economy and even national security [1, 2]. Especially against the backdrop of the recent developments during 2020, considering the Coronavirus pandemic, which forced many people around the world to switch to a remote office environment, the ever-increasing importance of cybersecurity in all sectors of life and industry has been further highlighted [3].

Throughout recent years, with the increasing complexity of IT solutions, we bore witness to the growing sophistication of cyber threats and attacks, as well as the dire consequences, following the exploitation of vulnerabilities. The evolving threat landscape makes security management within an organization ever so complex, let alone within a household.

Looking back at 2019, attacks against web-based services, including DNS hijacking [4], Distributed Denial of Service attacks, Unauthorized Scanning activities, and exploitation of known vulnerabilities in obsolete Content Management Systems were already on the rise [5]. The FBI's Internet Crime Complaint Center (IC3) revealed that in 2019 alone, they have received a total of 467,361 complaints with reported losses exceeding $3.5 billion [6]. The National Defense Industrial Association, on the other hand, confirmed that attacks against small and medium-sized enterprises are on the rise, however, still, they use security measures such as firewalls and multi-factor authentication at a much lower rate than large companies, as applicable security solutions are often behind a paywall, quite steep for a small company [7].

And the year 2020 was, for the lack of a better word, extraordinary in every regard, including in terms of cybersecurity. Being forced by the circumstances to work, shop, bank, communicate, and seek medical help remotely more than ever before in history, underlined the importance of cybersecurity. By the same token, these unprecedented circumstances have resulted in the need to quickly develop and adopt new ways to enable services from all sectors of the economy to be provided online, leaving little time for vulnerability testing, with cybersecurity incidents and attacks against web bases services becoming pervasive within the healthcare industry [8]. The pandemic put the topic of cybersecurity in the forefront of the media with the unprecedented number of scams and attacks, not only against individuals but entire companies and industry sectors alike [9], with increasing numbers of attacks against the healthcare and the education sectors, which are rich in personal data of value for criminals [10].

Early within the onset of the Coronavirus pandemic, in April, the World Health Organization reported a dramatic increase of cyber-attacks against its staff, against its public, and finally, against its web-based systems [11]. Facilities treating COVID-19 patients, experimental vaccines testing data, and various testing labs have been targeted by ransomware attacks, jeopardizing their activities to ensure citizens' health and safety [12]. Teleconference platforms, such as Zoom, have also been increasingly under attack and scrutiny since the onset of the pandemic [13].

Within the same context, newly developed telemedicine and IoT solutions, as well as a vast plethora of web-based services for the maximization of healthcare efficiency during the pandemic have surged throughout the pandemic, leaving not only limited time for their security testing but also limited resources for their maintenance, patching, and upgrading [14].

Notwithstanding, within our research, we have found that many healthcare, government, and educational web platforms and web-based services in Bulgaria in particular, are not following basic cybersecurity recommendations, when it comes to the maintenance of their services [15].

Said issue continuously and sustainably grows in importance nowadays, with the increasing interconnectivity and interdependence between web-based services [16, 17]. Due to entire economic sectors becoming intertwined in operational activity, the attack surface remains is constantly expanding [18]. As a result of this extensive interconnectivity, an increasingly worrisome perspective rises to the forefront, namely that harmful activities directed against online services might be deliberately employed to harm entire sectors alike [19]. Thus, for the sake of better cybersecurity and resilience capabilities, we face the need for concerted efforts to secure the integrity and availability of both individual systems and sophisticated composite systems-of-systems (SoS) [19].

Providing organizations from different sectors, with tools and instruments to add additional capabilities within their cyberspace, combined with a sector-specific cybersecurity situational awareness frame of reference, is proving to bring a plethora of benefits for organizations, especially within this context, as:

1. it enables cybersecurity centers of excellence, bodies of knowledge, and government agencies to provide structured and targeted recommendations, based on the overall cybersecurity specifics and posture of different economic sectors.
2. it supports organizations, with no cybersecurity traditions, to identify areas of improvement and provides them with the guidelines needed to seek cybersecurity expertise externally or develop it internally.
3. it empowers organizations under the pressure to quickly adapt to remote operations, with a baseline of cybersecurity requirements for their sectors, warnings, alerts, useful information, and recommendations, based on their cybersecurity deficiencies, triangulated with sector-specific insights and best practices and guidelines.
4. it encourages organizations with little capacity to maintain and monitor their web-based services to take a proactive stance in protecting their operations and their clients.
5. it increases the involvement of private cybersecurity companies within the protection of critical infrastructures, by providing them with the insight necessary to inspire innovation, based on the specific needs of different sectors.
6. it drives information exchange, active engagement with cybersecurity, and powers competitiveness and collaboration between industries.

In this contribution, we provide a detailed summary of our experience with the development and the pilot applications of MonSys, a flexible, robust, and scalable monitoring platform for situational awareness and monitoring of online services, developed by our team and implemented as a cloud-based platform and an on-premise solution, which is developed to do just that. We will further present key findings, related to the Bulgarian cyberspace, obtained through our work with the platform during this turbulent year and correlate them with historical data, we have collected, to shed light on the evolution of the Bulgarian cyber picture [27]. Last but not least, we will briefly overview our ongoing work and future directions for the development and contextual implementation of the platform.

2 Typical Application of Availability Monitoring Services

With the rapid increase of cybersecurity attacks and malicious activities online through-out recent years, and especially through the lens of this past year, many efforts have been put into the development of solutions for the intelligent monitoring and protection of web-based services and platforms [20]. Most commonly, these solutions are categorized under the terms Intrusion Detection Systems (IDS) and Intrusion Prevention Systems (IPS). The role of such systems is to, in broader terms, monitor a given infrastructure and based on predefined sets of criteria, report any anomalies, intrusion attempts, etc. Those events are reported through various channels and to various stakeholders, based on another set of predefined rules and alert customizations.

Research into Intrusion Detection Systems (IDS) and Intrusion Prevention Systems (IPS) began in the late nineteenth century and has advanced significantly since then. Currently, Intrusion Detection and Prevention Systems (IDPS) are traditionally separated into four distinct categories [21], as shown in Fig. 1 below:

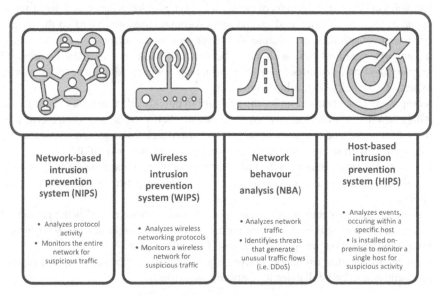

Fig. 1. Classification of IDPS by IDPS type.

The host-based intrusion prevention systems and the network-based intrusion detection systems have been commercially successful and widely recognized, which resulted in them being considered as the two main types of IDPS.

There are other ways to classify IDPS. Some researchers [22] classify them into either "passive" or "active", based on whether the system actively responds through changes in the environment to a potential intrusion, which is the case of active IDPS, or just maintains a log of events and alerts relevant stakeholders about these events, based on predefined criteria.

Others [23] categorize IDPS based on the detection method that they use to recognize an event as a malicious attempt, as shown in Fig. 2 below.

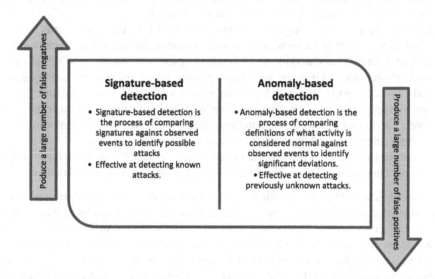

Fig. 2. Comparison between SBD and ABD, following Brandon Lokesak

Of course, other classifications exist, however for this current research, we follow these traditionally identified categories of IDPS. Besides, there are many shortcomings, associated with these traditional approaches to intrusion detection and prevention, a major one of which is the scaling ability of traditional systems.

Furthermore, considering the detection methods, a classic problem is the high rates of false negatives, associated with signature-based detection and, similarly, the high rates of false positives, associated with anomaly-based detection. The high rates of false positives and negatives (which need extensive manual filtering and human capital investment), as well as the requirement to administer and customize monitoring system environments [24]. Additionally, those intrusion detection systems are relatively complex and are typically targeted at large enterprises or specific infrastructures, making them profoundly inaccessible to small and medium-sized enterprises (SMEs), academic institutions, and not-for-profit organizations in terms of cost, administration, management, and even consideration of employing IDS/IPS in their context. Combined, these factors often produce several negative outcomes for SMEs, considering the adoption of monitoring services:

- a need for maintenance and manual filtering of logs – many small and medium-sized enterprises, educational institutions, such as high schools, medical facilities, etc., do not necessarily have the human and financial resources to perform these actions.

- complex for a non-traditionally IT-intensive company – the maintenance, customizations, and metrics are hard to understand and perform in some organizations, which cannot afford to employ people with the following expertise.
- a lack of dedicated resources – many of these solutions are tailored to fit the needs of large enterprises with dedicated IT departments and thus come with a high paywall, which could be steep or at the very least might prove discouraging, for smaller enterprises or organizations in some economical sectors.
- lack of context – not knowing how an organization fits within the cybersecurity context of its sector, might make some security recommendations feel vague or unrelated.
- lack of awareness about skills and knowledge gaps – of course, an IDPS is not a skills framework and it is not its primary purpose to inform customers about skills and knowledge gaps. However, for SMEs, recommendations, based on their context, easily digestible alerts and notifications, and easy customization based on proficiency levels, might make the difference in the overall cybersecurity situational awareness of these enterprises and their cybersecurity posture in the long run.
- low scalability – a lot of resources are often needed, especially when run on-premise, to scale the functionality of the system to fit the growing needs of the business.

Nevertheless, IDPSs play a critical role in enhancing an organization's overall existing knowledge and skills in cybersecurity defense and protection, and by extension, that of a whole sector or network of interconnected online services. An anomaly-detection intrusion prevention system, such as MonSys, would typically collect historical data on a service's normal baseline of activity and availability. Then, using settings, important metrics, and historical intelligence, such systems would monitor, identify, and warn the system's owner to key service failures, hostile or suspicious activity, and so on, with some systems even responding automatically to these behaviors [25]. **This setting necessitates efforts toward developing an accessible and intuitive platform that incorporates robustness, flexibility, and adaptability while also allowing for personalized testing, recommendations, and alerts** [27].

The current contribution proposes a method for rendering intrusion prevention and detection more attainable to organizations of various contexts, sizes, and lines of business to increase cyber-stability and overall cybersecurity posture on a larger scale, as well as to foster cyber-resilience, sectoral capabilities, and awareness about cybersecurity. Last but not least, through the integration of the same team's previously developed instrument, namely CyberMap Bulgaria, within the MonSys platform, the implementation team aimed to improve the cybersecurity situational awareness of organizations in both the public and private sectors by providing them with information and sector-relevant cybersecurity statistics, as well as research-informed and data-driven recommendations.

3   The MonSys Platform

To fill the gaps identified in the current context, we set out to develop an approach to making monitoring systems more widely accessible and share the lessons learned, and the key findings from the pilot implementation of a platform, specifically designed to address those needs – MonSys.

MonSys is a scalable, adaptable, and resilient monitoring platform available as a cloud-based service or on-premise solution. It is purpose-built to solve the demand for assuring the availability of digital services. It comprises both customized and conventional integrity and availability checks for services.

Furthermore, we will present some achievements, findings, and ongoing efforts concerning the planned integration of this platform, with the Early Warning System of the ECHO project, while ensuring long-term data storage, custom tests, and alerts, behavioral analysis, and information sharing with very little limitations, while preserving excellent scalability with thousands of ad-hoc tests for online services and devices, such as IoT and IIoT.

3.1 Overall Architecture

The architectural decisions behind the development of the MonSys platform, are based on the need to provide a scalable, robust and flexible monitoring platform, where particular attention is paid to the processes of metric collection, processing, storage, and querying of data and assuring the confidentiality, integrity, and availability of this data.

Designing the platform with scalability as a first requirement, significantly affected the application's architecture, as it implied that the general design of the platform will be based on interconnected microservices.

To provide a scalable foundation for the MonSys platform's implementation, the team chose the Kubernetes platform, which involves the integration of container infrastructure and yet thus provides a higher-level set of abstractions aimed at empowering and improving modern development and IT operations and their associated workflows.

Among the primary benefits of using the Kubernetes platform for the development of the MonSys platform are illustrated in Fig. 3:

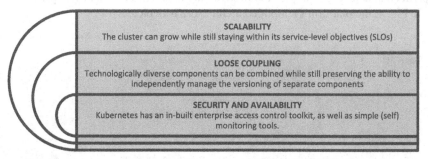

Fig. 3. The primary advantages of using Kubernetes as the foundation for developing the MonSys platform

The implementation team used the Function-as-a-Service (FaaS) computing model to ensure the platform's adaptability. With FaaS technologies, the service's "consumer" can offer bespoke source code to be executed in the service's defined runtime environment, which is typically a container running dynamically mounted code. This code must execute quickly (often between 5 and 15 min) and should have a granularity comparable to that of a function (thus explaining the name of the paradigm).

MonSys can execute custom availability tests for many types of infrastructure using the FaaS paradigm, including multiple black-box, grey-box, and white-box availability checks/metrics. The platform"s inherent flexibility and scalability enable MonSys to be employed in a variety of problematic domains, including the following:

- Data collection on availability and/or security across entire vertical or horizontal supply chain segments, combined with an ability to monitor a vast array of IoT devices, for instance, and rapidly process data, related to them.
- Real-time data extraction from highly specialized services that require a customized test setup, process, or infrastructure.

The existing architectural approach, however, has several notable disadvantages, namely.

- The platform has a high runtime cost "at rest." In practice, this means that even with a zero percent external load, a platform deployment will require significant funding to run (on a public cloud provider). However, as the load is increased (number of domains/services and test frequency), the cost per test drops significantly.
- Due to the informal knowledge base associated with the technologies, the best practices for integrating them are still being developed and pilot tested.

To enhance cybersecurity situational awareness inside the platform, the development team used capabilities from a previously built instrument called CyberMap Bulgaria [26].

CyberMap Bulgaria is a standalone platform collecting and visualizing data that can be used to analyze topics such as chronic vulnerabilities in the Bulgarian cyberspace by domain or sector, or identifying critical points in the Bulgarian public and private IT infrastructure. The implementation team created and implemented a system for the non-intrusive collecting of technical, geographical, organizational, and other data for the experimental database of over 55,000 Bulgarian domains and domain groups.

In Fig. 4, the platform's simplified architecture is depicted:

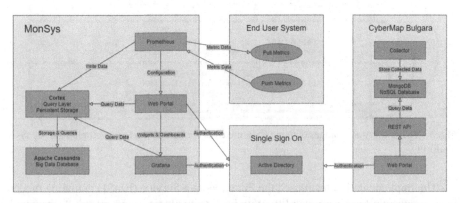

Fig. 4. MonSys's overall architecture and the integration of CyberMap Bulgaria

MonSys is built on the Prometheus monitoring platform. As a native monitoring solution for Kubernetes, it adds architectural and implementation cohesiveness owing to a large number of pre-developed plugins/extensions for connecting Prometheus to a variety of common infrastructure settings and products.

3.2 Key Functionalities

Alerting and Notifications

MonSys's primary feature includes an alerting system. The platform is built around the concept of user customization, and it is through this lens that MonSys collects, analyzes, and visualizes statistics with the goal of not only bringing situational awareness to the monitored service's cybersecurity context, but also alerting the organization to deviations from the standard line of behavior, suspicious activity, or the loss of critical services or functionalities.

The implementation team prioritized the customization of alerting and alerting methods when building the alerting capabilities. At the moment, MonSys notifies users through the platform's dashboard, e-mail, and/or SMS, depending on pre-defined and completely customizable sets of alerting criteria. This gives the user control over the number and type of alerts received, as well as the channels used to receive notifications with varying degrees of priority.

Custom alerts are built in a way that is very similar to custom tests—the alerts are executed within a FaaS environment and provide (alert request) response data through HTTPS.

By default, notifications contain automated informative and actionable elements. An informative item contains news and information on the security status or features of the monitored service's apps, services, and so on. On the other hand, an actionable item is used when the user's active participation is necessary, such as when upgrading a core service.

Finally, MonSys supports notifications issued by humans, such as those sent by the platform's maintenance crew. While such notifications are prioritized by default inside the platform above informational or actionable alerts, the user is fully empowered to create a personalized priority for various sorts of alerts.

Testing

Significant effort has been made to simplify and manage the process of servicing and organizing Black-box testing. Such tests are particularly pertinent to the quality of the end-user experience and satisfaction, as (contrary to what most monitoring systems presume), the real end-user is very seldom, if ever, present within the data center or server room, the domain of white-box testing. Actual service availability and quality are also contingent on the service supply chain and, to a lesser extent, on the end user's network infrastructure, such as their Internet service provider. White-box testing does not take any of those elements into consideration, as by definition, they monitor the service provider's infrastructure, which is only accessible to them.

To enhance the existing black-box testing facilities, the team addressed several underlying technology constraints, such as the execution time for FaaS tests (which is theoretically unlimited in MonSys, unlike most public cloud FaaS services). Additionally, the team engaged in the creation of many black-box tests and test tools that may be used to gain a better understanding of the individual services' availability.

We implemented the following tests and frameworks:

- In-Browser Black Box Testing Toolkit—built on top of Selenium, this framework enables the execution of user-supplied functional tests on Web sites and apps. Support for other in-browser testing platforms, such as cypress.io and puppet, is feasible but has not been deployed at the time of writing. Testing with Laravel/Forge is currently in progress.
- WordPress – being one of the most frequently used content management and blogging platforms [29], WordPress has a sizable user base that may benefit from more data openness.

Dashboarding

Additionally, the platform's development mandated the creation of a standard three-tier web application that acts as the platform's user interface. Due to the implementation team's internal preferences, the web application was created in Python and deployed as a FaaS application on the Kubernetes cluster, allowing for high resource usage and thereby lowering the 'at rest' cost.

The implementation team concentrated on a simple approach for the MonSys platform's frontend component to emphasize the platform's usability and intuitiveness. Users may quickly manage and adjust dashboards, services, alerts, and tests thanks to the basic design.

Visualization Dashboard

The platform's dashboard serves as the end user's monitoring and control panel, allowing them to monitor services, adjust the visualization of data, and conduct retrospectives. To ensure the organization's resilience, end-users required an easily customizable, and adaptable dashboarding service that allowed them to combine and refine metrics and visualizations in a clean and minimal environment while still expanding and researching metadata and contextual information for activity spikes, incidents, and customizable service monitoring metrics.

Service, Test, and Alert Management

The platform's users stressed the critical nature of being able to control the services they wish to dynamically monitor and test simply. This includes the ability to simply add and delete services, build and configure additional tests for distinct services, and adjust the metrics gathered, as well as alerts for specific services.

3.3 Integration with the ECHO Early Warning System

The ECHO Project (the European network of Cybersecurity centers and competence Hub for innovation and Operations) is one of the four pilot initiatives of the Horizon 2020 program of the European Union, established to gather expertise and share knowledge across multiple domains to develop a common cybersecurity strategy for Europe. As part of the initiatives under the ECHO Project is the development of an Early Warning System.

The ECHO Early Warning System (E-EWS) is developed with the purpose to provide a space for the safe exchange of information and coordination of incident response at a European level. The goal of the E-EWS is to provide its users with the opportunity to promptly respond to incidents, share intelligence and warnings, and create a cyber-security culture of proactiveness and prevention. This context provided a space for a bilateral exchange of anonymized and sanitized information between MonSys and the ECHO Early Warning System, thus bringing value to the users of both systems. This was made possible, due to the design of the E-EWS, which is developed to interface standard plugins and systems and allow multiple integrations with external systems through an ecosystem of plugins, offering additional capabilities to the E-EWS.

Since the beginning of 2020, it has been decided that MonSys will be piloted as an external monitoring system, to enter the Early Warning System of the ECHO project through the MonSys Bridge. Within the ECHO context, the MonSys Bridge is a plugin, which allows the integration of functionalities of external monitoring systems, such as (but not limited to) the MonSys platform, within the ECHO Early Warning System.

To allow the ECHO Early Warning System to be standardized and promote integrations such as the MonSys Bridge, the project consortium has built an interface that would allow us to both react to new data inside this system and to allow us to query modified data, contained within the ECHO Early Warning System. This allows the integration to subscribe to different events through plugin management. When those events happen, the system will inform any external system, by sending a webhook when the event has occurred. It is also possible to provide data to the system through a REST interface, however, as will be further discussed below, this is not the case with the MonSys Bridge. The ECHO project has developed a set of data transport models that allow to query, create, and update data within the system. These models are shared as SDK packages, which are used by the different plugins interfaced by the ECHO Early Warning System.

Therefore, the MonSys Bridge works by providing push notifications into the E-EWS to notify users of the E-EWS for events occurring or identified by MonSys, such as:

- Out-of-date security standards and protocols
- Attacks on RDP services and Remote Command Execution
- System misconfigurations
- Anomalous events of unknown origin in complex systems
- Brute-force attacks

The MonSys integration lies on the following functionalities, that MonSys or another monitoring system, through the MonSys Bridge, offers the E-EWS:

- On alert in MonSys, and based on predefined criteria, the bridge will **automatically create a ticket** in the CyberTicketModule of the E-EWS, which is responsible for providing client-side functionality surrounding tickets, templates, and workflows.
- Automatically **generate, upload, and dynamically update reports** from MonSys to the E-EWS based on a predefined schedule, template, and criteria.
- Automatically **upload and dynamically update visualizations** (graphs, charts, maps, etc.) from MonSys to the E-EWS.

These capabilities, as well as the systems that allow them, are depicted in Fig. 5:

The integration of the MonSys platform within the E-EWS, offers users of MonSys to subscribe or view selected intelligence from the E-EWS, such as different resources,

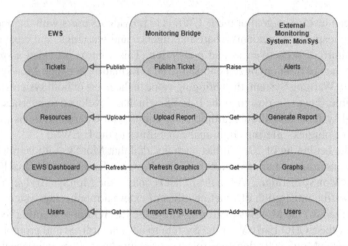

Fig. 5. The MonSys Bridge's overall architecture, as well as its interaction with ECHO's E-EWS

reports, analytics, and graphs, and will offer them the opportunity to subscribe to them, as well as to the ECHO Network.

This collaboration is a key milestone for the future development of the MonSys platform and enriching it with capabilities from external monitoring and early warning systems, offering further intelligence, knowledge, and expertise to extend the overall value of the platform. Likewise, anonymized data, shared across a large network, such as the ECHO network through the ECHO Early Warning System, offers an insight into the Bulgarian cybersecurity context, thus aligning Bulgaria to the European cybersecurity picture and offering the opportunities, at a strategic level, to develop appropriate initiatives, to address regional gaps in cybersecurity.

4   Core Findings and Use Cases

The MonSys integrated platform has been intensively applied, validated, and improved for more than 24 months in various pilot test cases and customer surveys covering both functional groups – services availability monitoring and alerting (MonSys) as well as screening and mapping with of the Bulgarian cyberspace with CyberMap. Some of the key typical findings and practical feedback from real use are presented below.

4.1   Monitoring Web Services Availability and Alerting

MonSys has been used for over 18 months to continuously monitor the availability of a preconfigured set of standard layer-7 services (such as HTTPS, HTTP, TCP, and DNS availability) for over 50 websites and critical information sources for government structures and public administration, as well as various major G2B, G2C, and B2B services (such as the national revenue agency and tax authorities, customs, traffic control, etc.). In light of the upcoming (at the time of writing this article) national elections, and in light of the negative experience and lessons learned from the unprecedented DDoS attacks during the 2015 local elections, relevant real-time information sources, including major media and news sources, have been closely monitored. The platform has proven to be easily scalable and expandable, as well as effective for early warnings of service disruptions and degradation.

A real-life observation of a typical DDoS attack against the website of a government institution is shown in Fig. 6. An unusually delayed HTTPS handshake response that gradually degraded over time was observed (the time shown in Fig. 6, which is examined and confirmed from two different testing locations, in Europe and the USA, respectively. Additional testing locations are also available worldwide for a better picture). This website was under a DDoS protection system, the log files of which show a similar attack pattern as the one, detected through MonSys.

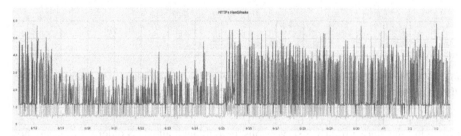

Fig. 6. A typical DDoS attack profile. The HTTPS handshake response times are shown in seconds. The data shown is obtained from two testing points, from the USA and Western Europe. Testing intervals could be customized (between 5 and 15 min in this case)

Another type of frequent observation is related to the improper configuration or inadequate system (or cloud) resources customization. MonSys detects such anomalies and warns against possible degradations in system performance or anticipated services disruption.

Such a case is observed and reported in Fig. 7. In Fig. 7, two different types of clear 24 h patterns in HTTPS handshake response have been identified, for two different websites. For clarity, results from only one test point were visualized, nevertheless, patterns from other testing locations have also been observed and shown to manifest similarly. In one of the cases shown in Fig. 7, the system overload during the daily hours is a direct result of the improper web services configuration. The other case is the result of heavy backup and replication activities during the night hours, thus inhibiting response, which may become problematic.

A third case of web services resources deficit with degrading performance leading to a complete DoS is shown in Fig. 8. As a result of MonSys alerting, a major redesign of the system services and implementation was initiated as a result.

In most of the cases observed, internal systems and web services monitoring were not signaling major performance issues, and only "observation from the outside" (i.e., the customers view of service availability from various test points around the world) as indicated by MonSys was producing early warnings, much before some service is down. Additional HTTPS-related warnings are embedded, such as dynamic monitoring of the validity of the server certificates, or the trusted type (e.g., security recommendations

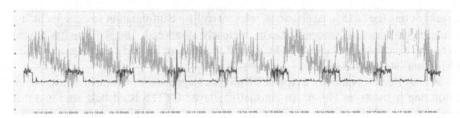

Fig. 7. Two types of system resources deficit or misconfiguration issues with clear 24h pattern, detected by MonSYs based on HTTPS handshake response times (in seconds)

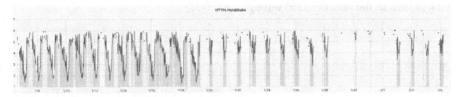

Fig. 8. A systematic system overloading with degrading performance to a complete service disruption (tests from one point are shown, HTTPS response in seconds, interval 15 min)

evolve in time, and currently SSL versions are outdated, and TLS older versions are not recommended anymore). Changes in configurations or other performance parameters could be also detected and alerted for validation.

Another use of MonSys as part of the test cases was to monitor the availability of complex interdependent services, such as for the advanced monitoring of the integrity of the supply chains and logistics services. By monitoring the availability and reaction times of "end-services" as well as a few essential interoperability services participating in the supply chain, a general and standardized behavior pattern may be established.

This enables the discovery of hidden dependencies or previously undisclosed attack routes with a possible cascade effect, as well as the implementation of tailored AI/ML approaches based on acquired actual observation data (which is typically difficult in restricted areas, such as military supplies and operations logistics). By using the Systems-of-Systems approach, MonSys can monitor the behavior of an entire complex and composite system, based on the interoperability of interconnected systems and business processes by looking at key services availability and responsiveness as expected by their "client". MonSys may also be beneficial for tuning the overall performance and potential compromise of web-accessible or internal (isolated services) services through a single integrated platform and dashboard.

Other use cases of MonSys platform include tailored implementations for monitoring services in isolated internal environments for industrial systems and cyber/hybrid exercises (such a Cyber Exercise Orchestrator and Cyber Range), in which a large number and variety of web or other specific services availability need to be simulated, such as ICS/SCADA, PLCs and IIoTs [27].

4.2 Screening the Cyberspace of a Country, Region, or Clusters with CyberMap Bulgaria

CyberMap is the more "static" part of the platform, which is designed to perform a larger-scale scanning and mapping for vulnerabilities at some predefined periods, rather than dynamic monitoring. It was in use for more than three years with continuously improving the tested parameters and the criteria for grouping and correlations. Numerous multi-faceted screenings and analyses have been conducted on subjects ranging from chronic vulnerabilities in Bulgaria's internet by area or industry to identifying crucial locations in the country's public and private IT infrastructure.

The non-intrusive techniques for collecting technical, geographic, organizational, and other data have been tested on an experimental database of approximately 55,000 domains and domain groups registered in Bulgaria (of the.bg TLD). It can serve for understanding better the vulnerabilities and ways of reducing cyber risk at the sectoral and sub-sectoral level, as outlined in [28]. Periodical or on-demand surveys support the identification of the progress of measures and initiatives at sectoral or territorial principles. A standard yearly based survey, performed for three years already, includes the following three groups:

- Central administration – websites of the central government, administration, and ministries (37 sites)
- Local administration – the sites of the municipalities and local/regional administrative services (around 220 sites)
- A reference group of "business organizations" – industry and services (around 260 sites)
- The total space of registered (and active) domains in the ".bg" top-level domain (around 47 000)
- "Big admin group" - a larger group of public administration services (agencies)

As shown in Fig. 9, the web platforms of the central and local administrations are gradually improving but still not sufficiently protecting their websites with TLS. Within the group of the private business organization, we could see a better-looking overall picture, showing that most of the analyzed web platforms are using TLS.

The global picture of the ".bg" top-level domain with aggregated results from 2018 and 2020 is quite troublesome, as no significant improvement is observed despite the initiatives and measures at a national level (such as "HTTPS only", declared in the National Cybersecurity Strategy of 2016).

A similar gradually improving trend can be observed with relation to the distribution of server versions, as shown in Fig. 10. A remarkable improvement of the share of outdated web servers in central administration is a positive sign and clear result of the systematic measures (e.g., the EU NIS Directive implementation and the Bulgarian Cybersecurity Act of 2018). The group of local administration demonstrates a low % of outdated web servers with known vulnerabilities, but there might be a considerably large hidden number of vulnerable platforms in the not-displayed versions.

In all groups, an increasing number of "supported" versions in 2019 and 2020 as compared to 2018 is a positive sign. With the business organizations, the platforms that

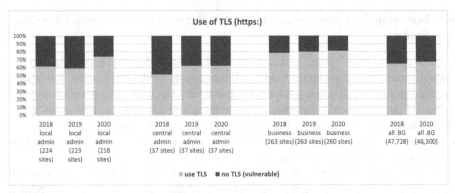

Fig. 9. Comparison of the distribution of TLS usage among local administration, central public administration, business organizations sample and the ".bg" top-level domain (2018, 2019, and 2020)

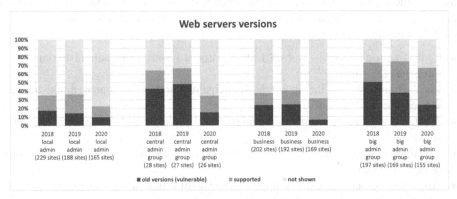

Fig. 10. Comparison of the distribution of outdated (known as vulnerable), new and not-displayed server versions used by the web platforms of the local administration, central public administration, business organizations, and a larger group of public administration services (agencies) in 2019–2020

are known to be running on outdated servers decreased from around 20% down to under 5%, however, we can see a tendency for the web server version information to be hidden.

Contrary to the expectation, there is no visible improvement between 2018 and 2019, but the significant change in 2020 might be a result of the quickly virtualized life due to the COVID-19 pandemic and the spotlight on cybersecurity. A separate study in the much larger business group provides a correlation with organization size, the profile of SMEs per sector, clusters, and territorial dependencies. Such surveys and analyses help in constructing a static picture of the overall state and well-being of the Bulgarian cyberspace, as it enables experts to come up with sectoral recommendations, actions, and supporting programs. Periodical scanning (at least yearly) and tracking various groups (clustered by organization type or size, sector, geography, or other parameters) would allow warnings and predictions about potential cyber threats and known vulnerabilities to be exploited and will serve as a baseline for further dynamic monitoring of the state by the combined MonSys platform.

5 Ongoing Research and Conclusions

Improved cyber-stability and achieving a stronger cybersecurity posture of individual organizations are paramount to maintaining resilience and security across multiple economic sectors, due to the interconnectivity and the reliability between digital services. Against this backdrop, intrusion prevention and detection systems are proven to be a powerful instrument for the intelligent monitoring and protection of web-based services and platforms. Regrettably, typical intrusion detection and prevention systems are frequently unavailable to small and medium-sized businesses (SMEs), academic institutions, and not-for-profit organizations, due to both a paywall on one hand and extensive maintenance requirements on the other.

With the development of MonSys, an intelligent availability monitoring, and alerting system, we aim to address this mismatch between supply and demand of robust, and scalable monitoring solutions and offer a flexible instrument, that supports customization towards a large variety of organizational and technological contexts and needs. To further address this need, we developed MonSys as a cloud-based service as well as an on-premises solution to make intrusion prevention capabilities more available to enterprises of varying backgrounds and capabilities.

Our ongoing research reflects our desire to engage a multi-stakeholder community of organizations from diverse challenging sectors, such as IoT and IIoT. Thus we aim at beginning a fruitful examination related to the adaptability and elastic resource management for the on-demand rapid extension of testing services across thousands of devices. Moreover, we are currently researching various approaches for the optimization of the service activation time through the FaaS approach, both through locally deployed lambdas on OpenWhisk and through lambda deployment on AWS. Through these efforts, we aim to underline the importance of the fact that all devices, connected to the Internet, are a factor for the overall cybersecurity posture of the local cyberspace, and thus there's a highlighted need to implement risk management and cybersecurity situational awareness mechanisms in place, that can react to the specific challenges, proposed by the IoT and IIoT devices and solutions.

To achieve a better alerting granularity, we are also currently experimenting with intelligent alerting through machine learning-based behavioral analysis, including machine learning methods for decreasing the number of false positives.

This contribution summarized our overall strategy for enhancing cyber-stability and the overall cybersecurity posture on a larger scale by providing accessible availability monitoring instruments to support the development of stronger sectoral capabilities and risk management practices, as well as raising overall awareness about cybersecurity. The implementation team's goal throughout the development of the MonSys platform was to increase organizations' cybersecurity situational awareness, by providing them with information and sector-relevant cybersecurity intelligence, as well as research-informed and data-driven recommendations, via the integration of the CyberMap Bulgaria software service, previously developed by the same implementation team, as part of MonSys.

Through the development of MonSys, we aim to support the development, maintenance, and refinement of accessible monitoring capabilities, which contribute to the betterment of the overall cybersecurity situational awareness of organizations, share relevant intelligence, set higher cybersecurity standards, and protect the web services, that drive our economy forward to strengthen the integrity and resilience of the security of the Bulgarian cyberspace.

Acknowledgments. The pilot version of MonSys is a project, financed under agreement № D-094 / 27.09.2019 by the Research and Development and Innovation Consortium (Sofia Tech Park JSC) and Nemetschek Bulgaria. The activities under the project were carried out within the period October 2019 - March 2020 by the Cybersecurity Lab at Sofia Tech Park JSC with the support of the European Software Institute - Center Eastern Europe (ESI CEE) and CyResLab of ESI CEE. The experimental results of MonSys shown were partially funded under an annual grant by the "Bulgaria National Roadmap for Research Infrastructure 2017–2023". Part of the pilot research and implementation of the system was performed under the ECHO Project, which has received funding from the European Union's Horizon 2020 Research and Innovation programme, under grant agreement № 830943.

References

1. Abu-Taieh, E.M.: Cyber security body of knowledge. In: 2017 IEEE 7th International Symposium on Cloud and Service Computing (SC2), pp. 104–111 (2017). Kanazawa. https://doi.org/10.1109/SC2.2017.23
2. Davis, N., Schwab, K.: Shaping the Future of the Fourth Industrial Revolution. Penguin UK. 0241366399 (2018)
3. Cisco Cybersecurity Report Series, Simplify to Secure (2020). https://www.cisco.com/c/dam/en/us/products/collateral/security/simplify-to-secure-report-cybersecurity-series-june-2020.pdf
4. Cisco Cybersecurity Report Series, Threats of the Year: A look back at the tactics and tools of 2019, Threat Report (2019). https://www.cisco.com/c/dam/en/us/products/collateral/security/2019-threats-of-the-year-cybersecurity-series-dec-2019.pdf
5. APCERT. Asia Pacific Computer Emergency Response Team (APCERT) Report 2019. White Paper, APCERT (2019). https://www.apcert.org/documents/pdf/APCERT_Annual_Report_2019.pdf
6. Federal Bureau of Investigation's Internet Crime Complaint Center (IC3), 2019 Internet Crime Report. https://pdf.ic3.gov/2019_IC3Report.pdf
7. National Defense Industrial Association, Beyond obfuscation: The Defense Industry's Position within Federal Cybersecurity Policy. A Report of the NDIA Policy Department (2019). https://www.ndia.org/-/media/sites/ndia/policy/documents/cyber/beyond-obfuscation_final.ashx
8. Jalali, M.S., Kaiser, J.: Cybersecurity in hospitals: a systematic, organizational perspective (January 11, 2018). MIT Sloan Research Paper No. 5264–18, J. Medical Internet Res. **20**(5), e10059 (2018). SSRN: https://ssrn.com/abstract=3100364 or https://doi.org/10.2139/ssrn.3100364
9. The 2020 Official Annual Cybercrime Report. Herjavic Group (2020). https://tinyurl.com/y56trmgv
10. Argaw, S.T., Troncoso-Pastoriza, J., Lacey, D., Florin, M., Calcavecchia, F., Anderson, D., et al.: Cybersecurity of hospitals: discussing the challenges and working towards mitigating the risks. BMC Med. Inform. Decis. Mak. **20**(1), 146 (2020)

11. WHO reports a fivefold increase in cyber-attacks, urges vigilance. World Health Organization (2020). https://www.who.int/news/item/23-04-2020-who-reports-fivefold-increase-in-cyber-attacks-urges-vigilance

12. NJCCIC Advisory. Cyber Threats & Cybersecurity for Healthcare During COVID-19 (2020). https://www.cyber.nj.gov/alerts-advisories/cyber-threats-cybersecurity-for-health care-during-covid-19

13. The Hacker News, COVID-19: Hackers Begin Exploiting Zoom's Overnight Success to Spread Malware (2020). https://thehackernews.com/2020/03/zoom-video-coronavirus.html

14. Jalali, M.S., Kaiser, J., Siegel, M., Madnick, S.: The internet of things (IoT) promises new benefits — and risks: a systematic analysis of adoption dynamics of IoT products (August 18, 2017). MIT Sloan Research Paper No. 5249–17, SSRN: https://ssrn.com/abstract=3022111 or https://doi.org/10.2139/ssrn.3022111

15. Sharkov, G., Todorova, C., Papazov, Y., Koykov, G., Zahariev, G.: Cybersecurity tools for threat intelligence and vulnerability monitoring for national and sectoral analysis. Information Security in Education and Practice, Edition 1, Chapter 1, Cambridge Scholars Publishing (2020)

16. Sforzin, A., Marmol, F., Conti, M., Bohli, J.: RPiDS: Raspberry Pi IDS - a fruitful intrusion detection system for IoT. 2016 Intl IEEE Conferences on Ubiquitous Intelligence & Computing, Advanced and Trusted Computing, Scalable Computing and Communications, Cloud and Big Data Computing, Internet of People, and Smart World Congress (2016)

17. Da Veiga, A., Astakhova, L., Botha, A., Herselman, M.: Defining organisational information security culture - perspectives from academia and industry. Comput. Secur. **92**, 101–713 (2020). https://doi.org/10.1016/j.cose.2020.101713

18. Wing, J., Manadhata, P.: An attack surface metric. IEEE Trans. Software Eng. **37**, 371–386 (2011). https://doi.org/10.1109/TSE.2010.60

19. Suryotrisongko, H., Musashi, Y.: Review of cybersecurity research topics, taxonomy, and challenges: interdisciplinary perspective. In: 2019 IEEE 12th Conference on Service-Oriented Computing and Applications (SOCA), pp. 162–167 (2019). Kaohsiung, Taiwan

20. Zhao, H., Feng, Y., Koide, H., Sakurai, K.: An ANN based sequential detection method for balancing performance indicators of IDS. In: 2019 Seventh International Symposium on Computing and Networking (CANDAR), pp. 239–244 (2019). Nagasaki, Japan. https://doi.org/10.1109/CANDAR.2019.00039

21. Scarfone, K., Mell, P.: Special publication 800–94: a guide to intrusion detection and prevention systems (IDPS), National Institute of Standards and Technology (NIST) (2007). https://nvlpubs.nist.gov/nistpubs/Legacy/SP/nistspecialpublication800-94.pdf

22. Scarfone, K., Mell, P.: Intrusion detection and prevention systems. In: Stavroulakis, P., Stamp, M. (eds) Handbook of Information and Communication Security. Springer, Berlin, Heidelberg (2010). https://doi.org/10.1007/978-3-642-04117-4_9

23. Brandon Lokesak. A Comparison Between Signature Based and Anomaly Based Intrusion Detection Systems (2008)

24. Liu, Y., Xiangdong, C., Lakkaraju, S.: Understanding Modern Intrusion Detection Systems: A Survey (2017)

25. Liao, H., Lin, C., Lin, Y., Tung, K.: Intrusion detection system: a comprehensive review. J. Netw. Comput. Appl. **36**(1), 16–24 (2013). https://doi.org/10.1016/j.jnca.2012.09.004

26. Sharkov, G., Papazov, Y., Todorova, C., Koykov, G., Georgiev, M., Zahariev, G.: Cyber threat map for national and sectoral analysis. Workshop on Information Security 2019, 9th Balkan Conference in Informatics, 26–28 September 2019. Vol. 13, No. 2/2019, pp. 29–33 (2019). Computer and Communications Engineering, Sofia

27. Sharkov, G., Papazov, Y., Todorova, C., Koykov, G., Zahariev, G.: MonSys: a scalable platform for monitoring digital services availability, threat intelligence, and cyber resilience situational

awareness. Information & Security: An International J. **46**(2), 155–167 (2020). https://doi.org/10.11610/isij.4611

28. Tagarev, T., Pappalardo, S.M., Stoianov, N.: A logical model for multi-sector cyber risk management. Information & Security: An International J. **47**(1), 13–26 (2020). doi:https://doi.org/10.11610/isij.4701

29. "Content Management Systems: The Five Most Used Platforms." Jin Design. jin-design.com (2021). https://jin-design.com/content-management-systems-the-five-most-used-platforms/

Protecting Critical Infrastructures and Essential Services from Cyberattacks

Cyber Security Threats in the Public Hosting Services

Ivan Blagoev[✉]

Institute of Information and Communication Technologies - Bulgarian Academy of Sciences,
Acad. G. Bonchev Str., Bl.2, 1113 Sofia, Bulgaria
`ivan.blagoev@iict.bas.bg`

Abstract. In the digital transformation era where covid-19 leaves no time to slow down the digitization process, because this slowdown can cost human health and lives. The rapid switching to many digital solutions that technological advancement provides is the salvation from the growing covid threat that continues to take its toll. But Cybercrime embodied in terrorism, kidnapping, industrial and economic espionage can be no less dangerous to modern society. In this study, we focus on the Cyber security of widespread services, where we find problems and offer possible solutions. The subject of the analysis is the cryptographic protection and the generators for generating random numbers RNG and PRNG. The results of the proposed method are discussed and is a shown possibility increasing cryptographic protection of the information systems.

Keywords: Cybersecurity · cryptography · RNG · entropy · cryptography protocols · web hosting

1 Introduction

The normal development of humanity leads us to increasingly digitalization. More and more activities and processes are much more productive and effectively managed through technology. These processes even accelerated and proved their worth when the world was affected by the global pandemic COVID-19. Processes that would take years had to happen in months, and society had to look for a new way of life that was much more technology related. At first glance, it seems that the world is prepared for such a technological challenge. To some extent this is the case, but the number of cybercrimes has increased and the encroachment on personal data, money and loss of information, extortion due to loss of information has also escalated to unprecedented levels. All of this is a strong indicator that while technology and computing infrastructure have met the challenge, we are not ready for strong cyber security [1–3]. The aim of this study is to focus on cyber security issues in public services, which are easily accessible and widespread.

© The Author(s), under exclusive license to Springer Nature Switzerland AG 2024
T. Tagarev and N. Stoianov (Eds.): DIGILIENCE 2020, CCIS 1790, pp. 63–72, 2024.
https://doi.org/10.1007/978-3-031-44440-1_10

2   Random Number Generator

Each encryption system basically relies on a random number generator. Therefore, no matter how complex cryptographic algorithms we use, they are as strong as the random number generator that underlies on this system. There are two main types of random number generators in cryptography systems [4]:

- Random Number Generator (RNG): If necessary, RNG is applied at a given time by generating values that must be unique and must not be repeated on subsequent RNG calls. The numbers obtained with this type of RNG are applied to operations that require unique and non-repeating numerical values generated over time. An example of such a situation is the generation of a cryptographic key for encoding or decoding data, initialization vectors, initial numerical values for controlled RNG, and others.
- Pseudo Random Number Generator (PRNG): The initial SEED number is used as the basis for this generator. All randomly generated random numbers originate from this value by means of an algorithm. These values in their order are re-reproducible. The only unexpected and secret value that should be as unpredictable as possible is the SEED number, which is the "root" at the base of this number sequence and the basis for generating the entire number range [4]. This technology is most often used for One Time Password (OTP) authentication, the generation of cryptographic keys derived from the Master Root Key, which is used in the compilation of portfolios in Block Chain - distributed ledger technology, authentication via HMAC, etc.

The effectiveness of RNG is measured by the degree of entropy for the generation of random numbers [5]. The complexity of analyzing a given RNG is a function of the quality of its entropy.

The quality of the RNG entropy is ensured by the researched service, namely, - shared web hosting. What is special for this service is that platforms of this type share the entire hardware resource between many users and their web service applications [6]. We still do not know if this shared hardware has real RNG. But if True RNG exists on the server and many users simultaneously "drain" this shared RNG resource through their web applications, then it can be assumed that the RNG entropy may crash. Therefore, the entire RNG entropy will be compromised, but this fact will remain hidden from the average user of shared hosting. This for a malicious cybercriminal with enough knowledge will be the perfect time for any attacks due to the breakthrough in cryptographic protection.

3   Study of the State of Public Hosting Service

The following is a study on the state of the service, which includes:

- IP address;
- TCP ports;
- Web service;
- cPanel service;
- DNS administration panel;
- Mail service.

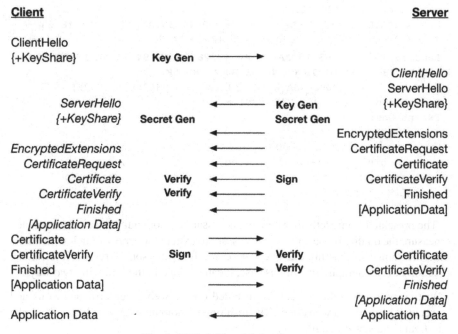

Fig. 1. TLSv1.2 handshake diagram.

To be protected when transmitting data over HTTP, the channel between the client (usually a web browser) and the server is encrypted by a TLS tunneling protocol, which at the packet level envelops the data transmitted in pure form. TLS consists of 2 phases - handshake and channel establishment via session key. [2, 3] The level of information security is determined by the agreed set of cryptographic algorithms, key lengths and generated random numbers that are exchanged between server and client in the handshake phase (Fig. 1).

The unpredictability of obtaining random numbers from the system significantly affects the initial results of cryptographic operations. The TLS session key is formed after transformations with random numbers generated by the server and the client. Because the client does not always have a reliable method for obtaining real random numbers, this default task is always given on the server side. [1] Here is an example of Hello shaking hands and getting a random number from a server:

```
   Version: 3.3 (TLS/1.2)
   SessionID: 23 6C F0 EA 52 FA 7A E9 40 35 AA 23 17 55 1E 24 6C
9D C8 81 59 F5 CF 92 30 D2 11 1D 12 F9 2A 33
   Random:      95 C6 63 18 AA 32 44 47 28 00 4B 94 2D AA F9 3B 12
9D 69 54 4B 45 1A B1 1E CA 4D DE B0 A3 86 5F
   Cipher:      TLS_ECDHE_RSA_WITH_AES_128_GCM_SHA256 [0xC02F]
   CompressionSuite:  NO_COMPRESSION [0x00]
   Extensions:
       server_name empty
       renegotiation_info 00
       ec_point_formats uncompressed              [0x0],           an-
siX962_compressed_prime [0x1], ansiX962_compressed_char2 [0x2]
       ALPN  http/1.1
```

The presented frame tells us where the necessary random numbers can be extracted to measure the quality of entropy. It is necessary to extract the array of random numbers (which is shown in the frame above) and come from the source responsible for the operation of cryptography [6]. In this case, it can be done in the following two ways:

1. Writing program code that can be installed on the web space provided to us and executed by calling a web client. The resulting random numbers can be received like a stream and saved in a file.
2. Even if you have not web hosting control, it can be done as client when making HTTPS web requests to the hosting service. Again, a computer program written in Python is used that establishes a TLS connection like a normal web client. Then, in the Server Hello and TLS handshake phases, the data from the random number generator is extracted and saved to a file. When this operation is repeated sufficiently, the data needed to study the quality of random numbers will be collected. However, if this approach is used, some delay between sessions should be provided so as not to over-open an excessive number of connections to the server. This will lead to slower data collection compared to approach 1, but it will be safer [6].

Following one of the above two methods, a binary array is compiled, which is written to a file in the form of data. These data with random numbers can be subjected to high-intensity computational analysis, which will assess the quality of their entropy.

In our study, the specialized open-source software "Dieharder" was used [7]. The quality of an array of random numbers can be described by mathematical analysis.

The simulation of 114 tests and various cryptographic operations were conducted. The quality of the values applied in the cryptography by the hosting server is below the levels of reliable cryptographic and cyber security of FIPS-140 and other world laboratories.

A summary of the data from the random number simulation test shows:

- Only 25 tests passed successfully,
- 76 tests failed, because they had compromised or predictable value and therefore detectable cryptography,
- 13 tests were vulnerable; this means cryptography can be detected with relatively good computer hardware.

From the presented results it can be considered that due to the weaknesses in the random numbers and the established violation of cryptographic protection, the hosting service can become a victim of various types of hacker attacks. Some of the well-known ones are such as content substitution and misleading the user, which can lead to various consequences, such as fake news, personal data leaks, access to other systems used by the user, encroachment on server resources, etc. [8]. Unfortunately, the problem is that with such a technological implementation, the provided public hosting services will always have the presented fundamental shortcomings. The advantage is that they are extremely affordable, easy to configure and cheap [6]. Their benefits should not be overlooked. From the presented results it can be concluded that services with such a level of cyber protection are not desirable to use for systems with critical functionality or working with personal data. In this case it is better to provide hosting on their own server or a leased virtual private server (VPS), where the number of concurrent systems will not exceed the capabilities of the shared system resources used to secure the cryptography.

Another type of solution would be to try to increase the entropy quality of the hosting server through specialized software. However, often it is more difficult for such systems to collect entropy by software way than other types of systems, because they lack peripherals and some other activities that would help, and often the activity of the hardware is not enough to enrich the entropy of random numbers faster. For this reason, it is recommended such systems to be supported by some additional hardware activity.

4 Software Way to Enrichment of Entropy Collection

Here is an example of such a configuration of a sample virtual machine with Debian 10 operating system.

In the entropy buffer, the value is extremely insufficient for the needs of a system:

```
$ cat /proc/sys/kernel/random/entropy_avail
108
```

Another check with the command pv:

```
# pv /dev/random > /dev/null
   40 B 0:00:15 [    0 B/s] [                    <=>
]
   52 B 0:00:23 [    0 B/s] [                    <=>
]
   58 B 0:00:25 [5.81 B/s] [           <=>        .
]
   64 B 0:00:30 [6.05 B/s] [                    <=>
]
^C
```

Installing software designed to enrich the entropy in a software way:

```
# apt install haveged
# systemctl start rngd
# update-rc.d haveged defaults
# rngd -r /dev/urandom
# systemctl start haveged
```

Here are the experimental results after the proposed changes:

```
$ cat /proc/sys/kernel/random/entropy_avail
3226

# pv /dev/random > /dev/null
7.12MiB  0:00:05  [1.43MiB/s]  [                                    <=>
]
15.7MiB  0:00:11  [1.44MiB/s]  [                                    <=>
]
27.2MiB  0:00:19  [1.46MiB/s]  [                                    <=>
]
  43MiB  0:00:30  [1.47MiB/s]  [                                    <=>
]
^C
```

The results show that the buffer has accumulated entropy capacity. The results with the pv command are no less impressive. It can be seen before starting the haveged speed is 2.1 bits per second (B/s), while after starting the haveged and adding CPU jitter to the Entropy pool you get ~1.5 MB/s. There is also a slightly more non-standard measure that can be applied. It can be done by adding an additional software solution that creates hardware activity that enriches entropy collection. For this case, a script is used that is suitable for server systems that do not have peripherals:

```
#!/bin/sh
## list of sites using round-robin DNS
ROUND_ROBINS="www.yahoo.com          google.com          twitter.com
outlook.com"
## Entropy stard and end value limits
STOP_LIMIT="3500"
START_LIMIT="3800"

until [ "$(cat /proc/sys/kernel/random/entropy_avail)" -gt
"$STOP_LIMIT" ]
  do while [ "$(cat /proc/sys/kernel/random/entropy_avail)" -lt
"$START_LIMIT" ]
      do for thing in "/tmp/loyeyoung" "/tmp/sueellen"
"/tmp/rootdev" "/tmp/files"
            do echo $thing ===================================
                touch /tmp/toss
                for robins in $ROUND_ROBINS
                    do nslookup "$robins" 8.8.8.8 > /tmp/toss
                        nslookup "$robins" 9.9.9.9 >> /tmp/toss
                        nslookup "$robins" 192.168.2.3 >> /tmp/toss
                        nslookup "$robins" >> /tmp/toss
                        cat /tmp/toss
                        mkdir $thing -p
                        cp /tmp/toss $thing/toss
                        cat $thing/toss
                        rm -f /tmp/toss
                        rm -f $thing/toss
                    done
                done
            done
        done
```

This script is quite basic and could be enriched and even written in other programming or scripting languages. But for the purposes of this study, it was able to give the expected results by improving the rate of entropy accumulation, which contributes to the system in question to withstand greater loads on the generation of RNG values. The code shows that the execution of the operations in the memory, processor, disk and network will be activated when the value reaches 3500 in the entropy pool. The process will stop when it reaches a value higher than 3800:

```
$ cat /proc/sys/kernel/random/entropy_avail
3820
```

The solution presented so far gives good results, but it would not be enough with an overloaded server for shared hosting. It will indeed improve the results to some extent, but it cannot solve the problems, because entropy-consuming sources would exceed the entropy collecting speed in the buffer.

This solution could also be supported by a hardware solution that Intel offers for its processors. The name of the module is Intel Secure Key, its previous code name was Bull Mountain Technology. With this name, Intel defines the extension in its Intel64 and IA-32 RDRAND processors and the related hardware implementation of the Digital

Random Number Generator (DRNG). Among other things, DRNG using the RDRAND instruction can be extremely useful in generating high-quality cryptographic protocol keys. Therefore, in order to be able to use this solution, it is necessary to check whether the processor used offers this extension:

```
$ cat /proc/cpuinfo | grep -i rdrand | echo $?
0
```

The result 0 means that the rdrand flag is present and the processor can be turned on to improve the cryptographic functions of the system as follows:

```
# apt install rng-tools-debian
# /etc/init.d/rng-tools-debian start
# /etc/init.d/rng-tools-debian status
* rng-tools-debian.service - LSB: rng-tools (Debian variant)
    Loaded: loaded (/etc/init.d/rng-tools-debian; generated)
    Active: active (running) since Fri 2020-11-28 17:30:54 EET;
3min 10s ago
      Docs: man:systemd-sysv-generator(8)
     Tasks: 4 (limit: 4915)
    Memory: 1.3M
    CGroup: /system.slice/rng-tools-debian.service
            `-3597 /usr/sbin/rngd -r /dev/hwrng

$ cat /proc/sys/kernel/random/entropy_avail
4096
```

The results show that the rate of entropy collection in our case exceeds the rate of its consumption. But the machine used for the present study has a modern Intel Xeon processor and the applications hosted on it do not exceed the capacity of the random number generator and entropy collection means. With a multi-application and shared server system, it would be appropriate to monitor the rate of random number flow. Then, if the values are insufficient, despite all the settings on the hardware and software optimization for this, more machines will have to be provided for the distribution of customer services and applications on them or the addition of an additional hardware module for random number generation (TRNG).

5   Hardware Random Number

A hardware random number generator (HRNG) or real random number generators (TRNG) are devices that generate random numbers from a physical process, not through an algorithm. This makes them radically different from the possible solutions considered so far. Because such devices are often based on microscopic phenomena that generate low-level, statistically random signals for "noise", such as thermal noise, a photoelectric effect involving a beam splitter, and other quantum phenomena. These stochastic processes are considered completely unpredictable in theory. This contrasts with the paradigm for generating pseudo-random numbers, often used in computer programs. In general, two main sources of practical quantum-mechanical physical chance are known: quantum mechanics at the atomic or subatomic level and thermal noise (some of which are of quantum-mechanical origin). Quantum mechanics predicts that some physical phenomena, such as the nuclear decay of atoms, are fundamentally random and generally unpredictable.

Since the result of quantum mechanical events cannot be predicted even in principle, they are the "gold standard" for generating random numbers. Quantum photon generators are considered to be one of the best random number generators for server systems, because they are compact enough and can fit on a computer board and have a very high performance. Most likely, such a hardware module of this type could power more than one such public hosting server with quality random numbers.

6   Conclusions

The study of the presented services and their level of cyber security is of key importance for a safer and faster transition to modern digital transformation. The rapid transfer of all social and economic activities to digital platforms proves that the existing technological infrastructure can meet today's challenges of digitalization [8, 9]. But in terms of cyber security, many of the current IT services are still lagging behind. Increasing the success rate of cybercrime would lead to a loss of confidence in technology and the obstruction of these processes, which will also affect scientific and technological progress. This will significantly slow down the development of many other related areas in the economy, security, technology and others. Therefore, it can be said that now it is absolutely necessary to make efforts to increase cyber resilience in all directions.

The focus on cyber security issues in public hosting services, which are easily accessible and widespread, is well-timed. The ways to improve the quality of random number generators, both software and hardware, are indicated. This investigation can be used for ensuring cyber protection of all technological activities and services.

Acknowledgement. This research is partially supported by the Bulgarian Ministry of Education and Science under the National Scientific Program "Information and Communication Technologies for a Single Digital Market in Science, Education and Security (ICTinSES)".

References

1. Jang-Jaccard, J., Nepal, S.: A survey of emerging threats in cybersecurity. J. Comput. Syst. Sci. **80**(5), 973–993 (2014)
2. Kostadinov, G., Atanasova, T.: Security policies for wireless and network infrastructure. Prob. Eng. Cybern. Rob. **71**, 14–19 (2019)
3. Dineva, K.; Atanasova, T.: Security in IoT systems. In: 19th International Multidisciplinary Scientific GeoConference SGEM 2019, book 2.1, pp. 569–578 (2019)

4. Pseudo-Random Number Generators. https://crypto.stanford.edu/pbc/notes/crypto/prng.html
5. Blagoev, I.: Method for evaluating the vulnerability of random number generators for cryptographic protection in information systems. In: Dimov, I., Fidanova, S. (eds.) Advances in High Performance Computing: Results of the International Conference on "High Performance Computing" Borovets, Bulgaria, 2019, pp. 391–397. Springer International Publishing, Cham (2021). https://doi.org/10.1007/978-3-030-55347-0_33
6. Blagoev, I.: Neglected cybersecurity risks in the public internet hosting service providers. Inf. Secur. J. **47**(1), 62–76 (2020). https://doi.org/10.11610/isij.4704
7. Brown R. G.: Dieharder: A Random Number Test Suite. https://webhome.phy.duke.edu/~rgb/General/dieharder.php
8. McKinsey & Company: Perspectives on transforming cybersecurity. Digital McKinsey and Global Risk Practice (2019)
9. Balabanov, T., Zankinski, I., Tomov, P., Petrov, P., Kostadinov, G.: Distributed computing cybersecurity in donated computing resources for evolutionary algorithms. In: Scientific Conference on Actiual Security Issues, Veliko Tarnovo, Bulgaria, pp. 697–704 (2020)

Big Data and Artificial Intelligence
for Cybersecurity

Towards Data-Centric Security for NATO Operations

Konrad Wrona[(✉)]

NATO Cyber Security Centre, Oude Waalsdorperweg 61, 2597 Ak The Hague,
The Netherlands
`konrad.wrona@ncia.nato.int`

Abstract. Providing efficient data protection and information sharing
capability across different security domains, belonging to NATO, the
Nations and specific Communities of Interest (COI), is of paramount
importance for effective execution of NATO operations. Current information protection practices rely to a large extent on a network-layer mechanism for compartmentalization of information and separation between
different COIs. This leads to segregation of networks into separate network domains and the implementation of perimeter defence at the boundaries of these domains. Data-centric security (DCS) architecture rather
than focusing on network perimeter defence focuses on securing access
to the data itself. DCS represents a new concept for protection of data
within IT systems. It introduces a comprehensive set of security measures, involving both passive and reactive measures, which can be configured to address various data protection and information sharing scenarios
relevant to NATO in both short and long term. The proposed generic
architecture is based on the NATO C3 Taxonomy and the NATO Communication and Information System Security Capability Breakdown.

Keywords: Data-centric security · Data protection · Information
Clearing House · Information sharing · Security architecture

1 Introduction

Providing efficient data protection and information sharing capability across
different security domains, belonging to NATO, the nations and specific communities of Interest (COI), is of paramount importance for effective execution of
NATO operations. The modern battlespace calls for flexible and efficient information sharing capabilities that support the commanders' ability to project
military force and provide force protection. Cross-domain information sharing
is particularly relevant to the implementation of Civilian-Military Cooperation
and new operational concepts, such as Federated Mission Networking (FMN).
In context of this paper a cross-domain information sharing is defined as sharing
of information between any information domains governed by different security
policies or organizations and not only sharing of information between domains
operating on different classification levels.

© The Author(s), under exclusive license to Springer Nature Switzerland AG 2024
T. Tagarev and N. Stoianov (Eds.): DIGILIENCE 2020, CCIS 1790, pp. 75–92, 2024.
https://doi.org/10.1007/978-3-031-44440-1_15

Current information protection practice relies to a large extent on network-layer mechanisms for compartmentalization of information and separation between different COI and security domains. This leads to segregation of networks into separate network domains and the implementation of perimeter defence at the boundaries of these domains. This security design approach relies to a large extent on network-layer security measures and is sometimes referred to as the "fortress" approach [1]. In addition to being costly and time-consuming, the current approach to need-to-know and information protection through network compartmentalization complicates the effective implementation of other principles required for mission success, i.e., need-to-share and need-to-collaborate [2]. Moreover, relying predominantly on perimeter defence provides insufficient protection of data assets against an insider threat and sophisticated cyber-adversaries, as demonstrated by some of the recent high-profile data leaks [3] and breaches [4].

Improving data protection and information sharing relies on achieving efficient compartmentalization of information within a single network domain. Such compartmentalization requires the deployment of security measures internal to the network domain that enforce security policies at the data object level. These security measures are needed to support the whole lifecycle of data, including storing, transmitting and processing data. Furthermore, the enforced security policy needs to capture both need-to-know and responsibility-to-share requirements.

Data-centric security (DCS) represents a new concept for protection of data within IT systems. It introduces a comprehensive set of security measures, involving both passive and reactive measures, which can be configured to address different data protection and information sharing scenarios relevant to NATO in both short and long term.

Currently, both nations [5] and industry [9] preform intensive R&D activities related to various aspects of DCS. Within NATO, the activities or member nations are coordinated within the Allied Command Transformation (ACT) Technology for Information, Decision and Execution superiority (TIDE) community [10]. Recently, NATO has developed the DCS Vision and Strategy for the NATO Enterprise and Alliance Federation [11] as the first and essential step towards implementing the DCS approach within NATO during the next decade. This implementation will be guided by the DCS Implementation Plan that is currently under development within NATO.

2   Data-Centric Security in NATO

2.1   Principles

Modern communication and information systems (CIS) store, transport and process multiple heterogeneous types of data. These different types of data are used in a different context and require different levels of protection. Therefore, the current frequent inability to enforce fine-grained protection and released conditions on data stored within the system and only on its boundary is inefficient both from the cost and performance perspective [2]. DCS aims to address these issues by providing security measures specific to usage and protection requirements determined by a particular data element, thus optimizing level and cost of protection and supporting optimal dissemination to the intended users.

DCS is a system-wide standard approach to data protection [11]; it is built on two strategic principles:

1. Protection is applied to individual data objects (or portions thereof) instead of to a collection of data objects and systems; and,
2. Metadata is bound to data objects and is used by protection enforcement mechanisms to determine the protection requirements for a data object.

DCS also complements the cyber defence component of a cybersecurity architecture by supporting data leakage prevention and defence-in-depth. In particular, DCS capability strengthens resilience to unforeseen threats in the sense that if perimeter protection appears to be insufficient, then there is a second layer of protection at the data object level, especially when cryptographic access control is deployed. In particular, DCS aims to address three critical challenges to data protection, which are faced by all modern CIS, including ones used by NATO:

- The location and transmission paths of information are not always known at information system design time;
- Protection of information must be adaptable to operational and protection requirements that may vary over time or location; and,
- Operational effectiveness requires that information can be shared with all parties having a legitimate operational need for this information while enforcing the appropriate security policy.

2.2   Operational Impact

A DCS approach provides improved security during all lifecycle of information, including storage, transport and processing, leading to increased operational effectiveness and much-improved safeguarding while reducing requirements for human intervention. DCS supports the process of evolution towards a system architecture based on a single information domain. This single information domain architecture will enable effective collaboration between partners while protecting their information protection requirements. It allows a transition from an economically inefficient approach of operating and maintaining multiple single classification level networks to an approach where many of these networks can be collapsed in a single IT environment supporting multiple sensitivity and caveat levels. Data-centric solutions to command-and-control requirements no longer need direct stove-piped connections as DCS provides the interoperability points supporting an exchange of any data objects, and not only application-specific exchange measures. DCS enables increased automation of information sharing and improves reliability, ability to deliver time-sensitive information, and overall environmental resilience to external and insider cyber-attacks.

DCS also complements the cyber defence component of a cybersecurity architecture by supporting data leakage prevention and defence-in-depth. In particular, DCS capability strengthens resilience to unforeseen threats in the sense that if perimeter protection appears to be insufficient, then there is a second layer of protection at the object level, especially when cryptographic access control is deployed.

The integration of the DCS approach within the NATO enterprise would have three main benefits. Firstly, it would allow a more efficient collaboration with external partners and release of information beyond NATO domain. Much of email and data flows between NATO and external partners are currently mediated via gateways or/and manual registries, which perform a content inspection before releasing information to the outside domain. The automated parts of the process result in a high number of false positives, which needs to be dealt with by human analysts. Due to the scarcity of appropriately trained personnel, the human analysis is expensive and introduces substantial unpredictability and delay in delivering the information to external partners. Trusted labelling of information would help reduce the false positives while increasing accountability for accurate labelling of the content by originators. Secondly, it could enable re-use of infrastructure, especially if cryptographic separation would be applied to data with different sensitivity markings or release conditions. In particular, it would reduce the need to use the system high approach within NATO systems, enabling users with different clearance levels and need-to-know properties to access the same data stores and IT systems, without increasing risk of information leakage. Thirdly, use of cryptographic access control would improve defence-in-depth of NATO systems, particularly providing an additional layer of defence against information leakage and reducing the impact of any information extraction due to either external attacks or malware and insider activity.

The FMN environment would routinely include users with different levels of clearance, need-to-know and organizational affiliations. The DCS approach would allow the system to support this heterogeneous group of users while ensuring proper information protection. A basic DCS is already provided by the Information Clearing House (ICH) concept, which has been proposed for use within the FMN. The ICH can be incrementally extended in order to provide richer data-centric support in the federated mission environment.

3   Transformation Objectives

Over the next decade, NATO, working together with nations, aims at establishing a DCS environment, providing information protection at the level of individual data objects and enabling the implementation of a single information domain with adequate data protection mechanisms. In order to achieve this goal, several transformation objectives need to be reached, as discussed below. These transformation objectives can be broadly divided into three classes: availability of sufficiently rich characterization of data; formalization of fine-grained security policies; and effective enforcement of these policies.

3.1 Common Labelling Approach for All Content

When information is produced within a COI, national domain or organizational domain (such as NATO) that information is initially only shared within that domain. The labelling solutions are often specific to the domain. Users, applications, services and systems within that domain all support and understand the specific labelling method. When information is to be shared between different COIs or domains, then the domain-specific labelling method may not be understood or supported outside of that domain. A common interpretation of the labels and binding (i.e. 'where can the labels be located in the information', 'what does the label mean' and 'to which data does the label pertain') is required to facilitate information sharing [12]. The ubiquitous availability of trusted metadata characterizing data properties, e.g. sensitivity (confidentiality) marking, is a critical requirement for implementing a DCS architecture. Labelling of information introduces two primary challenges, which are currently being addressed by NATO and NATO nations within joint standardization activities.

The first challenge is a standard syntax for labels, enabling automated processing of the labels and information included in them. In particular, to facilitate information sharing, a common understanding of the labels, including metadata associated with the data object, is required. Standardization must cover such aspects as 'where can the labels be located in the information', 'what does the label mean' and 'to which data does the label pertain'. This challenge is addressed by STANAG 4774 [13].

The other challenge is the definition of mechanisms providing a binding between the labels and the data and assuring the integrity of that binding. This challenge is being addressed by the ongoing work on STANAG 4778 [14]. STANAG 4778 is currently focused on specifying the binding of labels to finite data, i.e. data with a known finite size and a known structure. Further work is required to standardize the binding of labels to streaming data, such as voice and video.

3.2 A Standardized Approach to Describing Security-Relevant Attributes of Content, Users and Equipment

DCS is reliant upon Identity Management (IdM). The IdM capability provides infrastructure, policies, procedures and mechanisms to support identification, authentication and authorization of entities within the information domain and within a federation of information domains. An IdM capability enables entities (for example; users, terminal or services) to present identity information attributes (as credentials) to authenticate each other. The validated identity information attributes can be further used to support authorization decisions.

Availability of a standardized way for identifying entities and their attributes within a DCS architecture is required to support consistent and coherent enforcement of protection policies. In this respect, STANAG 4774 specifies a standard format for describing clearances for entities. This allows for exact matching of clearances and confidentiality labels for access control decisions based on

STANAG 4774. The possible domain values for sensitivity labels (or clearances) are well known and for NATO are defined in [15]. The NATO Core Metadata Specification (NCMS) [16] can be used for describing other content properties. More effort needs to be invested in integrating the NCMS with the DCS architecture.

Availability of standardized metadata specifications is critical for implementing any more advanced access control policies, such as Role-Based Access Control (RBAC) [17] and Attribute-Based Access Control (ABAC) [18], which are required for effective implementation of DCS enforcement. An example of the ABAC policy is the Content-based Protection and Release (CPR) model [19], which was proposed for use within the FMN.

3.3   Support for End-Point Labelling of Information

As discussed earlier, DCS requires ubiquitous and trusted labelling of information. There are several implementation challenges related to end-point labelling capability.

Most of the existing applications do not support the labelling of information following STANAG 4774 and 4778. A labelling service, so-called NATO Metadata Binding Service (NMBS), offers a solution to this problem, by providing a capability within the network related to the verification and generation of Security Labels in compliance with STANAG 4774 and 4778. The NMBS offers multiple interfaces to consumers, based on, e.g., SOAP, REST, C# and Java API. The NMBS can be deployed as a remote service or as a plugin for a client application, such as JChat [20]. For legacy systems and applications that label information in a COI-specific approach, the NMBS provides a configurable mechanism for supporting conversion between COI-specific labels to STANAG 4778 and STANAG 4774 and equivalencies between different security policies.

Another challenge is related to a choice of correct values for the labels by the originator of the content. A set of tools supporting the user in choosing correct metadata values for labelling would be required. Such tools could be based on a semantic and statistical analysis of information [21,22].

NATO systems host a large amount of existing data that do not include machine-readable labels. In order to support DCS, this data would need to be labelled appropriately. Due to a sheer quantity of data, an automated pre-processing and pre-labelling of the data would be required. The controversial cases could be referenced to human analysts for final decisions. The automated pre-processing information could also support the ICH implementation and contribute to the reduction of load put on the ICH personnel.

Of course, DCS environments of different maturity level would need to co-exist (see also Sect. 4). Some of them would support only simple sensitivity labels and Bell-LaPadula policy. In contrast, other systems would support rich sets of content properties and sophisticated attribute-based access control, e.g. CPR, policies. Bridge predicates enable backwards compatibility between systems supporting only traditional sensitivity markings and CPR-enabled systems [23].

Bridge predicates offer a mapping between sets of content properties and sensitivity markings. This type of derived sensitivity markings can be calculated at the time of document creation, in order to reduce discretionary aspects of content marking, or dynamically during the data life cycle. The dynamically generated sensitivity markings can take into account changing context information, which may result in different sensitivity marking, e.g. depending on the time since the content creation or relation to ongoing military operations. Bridge predicates can also be instrumental in handling the physical representation of information, e.g. printouts or aggregated data displayed on the screen and potentially visible to multiple users.

3.4   DCS Security Policy Management Mechanisms

DCS potentially enables formulation and enforcement of much more fine-grained security policies. However, proper formulation and analysis of such policies could be challenging for both security administrators and accreditors. Thus appropriate tools are required to support the security personnel in their tasks.

An open specification for security policies simplifies widespread adoption and use. STANAG 4774 describes the use of the Open XML SPIF [24] as a standard format for describing security policies.

It is recommended to combine a high-level policy language with tools enabling the automated translation of these high-level policies to low-level policies enforced within the IT system. Such an approach would make it both more natural for humans to write the policies and would prevent the potential errors caused by a manual interpretation and translation process [19].

Automated tools providing validation of security policies would both increase assurance in proper formulation of the policies and provide means for testing and generating proof of the correctness of the security policies during the accreditation process. The validation could also be used to assess the impact of the changes in the security policies on preserving particular security properties of the system [25].

3.5   DCS Key Management Mechanisms

Key management includes the ability to generate, transmit, receive, store, deploy on equipment, account for, archive, revoke, recover and destroy cryptographic keys. The keys managed through this capability can be used for different purposes such as encryption, digital signatures, message authentication codes and verification of integrity and authenticity. In a DCS approach, asymmetric cryptography techniques underpin identity and access management capabilities, e.g. relying on a PKI.

The key management plays a twofold role in the DCS. Firstly, it can support trust relations related to binding of attributes to data (i.e. labelling) and entities (i.e. identity management). Secondly, key management can be used in combination with cryptographic access control (CAC) to enforce data access control policies. In this case, key management policy represents an access control policy, e.g. CPR policy.

3.6 Cryptographic Access Control

One of the promising approaches to the enforcement of DCS relies on the implementation of CAC. In CAC, every data object is encrypted, and the process of key management replaces the process of access control to data. The CAC encryption schemes can be broadly divided into symmetric key-based and public key-based. In the case of public key-based systems, particularly relevant for future applications are attribute-based encryption schemes [26].

Due to potentially very fine-grained access control rules, a careful choice of the cryptographic algorithms and the key management mechanism is required to provide appropriate scalability and resilience of the system, e.g. in respect to key revocation.

3.7 Cross-Layer Enforcement of Security Policies and Integration with Protected Core Networking

The ongoing evolution of modern IT systems into the direction of software-defined infrastructures opens an opportunity for consistent enforcement of security policies across multiple layers of the system and for the multiple dimensions of data protection (i.e. confidentiality, integrity and availability). A particularly relevant technology in this context is software-defined networking (SDN) [27]. The SDN technology also provides a suitable platform for implementing Protected Core Networking (PCN) [28], both within organizational clouds and in a federated environment, such as the one proposed for FMN.

3.8 Cross-Domain Information Sharing Concept

One of the critical components of the future DCS architecture is the provision of a next-generation of cross-domain information sharing solution applicable to multiple information sharing scenarios, including a variety of functional and security requirements. Such a new cross-domain information sharing concept (C-DISC) needs to address various cross-domain information sharing scenarios in both the short and long term.

In the short term, simple solutions relying on manual audit - originating from ACCTA solution [31,32] - can be adapted to modern technology to provide a reasonable trade-off between scalability and security and implementation cost. Within the NATO information sharing concept, we define such a C-DISC architectural pattern, which provides an abstraction of the ICH [33,34].

In the midterm perspective, the solutions such as ICH can be modified to support human operators by introducing an automated analysis based on artificial intelligence technology and, therefore, mitigating potential scalability and performance bottlenecks [35].

In the long term, the medium assurance solution can be extended to meet also high assurance requirements, introduced when interconnecting secret and restricted/unclassified domains or implementing so-called Information Exchange Gateway (IEG) [36]. However, achieving availability of affordable and flexible high assurance guards to NATO would require proactive involvement with industry, NATO nations and other partners to achieve a critical mass required to push forward the development of the required technology.

Introduction of cryptographic separation between different logical security domains using the same physical infrastructure implies a very different implementation of a cross-domain information sharing solution than a classical cross-domain guard concept. In such a scenario, enforcement of cross-domain information flow policies is enforced at the edge of the network or the user terminal. Thus, the concept of an IEG or a cross-domain guard as a network middle-box ceases to exist.

4   Evolution Strategy

To support NATO transformation towards the DCS environment, there is a need for coordination of the development of standard DCS components so that interoperability between systems and COIs at different stages of transformation can be achieved [37]. We propose an approach based on a concept of DCS evolution stages and related milestones. DCS evolution stages are maturity stages of DCS, whereas DCS milestones define implementation phases of a DCS evolution stage. Multiple milestones are defined per DCS evolution stage.

The advantage of using defined DCS evolution stages is that it becomes easier to coordinate a joint development of these DCS components in a federated or multi-COI environment. The use of evolution stages and milestones also allows for an unambiguous comparison of DCS implementations and gap analysis. Several concrete actions related to technology and NATO policy development need to be completed for every chosen milestone.

4.1   Evolution Stages and Milestones

The concept of DCS allows for variation in how the protection requirements are determined, how the enforcement of the protection policy is executed, and in the choice of the underlying access control model. The variation is driven by evolution in the following directions:

- The level of detail for describing information;
- The granularity of access control; and,
- The level of object protection.

Detail of Content Description. Information can be described using metadata. Protection mechanisms use the metadata to determine the protection requirements for that information. The level of detail with which information is described determines the precision with which the protection requirements can be formulated and enforced. The following three stages can be distinguished in this respect:

- *None*: protection mechanisms do not rely on any metadata. Instead, a protection policy is enforced at the system (or network) level and is applied to all data objects (e.g. the 'system high' approach). As there is no protection at the data object level in this state, it is not part of the DCS concept. However, it is included in the discussion in order to establish where the DCS concept begins.
- *Sensitivity Markings*: the metadata comprises a sensitivity marking. A sensitivity marking does not provide information on the contents of a data object; however, it is an expression of the protection requirements and release conditions that apply to a data object.
- *Content Properties*: the metadata describes the content represented by the information. Contrary to sensitivity markings, content properties do not express the protection requirements and release conditions. The correspondence between the protection requirements, the release conditions and the content properties are recorded and managed in separate protection and release policies [38].

The Granularity of Access Control. The information about the subject and its environment can have varying granularity depending on the targeted state and are distinguished by the following two stages:

- *Clearance-based*: the information about the subject and its environment is limited to the subject's clearance level or the classification of the system (or network) from which the subject requests access to a data object. This is equivalent to the enforcement of the Bell-LaPadula security model [39].
- *Attribute-based*: the use of clearance levels (and system/network classifications) and roles are expanded to include more detailed sets of attributes describing the subjects involved in accessing data objects and the technical capabilities of the systems used for access. RBAC has not been included as its own DCS evolution stage as any RBAC policy can be expressed as an ABAC policy [8,18,40].

Level of Object Protection. Enforcing a protection policy at the data object level requires the ability to apply a protection policy to an individual data object regardless of its location and the time. The extent to which this can be realized is referred to as the 'level of object protection', for which three general states are distinguished:

- *Information Domain Separation*: Information is protected based on its domain membership and must not be transferred to an information domain under a different protection policy. The protection policy is inherited by all systems that constitute the information domain. This is known as the "fortress design" and is not part of the DCS concept but is included to establish where the DCS concept begins.

– *Deny-or-Grant Access (DOGA)*: protection mechanisms are introduced to enforce a protection policy at the data object level. The enforcement of the protection policy can be coarse-grained, i.e. access control is enforced on the information as a whole, or fine-grained in the sense that information can be sanitized or redacted. If a subject is permitted access to the information, then access is granted by releasing the information to that subject (where the information is transferred from one domain to another). Once the information has been released, the originating information domain's protection policy can no longer be enforced. An example of this stage is a cross-domain guard [41, 42].

– *Cryptographic Access Control*: the protection policy is enforced by encrypting the information. The use of CAC increases the level of object protection because encrypted information is protected regardless of its location. For CAC, the access control decision is not enforced in direct response to a request for information. Instead, information is encrypted, and the access control decision is delayed until a decryption attempt is made [6,7,26,43].

The evolution stages of DCS, based on classification described above, are summarized in Table 1.

Table 1. Evolution stages of data-centric security

DCS Evolution stage	Content Description	Granularity of Access Control	Enforcement mechanism
Sensitivity-Marking-based Protection and Release (SMPR)	Sensitivity Markings	Bell-LaPadula policy	Deny-or-Grant Access
Content-based Protection and Release (CPR)	Content Properties	Attribute-based access control policy	Deny-or-Grant Access
SMPR with Cryptographic Access Control (SMPR-CAC)	Sensitivity Markings	Bell-LaPadula policy	Cryptographic Access Control
CPR with Cryptographic Access Control (CPR-CAC)	Content Properties	Attribute-based access control policy	Cryptographic Access Control

For every of these evolution stages, multiple concrete milestones can be defined as presented in Table 2. It is recognized that different nations, communities of interest or systems can target different stages of DCS and reach specific milestones at different times. In particular, it is envisioned that in order to minimize cost, the DCS transition will be aligned with the natural modernization and refresh cycle of the communication and information systems operated by NATO and the Alliance. The current target for most of the systems is SMPR-1 and SMPR-2, however there are several ongoing preparatory actions for transition towards CPR and CAC stages. It is also possible that during the progress

Table 2. Milestones of the data-centric security concept

Milestone	Features	Critical enablers
SMPR-1	Standard data formats and exchange protocols labelled using STANAGs 4774/4778	STANAGs 4774/4778 ratified; deployment of NMBS and C-DISC
SMPR-2	All finite data cryptographically labelled using STANAG 4774/4778	STANAG 4778 Profiles ratified; NMBS supports cryptographic binding and mapping between different policies; end-point labelling; PKI integration; cross-domain guards and federated identity management capability available; standard security policy format based on SPIFs; XACML protection policies based on clearance and labels
SMPR-3	All data cryptographically labelled using STANAGs 4774/4778	Profiles for streaming data, such as voice and video, added to STANAG 4778
CPR-1	Standard content properties attached to data using STANAGs 4774/4778	NCMS ratified; NMBS supports NCMS metadata; XACML protection and release policies based on user, terminal, and content attributes; assisted labelling for users
CPR-2	CPR model supported by boundary protection devices and guards; all data labelled with content properties using STANAGs 4774/4778	Federated identity management with standardized user and terminal attributes; assisted policy formulation and validation for administrators; automated labelling of legacy data; bridge predicates for backwards compatibility and physical handling of information;
CAC-1	Validated and approved symmetric and public-key data encryption	Experimental testing and validation of agreed encryption and key management (KM) schemes for data at rest and in transit
CAC-2	Validated and approved attribute-based encryption (ABE)	Experimental testing and validation of agreed and evaluated ABE and ABE KM for data at rest and in transit
CAC-3	Deployed cryptographic access control (CAC)	Same as SMPR-3 and CPR plus accredited encryption for data at rest and in transit; accredited KM and NMBS support for symmetric and public key data encryption
CAC-4	Deployed ABE CAC	Same as CPR-2 plus accredited ABE and ABE KM for data at rest and in transit; NMBS supports ABE; centralized ABE Authority

towards higher DCS maturity levels there will be a need to enhance some of the functionality achieved at the earlier stages, e.g., there might be requirements for specific attribute encoding in order to efficiently support attribute-based encryption.

4.2 DCS Architecture

One of the essential aspects of successful transformation towards DCS is developing a flexible system architecture, which could address a broad spectrum of functional and non-functional requirements. To be cost-effective and facilitate interoperability and coordinated development, the architecture should rely to the greatest extent possible on re-usable standard architectural building blocks (ABB). These blocks could be implemented once and re-configured as required to address various NATO operational use cases. The ABB need to be aligned with the NATO C3 Taxonomy [29] and the Communication and Information System (CIS) Security Capability Breakdown [30]. Presentation of a complete DCS architecture is outside of the scope of this work, however below we discuss an example of an architectural approach based on ABBs in a context of cross-domain information sharing capability (C-DISC).

Example: C-DISC Generic Architecture. As discussed in Sect. 3, one of the critical components of the future DCS architecture is a provision of a next-generation of cross-domain information sharing solution applicable to multiple cross-domain scenarios, including a variety of functional and security requirements. The generic C-DISC architecture, consisting of re-usable and re-configurable high-level ABBs is depicted in Fig. 1. The Configuration Management, Cyber Defense, Access Management, Data Protection, and CIS Protection ABBs can be further decomposed according to the NATO CIS Security Capability Breakdown as illustrated in Fig. 1 - for more details on their functionality, refer to [30]. The C-DISC architecture includes also two ABBs which are not included in the CIS Security Capability Breakdown. The first of them, Cryptographic Support, captures cryptographic mechanisms, which need to be applied to protect data at the application layer. The second, Data Exchange, includes the mediation functionality for the relevant services described in the NATO C3 Taxonomy [29].

The advantage of the ABB-based approach is that the individual building blocks can be combined in different configurations. These so-called architectural patterns can be used to address different use cases and security scenarios involving cross-domain information sharing. Below we present an example of such a pattern, the Information Clearing House (ICH) pattern. More patterns are to be defined in the future, based on various concrete use cases.

Information Clearing House pattern The ICH pattern provides a mapping of currently implemented proof-of-concept information sharing solution for FMN to the abstract C-DISC architecture building blocks. This pattern, illustrated in Fig. 2, demonstrates a short-term solution, which can be implemented using existing commercially available and internally implemented components. The used architectural building blocks represent a subset of the blocks depicted in Fig. 1. The grey blocks represent the physical components used in the current implementation of the ICH pattern, i.e., ICH, Release Server, Data Diode and Boundary Protection System.

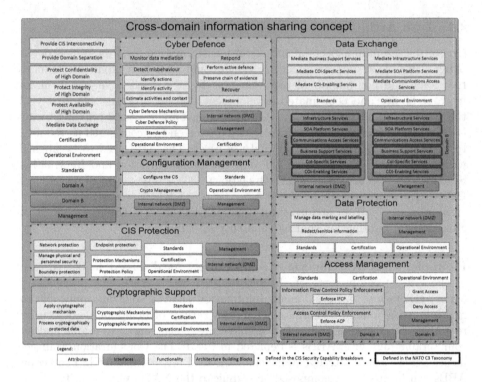

Fig. 1. C-DISC High-level ABBs.

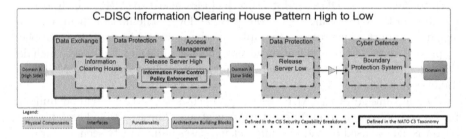

Fig. 2. Example of C-DISC pattern involving an Information Clearing House.

5   Conclusions and Future Work

In this paper, we have introduced the concept of data-centric security in the context of NATO operations. DCS implements security measures, which are specific to usage and protection requirements determined by a particular data element, thus optimizing level and cost of protection and supporting optimal dissemination of data to the intended users. We have presented main transformation objectives for implementing DCS within NATO and proposed an approach to the coordinated development of the DCS capability within NATO and NATO nations, based on a concept of evolution stages and related milestones. Finally, we have presented an example of an architectural approach to designing DCS by describing cross-domain information sharing capability, based on re-configurable and re-usable architectural building blocks. The ABBs can be used to compose different architectural patterns, meeting different information sharing and security requirements introduced by various NATO operational use cases. We have introduced briefly one of such patterns, the Information Clearing House.

Our work does not give answers to all the challenges related to design and implementation of practical DCS architecture. Instead, it aims to introduce the concept to a broader audience and stimulate further work and discussion on this topic. As presented in Sect. 3, DCS introduces several technical and procedural challenges, which need to be addressed before DCS can be widely adopted. Some additional challenges that were not discussed in detail in this paper are related to integrating the DCS with existing cyber defence infrastructure and procedures. For example, encryption of data objects may make it more challenging to analyze network traffic content by the boundary protection devices and sensor deployed within the network. To maintain the capability for such analysis, appropriate mechanisms would need to be deployed within the network. Also, although DCS, especially in the case of a CAC implementation, substantially increases the defence posture of a system, the protection of confidentiality and availability of metadata needs to be further investigated. In particular, rich content properties may constitute, in some cases, intentional or non-intentional side-channel resulting in information leakage. The existence of such side-channels needs to be controlled and prevented when required. Another important aspect is related to inclusion of some specific military and federation requirements in the new cryptographic schemes. For example, most of the current ABE systems are highly centralized with respect to key management. In order to enable an effective implementation of ABE Authority in the federated environment, we need to combine them with new approaches to implementation of trusted third parties [44,45].

The critical challenges are related to usability and acceptance of the proposed concept. We have discussed some of these challenges from a perspective of end-users (who need to label the data correctly) and security administrators (who need to configure the system correctly). However, the broader organizational perspective and compatibility with existing procurement and deployment procedures are often critical for successful innovation in the military environment [46].

References

1. Scully, T.: The cyber threat, trophy information and the fortress mentality. J. Bus. Continuity Emerg. Plann. **5**(3), 195–207 (2011)
2. Serena, C.C., Porche, I.R., Predd, J.B., Osburg, J., Lossing, B.: Lessons Learned from the Afghan Mission Network: Developing a Coalition Contingency Network, RAND Corporation (2014)

3. Toxen, B.: The NSA and Snowden: securing the All-Seeing Eye. Commun. ACM **57**(5), 44–51 (2014)
4. Lipton, E., Sanger, D. and Shane, S.: The Perfect Weapon: How Russian Cyber-power Invaded the US, The New York Times (2016)
5. Kiviharju, M.: Content-Based Information Security (CBIS): Definitions, Requirements and Cryptographic Architecture, Defence Forces Technical Research Centre Publications no. 21 (2010)
6. Kiviharju, M.: Attribute pooling for cryptographic access control: enabling cryptographical user-terminal policies for MLS content. In: Amanowicz, M. (ed.) International Conference on Military Communications and Information Systems - ICMCIS 2015, Krakow, Poland, May 18–19, 2015. Proceedings, pp. 1–12. IEEE (2015)
7. Kiviharju, M., Kurnikov, A.: Tactical CAC profile for NATO OLP - performance estimations for NATO OLP cryptographic evolution stage. In: Brand, J., Valenti, M., Akinpelu, A., et al. (eds.) Military Communications Conference - MILCOM 2016, Baltimore, MD, USA, November 1–3, 2016, Proceedings, pp. 533–538. IEEE (2016)
8. Kiviharju, M.: Enforcing Role-Based Access Control with Attribute-Based Cryptography in MLS Environments. 237p, Finnish Defence Research Agency's Publications no. 8 (2017)
9. Information Based Security Architecture, https://www.exsel-group.com/information-based-security
10. Allied Command Transformation (ACT) Technology for Information, Decision and Execution superiority (TIDE). https://tide.act.nato.int
11. NATO Allied Command Transformation, Data-Centric Security Vision and Strategy for the Alliance Federation, including the NATO Enterprise (2019)
12. Oudkerk, S. and Wrona, K.: Using NATO Labelling to support controlled information sharing between partners. In: International Conference on Critical Information Infrastructures Security (CRITIS) (2013)
13. North Atlantic Treaty Organization, Confidentiality Metadata Label Syntax, ADatP-4774 (2016)
14. North Atlantic Treaty Organization, Metadata Binding Mechanism, ADatP-4778 (2016)
15. NATO Consultation Command and Control Board, Guidance on the marking of NATO information, AC/322-N(2011) 0130 (2011)
16. NATO Consultation Command and Control Board (C3B), NATO Core Metadata Specification (NCMS) Version 1.0, Brussels, Belgium, AC/322-D(2014) 0010 (2015)
17. Sandhu, R.S., Coyne, E.J., Feinstein, H.L., Youman, C.E.: Role-based access control models. Computer **29**(2), 38–47 (1996)
18. Hu, V. C., et al.: Guide to Attribute-Based Access Control (ABAC) Definition and Considerations, NIST SP 800–162 (2014)
19. Armando, A., Oudkerk, S., Ranise, S., Wrona, K.: Content-based Protection and Release for Access Control in NATO Operations. In: Proceedings of the 6th International Symposium on Foundations & Practice of Security (FPS) (2013)
20. Johnsen, F.T., et al.: Collaboration services: Enabling chat in disadvantaged grids. In: Proceedings of the 19th International Command and Control Research and Technology Symposium (ICCRTS) (2014)
21. Wrona, K., Oudkerk, S., Armando, A., Ranise, S., Ferrari, L.: Assisted content-based labeling and classification of documents. In: Proceedings of the International Conference on Military Communications and Information System (ICMCIS) (2016)
22. Richter, M., Wrona, K.: Devil in the details: assessing automated confidentiality classifiers in context of NATO documents. In: Proceedings of the ITASEC (2017)

23. Armando, A., Ranise, S., Traverso, R., Wrona, K.: Compiling NATO Authorization Policies for Enforcement in the Cloud and SDNs. In: Proceedings of the Computer and Network Security Conference (CNS) (2015)
24. Open XML Security Policy Information File (SPIF). https://www.xmlspif.org
25. Armando, A., Ranise, S., Wrona, K.: SMT-based Enforcement and Analysis of NATO Content-based Protection and Release Policies. In: Proceedings of the 1st ACM Workshop on Attribute Based Access Control (ABAC), pp. 35–46 (2016)
26. Oudkerk, S., Wrona, K.: Cryptographic Access Control in support of Object Level Protection. In: Proceedings of the Military Communications and Information Systems Conference (MCC) (2013)
27. Wrona, K., Oudkerk, S., Szwaczyk, S., Amanowicz, M.: Content-based security and protected core networking with software-defined networks. IEEE Commun. Mag. **54**(10), 138–144 (2016)
28. Hallingstad, G., Oudkerk, S.: Protected core networking: an architectural approach to secure and flexible communications. IEEE Commun. Mag. **46**(11), 35–41 (2008)
29. NATO Allied Command Transformation: NATO C3 Taxonomy Perspective. Norfolk, VA, USA (2017)
30. Hallingstad, G., Dandurand, L.: CIS Security Capability Breakdown Revision 4, The Hague, The Netherlands, TR/2012/SPW008416/03 (2013)
31. Woodward, J.P.L.: Applications for multilevel secure operating systems. National Comput. Conf. **48**, 319–328 (1979)
32. Martins, G.R., Gaines, R.S.: Implementing message systems in multilevel secure environments: problems and approaches, Santa Monica (1982)
33. Domingo, A., Wietgrefe, H.: On the federation of information in coalition operations: building single information domains out of multiple security domains. In: Proceedings - IEEE Military Communications Conference MILCOM, pp. 1462–1469 (2013)
34. Domingo, A., Wietgrefe, H.: An applied model for secure information release between federated military and non-military networks. In: MILCOM Military Communications Conference, pp. 465–470 (2015)
35. Engelstad, P.E., Hammer, H., Yazidi, A., Nordbotten, N.A., Bai, A.: Automatic security classification with Lasso. In: Proceedings of the 16th International Workshop on Information Security Applications (WISA), pp. 399–410 (2015)
36. Hvinden, Ø., et al.: Information exchange gateway roadmap, The Hague, The Netherlands, Reference Document 2666 (2010)
37. Oudkerk, S., Wrona, K.: A common approach to the integration of object level protection in NATO. In: McCallam, D. and Luiijf, E. (eds.) NATO STO/IST-122 Symposium on Cyber Security Science and Engineering, Tallinn, Estonia, October 13–14, 2014. Proceedings, vol. 1. NATO STO (2014)
38. Wrona, K., Hallingstad, G.: Controlled information sharing in NATO operations. In: IEEE Military Communications Conference (MILCOM), pp. 1285–1290 (2011)
39. LaPadula, L.J., Bell, D.E.: Secure Computer Systems: mathematical foundations, MITRE Technical Report 2547, Vol. II (1973)
40. Jin, X., Krishnan, R., Sandhu, R.: A Unified Attribute-Based Access Control Model Covering DAC, MAC and RBAC. In: Cuppens-Boulahia, N., Cuppens, F., Garcia-Alfaro, J. (eds.) DBSec 2012. LNCS, vol. 7371, pp. 41–55. Springer, Heidelberg (2012). https://doi.org/10.1007/978-3-642-31540-4_4
41. Wrona, K., Hallingstad, G.: Development of High Assurance Guards for NATO. In: Military Communications and Information Systems Conference (2012)

42. Wrona, K., Oudkerk, S., Hallingstad, G.: Designing medium assurance XML-labelling guards for NATO. In: Proceedings of the Military Communications Conference (MILCOM), pp. 1794–1799 (2010)
43. Blundo, C., et al.: Managing key hierarchies for access control enforcement: heuristic approaches, Comput. Secur. **29**(5), 533–547 (2010)
44. Kanciak, K., Wrona, K.: Towards an auditable cryptographic access control to high-value sensitive data. Int. J. Electron. Telecommun. **66**(3), 449–458 (2020)
45. Xu, R., Joshi, J.: Trustworthy and transparent third-party authority. ACM Trans. Internet Technol. **20**(4), Article 31 (2020)
46. Kaplan, F.: The Pentagon's innovation experiment. MIT Technology Review (2016)

Challenges and Opportunities for Network Intrusion Detection in a Big Data Environment

Petya Ivanova[1](✉) ⓘ and Todor Tagarev[2] ⓘ

[1] Procon Ltd., 3, Razluka Str., ap. 20, Sofia 1111, Bulgaria
petya@procon.bg
[2] Institute of Information and Communication Technologies, Bulgarian Academy of Sciences,
Acad. G. Bonchev Str., Bl. 2, Sofia 1113, Bulgaria
todor.tagarev@iict.bas.bg

Abstract. Advanced network sensors, data storage, and processing technologies allow the accumulation of logs, network flows, and system events from various sources in terabytes of heterogeneous data. The abundance of data can be used to train and validate multiple machine learning approaches and algorithms to detect anomalies and classify network attacks. This paper presents the state of the art in data preprocessing, feature selection, and applying various machine learning methods for intrusion detection. It outlines the main challenges in big data analytics, the functional requirements to related tools and applications, and the opportunities provided by combining the outputs of several methods to increase the accuracy of detection and decrease the number of false alarms. Finally, the authors propose an architecture of an intrusion detection system combining offline machine learning and dynamic processing of data streams.

Keywords: Intrusion Detection · Big Data Analytics · Machine Learning · Heterogeneous Data · Feature Selection · Decision by Committee · Explainability · Cybersecurity · Situational Awareness · IDS Combo · ECHO project

1 Introduction

In developed countries, there is hardly an economic sector, administrative or social activity that is not dependent on databases, information systems, and uninterrupted communications. Moreover, these dependencies are growing globally. Lost or corrupt data, malfunctioning hardware, tampered software applications, or disrupted communications may not only decrease the efficiency but totally shut down the delivery of essential services and cause material damage. Thus, these dependencies create opportunities for malicious exploitation.

Networks, computer systems, data storage, and communications are the primary targets of attacks. However, dependent banking and financial systems [1], the generation [2] and delivery of electricity [3], oil and gas pipelines [4], transport [5], water supply and wastewater collection and treatment systems [6], among others, are all under the threat of abuse via cyberspace.

© The Author(s), under exclusive license to Springer Nature Switzerland AG 2024
T. Tagarev and N. Stoianov (Eds.): DIGILIENCE 2020, CCIS 1790, pp. 93–106, 2024.
https://doi.org/10.1007/978-3-031-44440-1_16

Cyberattacks are on the rise in terms of numbers, sophistication, exploited targets, financial, reputational, and even physical consequences. According to forecasts by "Cybersecurity Ventures," worldwide cybercrime costs are expected to reach $6 trillion annually by 2021 and $10.5 trillion by 2025. In the same timeframe, just the costs of ransomware damages will rise to $20 billion [7]. Given these trends, nations and individual organizations are willing to investigate any available opportunity to mitigate the risks of cyberattacks, strengthen the protection of primary targets, and increase the resilience of computer networks and information systems.

Advances in collecting, storing, and processing data and the increasing computational power accessible at reasonable costs, combined with the advances in machine learning, provide such opportunities.

As of 2020, the world daily generates 2.5 quintillion bytes, and by 2025, over 200 zettabytes of data will be stored in the cloud globally [8]. Moreover, the computational power continues to increase. Although Moore's law is not considered valid in strictly technical terms, the combined performance of the combination of CPUs with alternative processors is improving at a rate of more than 100 percent per annum [9]. This increase in computing capacity affords the application of ever more sophisticated methods and algorithms in processing huge amounts of data.

In the field of network and computer security, these trends allowed the transition from the traditional signature-based methods for intrusion detection [10] to the use of models learning to identify, classify, and predict intrusions on the basis of data, i.e., machine learning methods [11]. The machine learning methods are not limited to predefined attack signatures in network traffic [12] and thus have an indisputable advantage over the signature-based techniques in the rapidly evolving threat landscape.

This paper focuses on machine learning (ML) methods for network intrusion detection trained over big data and processing relevant data streams in real-time. The next section outlines the challenges in implementing ML approaches due to the quality, heterogeneity, and diversity of the data available for training, the changing threats, and the need to explain the classification of certain anomalies as an intrusion. Section 3 provides the problem formulation and a list of functional requirements in intrusion detection applications. Section 4 provides an overview of research and technology advances that allow exploring and designing ML-based intrusion detection systems (IDS). The fifth section briefly outlines the architecture of an ML-based intrusion detection tool currently under development by the authors. Finally, the paper concludes with a summary of the advantages of the ML approaches and the follow-on steps in our research.

2   Challenges

While advanced technologies allow for the collecting and storing large amounts of data, the available relevant data still poses challenges to applying data-based methods. Other challenges reflect the nature of machine learning and the evolving cyber threats.

2.1 Characteristics of Raw Data

Network traffic easily generates large amounts of data. Even a small network of 10 hosts can generate more than 100 GB of data for a single day. And this volume quickly grows with the expansion of the network and its usage.

The volume of data is not the only challenge. The "3Vs" description of big data, suggested at the beginning of the century, adds Velocity (the speed with which data accumulates) and Variety (high dimensionality, many sources of origin, different data structures). In the years since then, researchers have added to the description features like Veracity (data correctness, quality problems such as missing values or noise), Value (collecting and storing data not relevant to analysis), Validity, Variability, Viscosity, Viability, Volatility, etc. [13, 14].

The heterogeneity of data sources poses a particularly important challenge. Incorporating data from more diverse heterogeneous sources into intrusion detection holds the promise to enhance situational awareness and improve accuracy [15]. However, that requires collecting and fusing data from every security-relevant source, including traditional, e.g., firewall, database access, web access, and non-traditional sources, e.g., social media, blog posts, external threat feeds, domain registration.

Another data-related challenge reflects to need to respect privacy concerns in collecting security-relevant data, evaluate and account for the trustworthiness of each source, and preserve data integrity.

2.2 Evolving Network Technologies and Threat Landscape

Organizations readily incorporate new technologies to increase their effectiveness and efficiency and gain a competitive advantage, often without comprehensive testing to guarantee security. Vulnerabilities, appearing as a result, are readily exploited by hackers with various intents. Hence, any intrusion detection approach needs to account for the dynamic threat landscape, including new attack vectors, tactics, or procedures. That may require adding new data sources or retraining the whole machine learning pipeline to consider and learn to detect new types of attacks.

The two remaining challenges relate to the specifics of machine learning.

2.3 The Need for Supervised Training

The design and the tuning of machine learning models rely upon—entirely, or at least partially—the availability of labeled data, i.e. when each point in the dataset is related to normal behavior or an attack of a certain type. To provide for accurate intrusion detection, the dataset used for training needs to include samples of all known and relevant types of attacks. Further, the dataset needs to be balanced, i.e., it should not include a disproportionally high number of samples corresponding to one type of attack while other types are underrepresented.

Such data is not readily available in practice. Collecting intrusion data from a single network even over long periods cannot be expected to provide a rich dataset. Creating datasets suitable for training purposes requires information exchange between various organizations. However, organizations are often reluctant to share such data due to the sensitivity of the information (privacy issues, disclosure of vulnerabilities, etc.), legal or reputational reasons.

2.4 The 'Black-Box' Effect

The final challenge, selected for its impact on the design and usability of machine learning models for intrusion detection, relates to the readiness of a decision-maker to trust the ML-based findings. The workings of machine learning models are often too complicated for a human to grasp; hence, people are rarely inclined to rely on their output in making critically important decisions [16].

Therefore, the challenge in designing ML models is to deliver alerts, or predictions, along with the rationale for the prediction and the most relevant contextual information. Moreover, this information needs to be presented in easy to comprehend textual and visual formats.

3 Problem Definition, Requirements, and Working Hypothesis

To be effective, an network intrusion detection method, tool, or system (the abbreviation IDS will be used below for short) needs to be able to cope with the challenges described in the previous section, provide information to the users that is adequate to their needs and capacity, and interface with the wider community of cybersecurity stakeholders for a mutual benefit.

First, IDS needs to be able to collect, aggregate, store, and manage heterogeneous data related to the functioning of the network. That includes server and application logs, network traffic and events, user activities, and any other relevant data.

Second, the IDS must have the capacity to process historical data and incoming data streams in real- or near-real-time, detect anomalies, identify and classify intrusions. Processing typically includes techniques for handling missing values [17], removal of duplicates and incorrect data, data normalization, and others [18]. The incorporated methods and algorithms typically work better and faster on a sub-set of the input data. Hence, the IDS needs to extract or select a limited number of important features for subsequent data analysis. Furthermore, identification and classification methods and procedures need to be designed and tuned to maximize the accuracy and precision of classification, minimize false alarms, and prioritize alerts.

The output of ML methods is often seen as opaque, and that limits their application for practical purposes [19]. Hence, the 'black box' effect defines the third problematic area in applying big data and machine learning methods for intrusion detection. Therefore, an advanced IDS is expected to provide the rationale for a particular alert, explain it, and deliver the relevant contextual information to the user. It also needs to provide an explanation for prioritizing certain alerts above others. Researchers usually designate this problem in terms of explainability and interpretability [20].

Fourth, the IDS needs to reflect and adapt to changes in the network configuration, usage patterns, and the evolving attack tactics, techniques, and procedures. That would require the implementation of techniques for incremental training, estimation of concept drifts (data distributions), and respective adaptation of the applied machine learning algorithms [21].

The fifth and final area of requirements discussed here relates to the opportunities in going beyond the monitored network to exchange threat intelligence via trusted platforms [22–24]. For example, via dedicated communications channels, the IDS may share with partners operational information (i.e., information on ongoing or recent attacks). Further, it will receive and should be able to incorporate information on novel attacks and classes of attacks while, in parallel, providing information on unclassified and potentially unknown attacks. The sharing of cyber threat intelligence has the potential to facilitate the attribution of a cyberattack [25, 26], and contribute to the deterrence of malicious activities in cyberspace. Overall, advanced intrusion detection, sharing information on cyberattacks and other threat intelligence, and enhanced situational awareness are expected to increase cyber resilience at organizational, sectoral, and national levels [27].

Our working assumption is that by utilizing advances in big data technologies, computing power, and open software machine learning libraries, even a small team of researchers will be able to develop an advanced IDS meeting all requirements listed in this section. Our particular scientific interest is in the second and the third group of requirements presented above. The respective research hypothesis is that by combining the outputs of carefully selected machine learning methods, it is possible to considerably increase the accuracy of attack classification while reducing false alarms.

Before presenting the architecture of this ensemble-based approach to intrusion detection, the following section reviews the opportunities for resolving the main challenges in developing an advanced IDS.

4   Opportunities

4.1   Big Data Tools and Architectures

In parallel with the generation of increasing amounts of data, hardware and software industries develop novel and ever more powerful tools to handle big data.

In terms of local storage, HDDs continue the be of interest, while the NAND technology allows to increase the capacity and cost-effectiveness of SSDs. In addition, cloud services can also provide efficient storage solutions.

The processing power continues to be on the increase as well. Over the last 25 years, the available power per dollar has increased by a factor of ten roughly every four years. Recently, this trend started slowing down, with a ten-times increase every 10–16 years [28]. However, this slowdown is compensated by new processor technologies, allowing to incorporate parallelism in CPUs and GPUs. Furthermore, academic and company researchers have been working over the past decade to develop architectures tailored to speeding up network traffic processing and detecting intrusions in real-time. In one such example, researchers have managed to increase processing speeds substantially while avoiding data loss by parallelizing processes among multiple CPUs and GPUs and network interface controllers [29].

In terms of software, Apache Spark and Cassandra are among the proven big data technologies and continue to be in high demand. As of 2021, these five tools for handling big data are mostly used [30]:

- *Apache Storm* is a distributed tool for the real-time processing of data streams (unlike the batch processing in Apache Spark). It is scalable, open-source, flexible, and robust.
- *MongoDB* is an open-source document-oriented NoSQL database. It can store data of any type and run on several servers.
- *Cassandra* is preferred for processing structured data sets. It replicates the data on several nodes to avoid a single point of failure. Backing up and restoring data are built-in features.
- Initially developed as an open-source Apache Hadoop distribution, *Cloudera* is considered as one of the fastest and most secure big data technologies. In addition, it provides a built-in capability to create and train data models.
- *OpenRefine* is a powerful tool for cleaning data and converting it into different formats.

Of particular interest to our study are the examples of open software and open architectures, providing opportunities to add computational power when it becomes available and thus speed up the process of developing big data-based intrusion detection solutions.

4.2 Datasets

In 1998, DARPA launched a program aiming to evaluate intrusion detection methods and techniques. A year later, a competition was organized as part of the program. The organizers used a synthetically generated dataset with 4.8 million rows and 41 features that became known as the KDD Cup 1999 dataset. Although the dataset was later criticized for containing duplicate entries, being unbalanced, and other reasons, the approach proved its utility in providing labeled data for supervised learning and serving as a benchmark for comparing the performance of various methods [31].

That triggered a significant interest in providing labeled datasets accounting for new sources and types of attacks. The following datasets are of highest current interest [18]:

- NSL-KDD 2009, provided by the Canadian Institute for Cybersecurity and the University of New Brunswick and resolving some of the issues in the original 1999 dataset (this and other datasets of the Canadian Institute for Cybersecurity, listed below, are available at https://www.unb.ca/cic/datasets/index.html).
- UNSW NB15 IDS dataset, collected by the University of New South Wales, Sydney, Australia, with 49 features and over 2.5 million records representing nine types of attacks [32] (available at https://research.unsw.edu.au/projects/unsw-nb15-dataset).
- MAWILab is a database in place since 2010. It records daily datasets consisting of 15-min network traffic between two endpoints – in Japan and in the US. The process of labeling is automated, and labels fall into four broad categories – anomalous, suspicious, notice, and benign (available at http://mawi.wide.ad.jp/mawi/).
- The UGR'16 dataset is provided by researchers from the University of Granada in Spain. It combines real traffic from a provided of internet services with synthetically generated attacks and allows longitudinal studies (available at https://nesg.ugr.es/nesg-ugr16/).

- CIDDS-001 and CIDDS-002 flow-based datasets, generated by researchers from the Coburg University of Applied Sciences, Germany in 2017, simulate a small business environment. They represent respectively three types of attack and five types of port scans [33] (available at https://www.hs-coburg.de/forschung/forschungsprojekte-oef fentlich/informationstechnologie/cidds-coburg-intrusion-detection-data-sets.html).
- ISCX-IDS-2012, CIC-IDS-2017, and CIC-IDS-2018 are all generated by the Canadian Institute for Cybersecurity. The first dataset consists of seven days of network activity with four types of attacks (one being an insider threat). The second represents 14 attack types (several types are all DoS/DDoS attacks) in five-day traffic. The third dataset covers five classes of attacks. Since 2014, the Canadian Institute for Cybersecurity is publishing datasets representing particular attack classes or typical for an operating system, with a focus on Android.
- The LITNET-2020 dataset is collected by researchers from the Kaunas University of Technology, Lithuania. It includes real traffic among academic institutions in Lithuania, described by 85 network flow features and representing 12 attack types [34] (available at https://dataset.litnet.lt/).

Except for MAWILab and LITNET, all these datasets are, at least partially, synthetically generated. All of the listed datasets afford rigorous testing of novel methods and tools and benchmarking.

4.3 Methods, Algorithms, and Open Software

The most important contribution to the timely development of an ensemble-based intrusion detection system is the free access to software libraries, including codes of advanced and rigorously tested methods and algorithms. These realizations allow us to test and compare the performance of various machine learning methods over most steps of the IDS pipeline. In selecting the examples below, we gave preference to libraries available in Python.

A number of open-source libraries support data preprocessing. *Pandas* is one powerful open-source data analysis and manipulation tool (https://pandas.pydata.org/). It provides interfaces to all main data formats and allows for intelligent data alignment and integrated handling of missing data. Another package, *sklearn.preprocessing*, provides various utility functions and transformer classes to transform raw vectors into a representation suitable for the downstream estimators.

The next task is feature selection [35], intended to reduce the dimensionality of the input data and increase the performance of intrusion detection methods. BorutaPy (https://github.com/scikit-learn-contrib/boruta_py) is the Python version of Boruta – an open-access library initially written in R. It includes several methods that allow to identify all features relevant to a classification task and rank them. *FeatureSelector* is another tool for dimensionality reduction (https://github.com/WillKoehrsen/feature-selector). It enables the identification of missing values, single unique values, collinear features, features of zero of low importance that can be potentially removed. Further, it supports the visualization of the input data and its characteristics.

Numerous machine learning methods support the identification of anomalies and the classification of attacks. Among the best known are decision trees, gradient boosting techniques (e.g., CatBoost, XGBoost, Microsoft's LightGBM), bagging techniques (e.g., random forest), support vector machines (SVM), nearest neighbors, Bayesian methods, and various types of artificial neural networks. The realization of many of these methods is available in open-source libraries. *Scikit-learn* is one such library (available https://scikit-learn.org/), including realizations on practically all main methods for supervised and unsupervised machine learning. In addition, communities of developers and users appear around a particular ML method. One such example is the XGBoost community (https://xgboost.ai/).

Scikit-learn can also serve as a framework to optimize the performance of an individual classifier, as well as the combination of the outputs of an ensemble of classifiers. Other frameworks, such as *Optuna, Hyperopt, Ray-Tune, mlmachine, Polyaxon, BayesianOptimization, Talos*, and *SHERPA*, can be used in solving this task of hyperparameter optimization. Some of these frameworks may perform even better than *scikit-learn*.

Although the problem of *explainability* was formulated fairly recently [16], several open-source tools are already well known in the research community. Among them are:

- The Local Interpretable Model-agnostic Explanations for machine learning models (*LIME*), designed to explain any black-box classifier;
- *InterpretML* is a flexible and customizable tool with a wide range of explainers and techniques using interactive visuals;
- *ELI5* allows to explain weights and predictions of linear classifiers and regressors, show feature importances, and explain predictions of decision trees and respective ensembles;
- *SHAP* (SHapley Additive exPlanations) is a game-theoretic approach to explain the output of any machine learning model. *SHAPash* is a newer addition enhancing the tool's visualization capacity.

This sample of methods is drawn from the GitHub list at https://github.com/EthicalML/awesome-production-machine-learning#explaining-black-box-models-and-datasets. *DeepExplain* is another library of interest, supporting the interpretation of the output of perturbation and gradient-based attribution methods for deep neural networks (available at github.com/marcoancona/DeepExplain).

The last task under discussion here is the identification of and adaptation to concept drifts. *Evidently* (https://github.com/evidentlyai/evidently) is an open-source python package that estimates and explores data drift for ML models during validation and monitors them in production. It generates interactive visual reports facilitating ad hoc analysis. Other open-source frameworks, such as *River* (https://github.com/online-ml/river), *Massive Online Analysis* (MOA) and *Scikit-Multiflow* [36], also provide for detection and/or adaptation to concept drifts.

Finally, some open-source libraries combine tools for solving more than one of the listed tasks. One example is the *BorutaShap* package [37] that combines the Boruta feature selection algorithm with the SHAP (Shapley Additive exPlanations) technique.

5 Ensemble-Based Network Intrusion Detection

Utilizing the opportunities presented above, we embarked on research and consequent development on an intrusion detection system designated as IDS Combo (Intrusion Detection [System] Combined Methods Toolbox). IDS Combo instantiates a comprehensive framework based on advanced and proven developments in the field of artificial intelligence and big data analytics. This section presents some of the main architectural views with respective tasks, underlying technologies, components, and interfaces.

The main components of the system are presented in Fig. 1 (inspired by Fig. 24 in [38]). As input information, it uses flows from diverse sources that represent network activity, database activity, data on user behavior, the activation and performance of applications, cyber threat intelligence, and others. Several tools allow for capturing and collecting such information. The data preprocessing component provides data consolidation, handling missing values, removal of duplicates, data reduction, enrichment, and transformation. The feature engineering component is dedicated to the generation, transformation, and extraction of features and selecting those among them that would maximize the accuracy of the classification and enhance the computational performance. Realizing the machine learning detector requires selecting suitable methods and algorithms, optimizing the respective models, tuning model parameters, and creating an ensemble of models. Decision-making is based on anomaly detection and attacks classification by each individual model and combining the outputs of the ensemble of models. Finally, data post-processing includes applying techniques for reducing false alarms, correlating and ranking alerts, identifying concept drifts and adapting/retraining models to them, and storing data and results.

In terms of underlying technologies, we selected:

- Apache Spark and Hadoop HDFS for data management, parallelization of the computations, and adding additional storage and computational resources when feasible;
- Python and PySpark for software development;
- Kibana for the design of the graphic user interface.

The core of IDS Combo—the ensemble of methods and respective models—is in the center of Fig. 2. The output of all models is combined to maximize the accuracy of the classification of intrusions and reduce false alarms. During the development phase, the attack dataset is split into three parts. The first is used for training the IDS, the second part, not seen during training, is used for testing, and the third – to emulate an input data stream and test the system's capacity to perform in real-time. When deployed (as illustrated in Fig. 2), IDS Combo will exchange alerts and information on cyber incidents with partners via a trusted platform (on the figure – the Early Warning System developed within the ECHO project). In addition, IDS Combo will provide the platform alerts with the respective contextual information in cases it has been unable to classify an intrusion; such cases may indicate new types of cyberattacks. And vice versa, IDS Combo will take from the platform information on new types of attacks discovered by others and will adapt its classification algorithms accordingly.

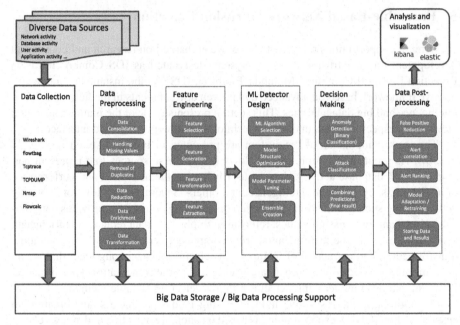

Fig. 1. IDS Combo component architecture.

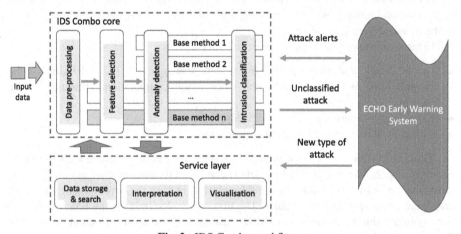

Fig. 2. IDS Combo workflow.

The main behavioral view on IDS Combo is presented in Fig. 3. It shows the developers and the network admins working jointly to deploy and test IDS Combo in the specific network environment and the threat analyst (or another appropriate expert in the organization running the network) as the main user.

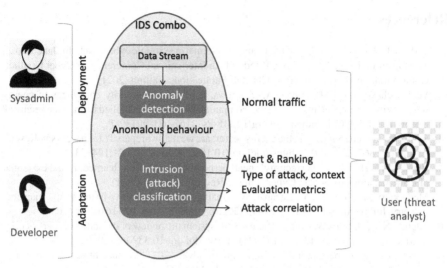

Fig. 3. IDS Combo behavioral view.

6 Conclusion

The increased capacity to collect, store, and process vast amounts of data on the functioning of computer networks provides opportunities to develop, test, and validate novel data-based machine learning methods for intrusion detection. There are, however, some obstacles to using the available data. This paper reviews the challenges related primarily to the quality of data and the unpredictable evolution of the threat landscape.

Fortunately, there is a parallel trend of intensive development of methods and technologies to overcome these obstacles, and many of them are tested rigorously and can be freely accessed. This allows even small research teams to realize innovative ideas.

One such idea is to use an ensemble of methods to increase the accuracy of intrusion detection while seeking to enhance the explainability of the outputs of machine learning methods and provide adaptation to concept drifts. This paper presented a respective tool called IDS Combo.

By the time of writing this paper, the research hypothesis has been confirmed – by combining the outputs of more than a dozen ML methods, we have been able to increase the accuracy of classification considerably. The NSL KDD dataset was used for this purpose. The current plan is to transition to larger datasets, add deep learning methods, and test the real-time performance over emulated network data streams. Among the medium-term tasks are to enhance the transparency of machine learning methods and provide for adaptation of the ensemble of methods to concept drifts. In the longer term, we will aim to demonstrate the applicability of IDS Combo in a real network environment and explore potential vulnerabilities [39] in the reliance on open-source software.

Acknowledgement. This work was supported by the ECHO project, which has received funding from the European Union's Horizon 2020 research and innovation programme under grant agreement no. 830943.

References

1. Vedral, B.: The vulnerability of the financial system to a systemic cyberattack. In: Jančárková, T., Lindström, L., Visky, G., Zotz, P. (eds.) 13th International Conference on Cyber Conflict: Going Viral, pp. 95–110. NATO CCDCOE Publications, Tallinn (2021)
2. Venkatachary, S.K., Alagappan, A., Andrews, L.J.B.: Cybersecurity challenges in energy sector (virtual power plants) - can edge computing principles be applied to enhance security? Energy Inf. **4**, 5 (2021). https://doi.org/10.1186/s42162-021-00139-7
3. Smith, D.C.: Cybersecurity in the energy sector: are we really prepared? J. Energy Nat. Resour. Law **39**(3), 365–275 (2021). https://doi.org/10.1080/02646811.2021.1943935
4. Reeder, J.R., Hall, T.: Cybersecurity's pearl harbor moment: lessons learned from the colonial pipeline ransomware attack. Cyber Defense Rev. **6**(3), 15–39 (2021)
5. Mednikarov, B., Tsonev, Y., Lazarov, A.: Analysis of cybersecurity issues in the maritime industry. Inf. Secur. Int. J. **47**(1), 27–43 (2020). https://doi.org/10.11610/isij.4702
6. Tuptuk, N., Hazell, P., Watson, J., Hailes, S.: A systematic review of the state of cyber-security in water systems. Water **13**(1), 81 (2021). https://doi.org/10.3390/w13010081
7. Sobers, R.: 134 Cybersecurity Statistics and Trends for 2021. Varonis. https://www.varonis.com/blog/cybersecurity-statistics/. Accessed 16 Mar 2021
8. Bulao, J.: How Much Data Is Created Every Day in 2021?. Techjury. https://techjury.net/blog/how-much-data-is-created-every-day/. Accessed 06 Aug 2021
9. Vellante, D., Floyer, D.: A new era of innovation: Moore's Law is not dead and AI is ready to explode. SiliconAngle. https://siliconangle.com/2021/04/10/new-era-innovation-moores-law-not-dead-ai-ready-explode/. Accessed 10 Apr 2021
10. Stetsenko, I.V., Demydenko, M.: Signature-based intrusion detection hardware-software complex. Inf. Secur. Int. J. **47**(2), 221–231 (2020). https://doi.org/10.11610/isij.4715
11. Kok, A., Mestric, I.I., Valiyev, G., Street, M.: Cyber threat prediction with machine learning. Inf. Secur. Int. J. **47**(2), 203–220 (2020). https://doi.org/10.11610/isij.4714
12. Alzahrani, A.O., Alenazi, M.J.F.: Designing a network intrusion detection system based on machine learning for software defined networks. Future Internet **13**(5), 111 (2021). https://doi.org/10.3390/fi13050111
13. De Mauro, A., Greco, M., Grimaldi, M.: A formal definition of Big Data based on its essential features. Libr. Rev. **65**(3), 122–135 (2016). https://doi.org/10.1108/LR-06-2015-0061
14. Firican, G.: The 10 Vs of Big Data. tdwi, February 8 (2017). https://tdwi.org/articles/2017/02/08/10-vs-of-big-data.aspx
15. Zuech, R., Khoshgoftaar, T.M., Wald, R.: Intrusion detection and big heterogeneous data: a survey. J. Big Data **2**, 3 (2015). https://doi.org/10.1186/s40537-015-0013-4
16. Rudin, C.: Stop explaining black box machine learning models for high stakes decisions and use interpretable models instead. Nat. Mach. Intell. **1**, 206–215 (2019). https://doi.org/10.1038/s42256-019-0048-x
17. Rostami, S., Kleszcz, A., Dimanov, D., Katos, V.: A machine learning approach to dataset imputation for software vulnerabilities. In: Dziech, A., Mees, W., Czyżewski, A. (eds.) MCSS 2020. CCIS, vol. 1284, pp. 25–36. Springer, Cham (2020). https://doi.org/10.1007/978-3-030-59000-0_3
18. Chou, D., Jijang, M.: Data-Driven Network Intrusion Detection: A Taxonomy of Challenges and Methods. arXiv preprint https://arxiv.org/abs/2009.07352v1 (2020). Accessed 03 May 2021
19. Zednik, C.: Solving the black box problem: a normative framework for explainable artificial intelligence. Philos. Technol. **34**(2), 265–288 (2019). https://doi.org/10.1007/s13347-019-00382-7

20. Linardatos, P., Papastefanopoulos, V., Kotsiantis, S.: Explainable AI: a review of machine learning interpretability methods. Entropy **23**(1), 18 (2021). https://doi.org/10.3390/e23 010018
21. Mehmood, H., Kostakos, P., Cortes, M., Anagnostopoulos, T., Pirttikangas, S., Gilman, E.: Concept drift adaptation techniques in distributed environment for real-world data streams. Smart Cities **4**(1), 349–371 (2021). https://doi.org/10.3390/smartcities4010021
22. Rajamäki, J., Katos, V.: Information sharing models for early warning systems of cybersecurity intelligence. Inf. Secur. Int. J. **46**(2), 198–214 (2020). https://doi.org/10.11610/isij. 4614
23. Yucel, C., Chalkias, I., Mallis, D., Karagiannis, E., Cetinkaya, D., Katos, V.: On the assessment of completeness and timeliness of actionable cyber threat intelligence artefacts. In: Dziech, A., Mees, W., Czyżewski, A. (eds.) MCSS 2020. CCIS, vol. 1284, pp. 51–66. Springer, Cham (2020). https://doi.org/10.1007/978-3-030-59000-0_5
24. Sharkov, G., Papazov, Y., Todorova, Ch., Koykov, G., Zahariev, G.: MonSys: a scalable platform for monitoring digital services availability, threat intelligence and cyber resilience situational awareness. Inf. Secur. Int. J. **46**(2), 155–167 (2020). https://doi.org/10.11610/isij. 4611
25. Rid, T., Buchanan, B.: Attributing cyber attacks. J. Strateg. Stud. **38**(1–2), 4–37 (2015). https:// doi.org/10.1080/01402390.2014.977382
26. Goel, S.: How improved attribution in cyber warfare can help de-escalate cyber arms race. Connect. Quart. J. **19**(1), 87–95 (2020). https://doi.org/10.11610/Connections.19.1.08
27. Sharkov, G.: Assessing the maturity of national cybersecurity and resilience. Connect. Quart. J. **19**(4), 5–24 (2020). https://doi.org/10.11610/Connections.19.4.01
28. Trends in the Cost of Computing, AI Impacts. https://aiimpacts.org/trends-in-the-cost-of-com puting/. Accessed 15 May 2021
29. Vasiliadis, G., Polychronakis, M., Ioannidis, S.: MIDeA: a multi-parallel intrusion detection architecture. In: Proceedings of the 18th ACM Conference on Computer and Communications Security CCS'11, pp. 297–308 (2011). https://doi.org/10.1145/2046707.2046741
30. Sharma, R.: Top 5 Big Data Tools [Most Used in 2021], upgrade, January 3, 2021. https:// www.upgrad.com/blog/big-data-tools/
31. Siddique, K., Akhtar, Z., Khan, F.A., Y, F.A.: Kdd cup 99 data sets: a perspective on the role of data sets in network intrusion detection research. Computer **52**(2), 41–51 (2019). https:// doi.org/10.1109/MC.2018.2888764
32. Moustafa, N., Slay, J.: UNSW-NB15: a comprehensive data set for network intrusion detection systems (UNSW-NB15 network data set). In: Military Communications and Information Systems Conference MilCIS, pp. 1–6 (2015). https://doi.org/10.1109/MilCIS.2015.7348942
33. Ring, M., Wunderlich, S., Grüdl, D., Landes, D., Hotho, A.: Creation of flow-based data sets for intrusion detection. Inf. Warfare **16**(4), 41–54 (2017)
34. Damasevicius, R., et al.: LITNET-2020: an annotated real-world network flow dataset for network intrusion detection. Electronics **9**(5), 800 (2020). https://doi.org/10.3390/electroni cs9050800
35. Umar, M.A., Chen, Z., Liu, Y.: A hybrid intrusion detection with decision tree for feature selection. Inf. Secur. Int. J. **49** (2021). https://doi.org/10.11610/isij.4901
36. López, J.: The ravages of concept drift in stream learning applications and how to deal with it. KDnuggets. https://www.kdnuggets.com/2019/12/ravages-concept-drift-stream-learning-applications.html. Accessed 30 May 2021
37. Keany, E.: Is this the Best Feature Selection Algorithm 'BorutaShap'?. medium.com. June 1, 2020. https://medium.com/analytics-vidhya/is-this-the-best-feature-selection-algorithm-bor utashap-8bc238aa1677

38. Ullah, F., Babar, M.A.: Architectural tactics for big data cybersecurity analytics systems: a review. J. Syst. Softw. **151**, 81–118 (2019). https://doi.org/10.1016/j.jss.2019.01.051

39. Zhang, C., Costa-Perez, X., Patras, P.: Tiki-taka: attacking and defending deep learning-based intrusion detection systems. In: Proceedings of the 2020 ACM SIGSAC Conference on Cloud Computing Security Workshop (CCSW'20), pp. 27–39 (2020). https://doi.org/10.1145/341 1495.3421359

Cybersecurity in Donated Distributed Computing for Evolutionary Algorithms

Petar Tomov, Iliyan Zankinski, and Todor Balabanov$^{(\boxtimes)}$ (ID)

Institute of Information and Communication Technologies - Bulgarian Academy of Sciences, Acad. Georgi Bonchev Str., Block 2, 1113 Sofia, Bulgaria
p.tomov@iit.bas.bg, iliyan@hsi.iccs.bas.bg, todorb@iinf.bas.bg

Abstract. Donated distributed computing, also known as volunteer computing, is a form of distributed computing that is organized as a public donation of calculating resources. Donated calculating power can involve thousands of separate CPUs and it can achieve the performance of a supercomputer. In most of the cases donated distributed computing is organized by open source software, which can lead to the involvement of many more volunteers. This research focuses on cybersecurity issues when donated distributed computing is used for optimization with evolutionary algorithms.

1 Introduction

A subset of calculating problems has the characteristic that different computation steps are not strongly connected to each other and those steps can be calculated separately. In such problems, parallel programming is used and computation time is usually reduced by involving more calculating units. According to who owns and administers the calculating resources there are two groups of parallel computing - calculating devices under your own control and calculating devices under somebody else control. Part of the first group (private owned) is single machines with multi-cores or multiprocessors, supercomputer with many identical modules, a grid [1] of identical single machines and a cluster of different single machines. It does not matter what is the hardware specification in the first group, which is common for the first group is that the organizer of the parallel computations has full access and full control over the hardware. This situation is very important when cybersecurity in massive computing is discussed. In the second group different type of computing hardware is organized to compute a common task, but calculating devices are not under the control of the person or the organization who/which is doing the computations. When the involved devices are participating in a volunteer principle there is no control of any kind over the donated calculating power. The biggest advantage of the donated distributed computing is that it comes at a very low price [2]. The biggest disadvantage of the donated distributed computing is that it comes with a wide list of security and reliability issues.

Fig. 1. FOREX data for EUR/USD currency pair.

General cybersecurity does not differ in donated distributed computing than the other network communication software solutions. What is more, in donated distributed computing is related to calculation accuracy and reliability of the results. Numerical calculations that are done on different hardware can lead to different results just because of the machine word, floating-point numbers presentation and different error handling. Such differences are not human provoked and are directly math dependent. A bigger problem are human interventions with calculation instructions executed on the device and the information exchanged with the central distributed computing infrastructure. Even that it is relatively complicated a malicious user is capable to change what is calculated on his/her device directly in the device memory. A malicious user is capable to change the input data and to manipulate the output data. The general problem for the organizer of the donated distributed computing infrastructure is that he/she can not trust any of the volunteer participants.

This study is devoted to cybersecurity issues in donated distributed computing when it is used for evolutionary algorithms. After the introductory part, the paper is organized as follows: Evolutionary algorithms in donated distributed computing are discussed; After that, some examples of damaged reliability are presented; And finally, conclusions and some further research are proposed.

2   Evolutionary Algorithms

There are many evolutionary algorithms. The keyword in this subset of optimization algorithms is evolutionary. It means that some kind of evolution is applied. Most of the evolutionary algorithms are organized on the top of some population kind. Their application is mainly in global optimization problems. When population is used it is formed by vectors into solution space. Each individual is treated as a potential candidate for an optimal or suboptimal solution.

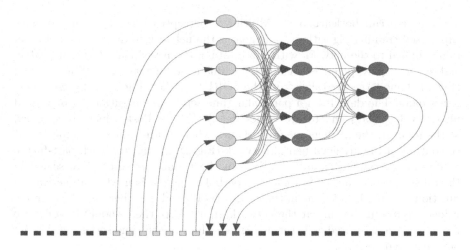

Fig. 2. Three-layer perceptron organized for time series forecasting.

Individuals are evaluated according predefined fitness function and the achieved fitness value is used in the process of evolution. The basic idea is that better-fitted individuals should have better chances to evolve with the hope that evolved individuals will offer better solutions.

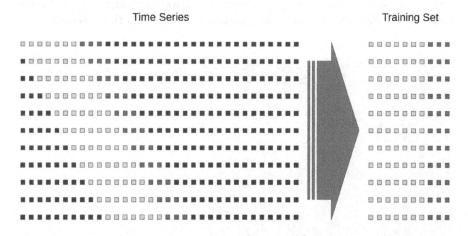

Fig. 3. Artificial neural network training set.

In this research, the focus is over genetic algorithms and differential evolution used for artificial neural networks training in financial forecasting problems [3,4]. Artificial neural networks are a well-known tool for classification and forecasting. Most of the artificial neural networks are organized as nodes (of neurons) and some kind of weights between the nodes. Some of the artificial neural networks are organized in layers and it is proven that with a three-layer perceptron any function can be learned [5]. Multilayer perceptrons are used mainly with supervised training algorithms. The goal is the network to approximate a function supplied to the network with subset of input-output pairs. In this research, a three-layer perceptron is organized for financial time series [6–8] forecasting (Fig. 2). Time series are taken from the FOREX market (Fig. 1) and present currency pairs. The data from a particular time series are conditionally organized in past values (lag) and future values (lead) (Fig. 3). Past values are supplied at the input of the artificial neural network when future values are expected at the output of the artificial neural network (Fig. 2). In this way each past-future pair forms a training example. Values in the training examples are scaled in the range of −0.9 and +0.9 because hyperbolic tangent is used as an activation function. Scaling is not done in the range of −1.0 and +1.0 because the extreme values are too influencing at the network input. Also, there should be a chance for the network to predict lower or higher values in the time series which were not presented yet.

In a classical multilayer perceptron layers are fully connected. It means that each neuron has connections with all neurons from the next layer. The size of the input layer is problem dependant and it is adjusted manually or with some kind of self-adapting algorithm. The size of the output layer depends on how many values ahead are needed as a forecast. The size of the hidden layer can be set as the average of the input and output sum, but in most cases, it is experimentally adjusted. The pruning algorithm also can be used for the estimation of the hidden layer size. The topology of the artificial neural network can be put under heuristic optimization, but such an approach is not used in this research.

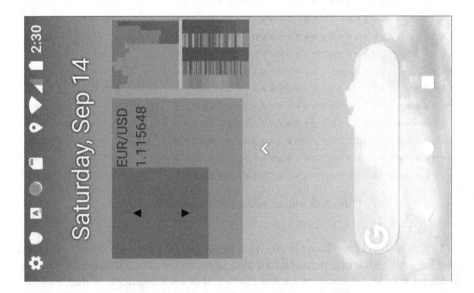

Fig. 4. Mobile application for donated distributed computing in financial forecasting.

Weights of the artificial neural network can be presented as vector of real numbers. Each vector of weights is loaded into the artificial neural network structure and it is trained with classical back-propagation until there is no prediction improvement with prespecified epsilon level. A group of weights vectors forms a local evolutionary population. The evolutionary process is applied locally and the best-found solutions are sent to the remote server in such a way that to become a part of the global population. The security problem rises exactly at this point when calculation results are sent to the remote server. There is no guarantee that what is sent is accurate and it is not manipulated by the owner of the calculating device.

A major species of the evolutionary algorithms is that the optimization process goes across many intermediate calculations which are not used as part of the final result. If malicious user manipulates the reported results in the global population low-quality evolutionary individuals will be reported. One strategy to fight with such a cybersecurity issue in the evolutionary donated distributed computing is by checking the individual on the server-side as part of the global population. Even such a strategy is possible it is not rational and cost-efficient. The main idea of the donated computations is to lower the expenses for server operation. Keeping the cost of the calculation low on the server-side is a common goal in donated computations. Because of this, it is not preferable individuals checking to be done on the server-side. The other strategy, which is much more efficient is to keep compromised individuals as part of the global population. From one side extra server time will be kept and from another side, the checking will be done on other donated devices during the next distribution of global population subsets as local populations. By implementing aging for the individuals in the global population the compromised individuals will be removed with the time goes on. Aging also will protect server storage capacity. As an additional positive side effect, the compromised individuals act as genotype diversity into the local populations, which indirectly can work as an improvement of the evolutionary process.

With the exponential spread of smart mobile devices donated distributed computing offers infinite possibilities for practical implementations. Such a project is developed at IICT-BAS under the name VitoshaTrade [9]. It is an Android Active Wallpaper (Fig. 4) organized for artificial neural networks training with the Encog AI framework and Apache Commons genetic algorithms library.

3   Conclusions

With its cost-efficiency and with the almost infinite scaling capabilities donated distributed computing is one of the most promising areas of scientific researches. It has applications in all areas with big data and a huge amount of heavy calculations which should be done. Of course, there is a limitation that calculations should be possible to be divided and to be done simultaneously on separate machines [10]. When donated distributed computing is needed for population-based evolutionary algorithms the security issues can be even positive as a side effect than negative as it is in the other types of donated calculations. As further research it will be interesting how cybersecurity will be influenced if users are allowed to vote [11,12] with their subjective opinion about future financial situations.

Acknowledgments. This research is funded by Velbazhd Software LLC and it is partially supported by the Bulgarian Ministry of Education and Science (contract D01-205/23.11.2018) under the National Scientific Program "Information and Communication Technologies for a Single Digital Market in Science, Education and Security (ICTinSES)", approved by DCM # 577/17.08.2018.

References

1. Chokesatean, P.: Credibility-based Binary Feedback Model for Grid Resource Planning. University of Pittsburgh (2008)
2. Chang, C., Narayana, S.S., Buyya, R.: Indie fog an efficient fog-computing infrastructure for the Internet of Things. Computer **50**(9), 92–98 (2017)
3. Bohn, A., Guting, T., Mansmann, T.: MoneyBee Aktienkursprognose mit kunstlicher intelligenz bei hoher rechenleistung. Wirtschaftsinf **45**, 325–333 (2003)
4. Donate, J.P., Li, X., Sanchez, G.G., Miguel, A.S.: Time series forecasting by evolving artificial neural networks with genetic algorithms, differential evolution and estimation of distribution algorithm. Neural Comput. Appl. **22**, 11–20 (2013)
5. Irie, M.: Capabilities of three-layered perceptrons. In: Proceedings of IEEE International Conference on Neural Networks, vol. 1, pp. 641–648 (1988)
6. Bandt, C., Pompe, B.: Permutation entropy a natural complexity measure for time series. Phys. Rev. Lett. **88**(17), 174102 (2002)
7. Salvador, S., Chan, P.: Toward accurate dynamic time warping in linear time and space. Intell. Data Anal. **11**(5), 561–580 (2007)
8. Lan, Y.: Computational approaches for time series analysis and prediction datadriven methods for pseudo-periodical sequences. University of Bradford (2009)
9. Zankinski, I., Barova, M., Tomov, P.: Hybrid approach based on combination of backpropagation and evolutionary algorithms for artificial neural networks training by using mobile devices in distributed computing environment. In: Lirkov, I., Margenov, S. (eds.) LSSC 2017. LNCS, vol. 10665, pp. 425–432. Springer, Cham (2018). https://doi.org/10.1007/978-3-319-73441-5_46
10. Megiddo, N.: Applying parallel computation algorithms in the design of serial algorithms. J. Assoc. Comput. Mach. **30**(4), 852–865 (1983)
11. Leppanen, T., Alvarez Lacasia, J., Tobe, Y., Sezaki, K., Riekki, J.: Mobile crowdsensing with mobile agents. Auton. Agent. Multi-Agent Syst. **31**, 1–35 (2017)
12. Laukkanen, S., Kangas, A., Kangas, J.: Applying voting theory in natural resource management a case of multiple-criteria group decision support. J. Environ. Manage. **64**(2), 127–137 (2002)

Modelling a Multi-agent Protection System of an Enterprise Network

Alla Hrebennyk[1] ⓘ, Elena Trunova[2](✉) ⓘ, Volodymyr Kazymyr[2] ⓘ,
and Alexander Tarasov[2]

[1] Institute of Mathematical Machines and Systems Problems, 42 Ac. Glushkov Ave.,
Kyiv 03680, Ukraine
[2] Chernihiv National University of Technology, 95 Shevchenko Str., Chernihiv 14035, Ukraine
e.trunova@gmail.com

Abstract. This paper considers approaches to distribute functions of a corporate network protection system between a set of informational modules – agents, that will ensure mobility, adaptability and fault tolerance of a multi-agent protection system (MAS). The analysis of classes of MAS agents by their functionality is conducted. The integration of MAS in corporate networks is based on the distribution of corporate network components between agents which are responsible for their protection. Internal and external information flows caused by user and attacker actions are used to reproduce network activity processes. By involving sets that simulate the behavior of a regular user, an attacker and a component, the set of MAS agents has been extended to include the following sets: user agent; intruder agent; agent component. The modeling of the MAS agents was conducted with using of the Unified Modeling Language, in particular, the state diagram is constructed and the algorithms of classical agents are described in details: protection agent and counteraction agent, and new ones: user agent, intruder agent, component agent.

It is noted that the proposed approach has a number of advantages, namely: the components of a typical corporate network are distributed across several nodes, so MAS agents will also operate on different nodes, which will ensure the saving and mobility of computing resources; the use of MAS will allow to adapt to changes in the network architecture easily; the creation of new agents provides flexibility of the solution and high scalability; due to the distributed work of agents, the fault tolerance of the system increases: it is harder to attack and disable than systems with a single security server; management of the entire corporate security system can be organized centrally by combining multiple agents using an integration information bus.

Keywords: Multi-agent system (MAS) · Corporate network · Security system

1 Introduction

The rapid growth of the computing abilities of computers, along with their reduction in price, has led to the mass implementation of various software systems in all spheres of human activity: education, medicine, financial sector and so on. Corporate networks

T. Tagarev and N. Stoianov (Eds.): DIGILIENCE 2020, CCIS 1790, pp. 113–122, 2024.
https://doi.org/10.1007/978-3-031-44440-1_18

(CNs) are no exception. CNs are structures, the main purpose of which is to ensure efficiency, ergonomics and security of work and internal processes of a particular corporation or organization.

The quality of CN directly influences on the efficiency of corporations and organizations, and is one of the indicators of their security [9]. Today, the protection of CN and the data stored in them is one of the most critical tasks faced by information security professionals, so the exploring of methods for solving problems of security control (SC) is a very promising area. The most promising modern field for research is artificial intelligence (AI). Among the methods of AI can be identified production systems, neural networks, multi-agent systems (MAS) [9]. Classical AI theory in the process of solving the problem creates a single intelligent system, which is sometimes called an intelligent agent. Such a system, having access to the necessary knowledge and computing resources, solves some global problem. In contrast, MAS theory uses the opposite approach – the whole system is divided into many agents, each of which can solve only some local problem, because it does not have comprehensive knowledge of the global problem [10].

The purpose of the work is to distribute functions of the Corporate networks (CNs) between the set of information modules – agents, that will ensure mobility, adaptability, fault tolerance of multi-agent protection system, and modeling of the selected classes of agents considering requirements for their functionality and principles of interaction in the general protection system.

2   Multi-agent System for Corporate Network Protection

According to the principles of MAS theory, each component of the CN is being assigned a set of agents, and each of the agents is responsible for a set of components. Therefore, the solution is to implement a set of agents and organize effective interaction between them [2].

Based on the requirements for the functionality of the CS system, when constructing it according to the principles of MAS, the following classes (sets) of agents can be distinguished:

1. Analysis agents (AnA) – monitor the information flows of the network, identify vulnerabilities of the CN components, assess the current situation and report it to other agents that belong to the MAS. In particular, information about the vulnerability goes to the configuration agent, which is responsible for the component in which it was detected. The result of the analysis of information flows is transmitted to the protection agent (PA) for the further evaluation. AnA functions also include processing the results of responses of all other MAS agents [5].
2. Configuration agents (ConfA) – eliminate vulnerabilities and confirm their absence. If it is necessary, ConfA may initiate an unregulated additional AnA inspection. The work of ConfA requires information about subordinate and surrounding components, its relevant protection agents and about configuration agents of other nodes of the CN. The system administrator can act as a more "intelligent" CA.
3. Protection agents (PA) – provide calculation of coefficients of deviations (CD) of separate components or all topology of CN as a whole. Detect suspicious actions.

Protect agents in the process of their work using ontologies of normal behavior, which can be formed by training agents and receive ontologies of the dynamic state of CN from AnA for both one component and the CN as a whole. When deviations are detected, the work of the counteraction agent is initiated and the results of the operation are expected to be notified.

4. Counteraction agents (CountA) – if it is possible, stop the processes of unauthorized actions, identify their source, and eliminate the consequences. The results of the triggers must be available to other MAS agents.

5. Teaching agents (TA) – collect and process data to form an ontology of normal network behavior. The TA can receive information from a person, use its own learning algorithms based on data presented in different databases, or work in conjunction with PA (detecting an attack through its adapted mechanism, PA shares "knowledge" with TA, and TA with AnA). TA share training data to other agents. The data include schemes of known and new attacks, their signatures, vulnerabilities inherent in certain types of attacks or system components, and so on. TA is a common interface for training other agents, which accelerates the detection of new types of attacks and allows to increase the mobility and adaptability of MAS in general.

Formally in general, the MAS can be defined as follows [1, 6]:

$$MAS = (A, E_A, I_A),$$

where MAS – multi-agent system;

A – a set of agents;

E_A – a set of environments, in which agents operate;

I_A – a set of interactions.

The set of agents, as stated above, contains the next sets:

$$A = ((AnA), (ConfA), (PA), (CountA), (TA)),$$

where (AnA) – a set of analysis agents;

$(ConfA)$ – a set of configuration agents;

(PA) – a set of protection agent;

$(CountA)$ – a set of counteraction agents;

(TA) – a set of teaching agents.

Let us implement the MAS adaptation process to protect corporate networks, complementing it with the following sets:

BOS – a set of components the CN (corporate network) consists of;

S – a set of internal and external information threads, that are the sources of attacks;

AC_{us} – a set of user actions;

AC_{at} – a set of attacker actions.

So, the model of multi-agent system is the following:

$$MAS = (A, E_A, I_A, BOS, S, AC_{us}, AC_{at}).$$

Let us widen the set of MAS agents involving the sets modeling a behavior of a regular user, an intruder and a component of CN, in which the MAS operates, namely:

116   A. Hrebennyk et al.

(UA) – a set of user agents;
(IntA) – a set of intruder agents;
(CompA) – a set of component agents.
Then, the set of agents will be defined as follows:

$$A = ((AnA), (ConfA), (PA), (CountA), (TA), (UA), (IntA), (CompA)).$$

According to the topic of CN protection, the greatest attention is paid to protection and counteraction agents. Thus, a simplified composition of agent classes and modules that reproduce the structure and behavior of the CN were used to model the MAS. The analysis involves protection agents, countermeasures, as well as agents that simulate the behavior of a regular user, an intruder and a component of CN – a user agent, an intruder agent and an agent component, respectively.

A general view of the conceptual scheme of the simulated MAS with the selected set of agents and the interactions between them is presented in Fig. 1.

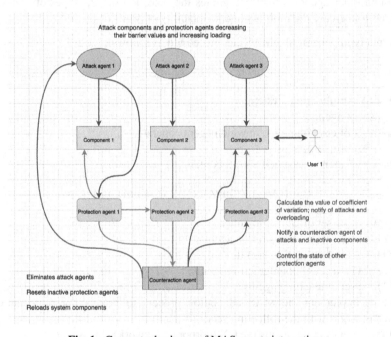

Fig. 1. Conceptual scheme of MAS agents interaction

Let us model the MAS agents using Unified Modeling Language (UML), constructing state diagrams corresponding to the agents [3, 4].

2.1 Protection Agent (PA)

Let us consider in details the work of a protection agent. The purpose of its work is to identify threats in real time (Fig. 2).

The work of this agent is based on determining the coefficient of deviation (C_{dev}) of real-time dynamic processes using the ontology of normal behavior of the subordinate agent component of the CN [8].

C_{dev} calculation algorithm depends on the specifics of the certain component of the CN. For the modeled system, the calculation of C_{dev} is based on the load of the components of the CN.

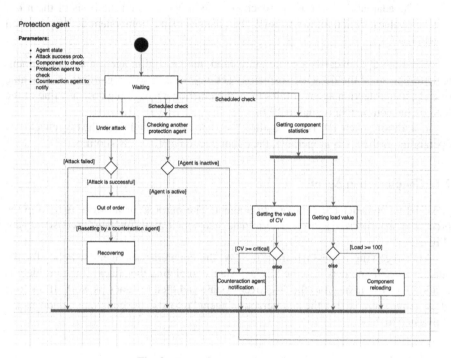

Fig. 2. Protection agent state diagram

The approach chosen for calculation C_{dev} is an analysis of the angle between two straight lines and is performed using the following algorithm:

1. Protection agent takes n load indicators.
2. Taken indicators form the points:
   (t_1, y_1), where t_1 – the time of the first taking, y_1 – its value;
   $(\bar{t}, \bar{y})$, where $\bar{t}$ – the average time of n-taking, $\bar{y}$ – the average value of n-taking;
   (t_n, y_n), where t_n – the time of the last taking, y_n – the relevant value.
3. For the obtained three points, two lines are constructed, each of which is described by an equation (by a point and an angular coefficient). The first line passes through the first and second points, the second – through the second and third.
4. The relevant angular coefficients are calculated by formulae:
   $$k_1 = \frac{\bar{y}-y_1}{\bar{t}-t_1}, k_2 = \frac{y_n-\bar{y}}{t_n-\bar{t}}.$$

5. The tangent of the angle between the lines:

$$tg\left(\frac{k_2 - k_1}{1 + k_1 \bullet k_2}\right).$$

6. The deviation coefficient is calculated:
$$C_{dev} = \text{arctg}\left(\frac{k_2 - k_1}{1 + k_1 \bullet k_2}\right).$$

The adaptability of this approach consists in working on the basis of the n last taken values, which allows to track the changes of the component activity level in real time.

When the C_{dev} exceeds a certain threshold, the protection agent notifies the counteraction agent of the detected suspicious activity. In addition, regardless of the value of C_{dev}, the protection agent notifies the counteraction agent of the critical value of the load on the component (equal to 100).

In addition, each PA is an "auditor" of another PA and periodically checks its operability. If the PA is inoperable, the counteraction agent is also notified.

2.2 Counteraction Agent

Next, let us consider the counteraction agent. The purpose of its work is to stop the process of unauthorized actions, determinate their source and eliminate the consequences (Fig. 3).

After receiving a message from the PA, the counteraction agent searches for the attacking agent and puts it in the "Delay" state completing the attack. If the problem is a failed PA, it switches it to the "Recovery" state and then resumes its work. If the load of the component is 100, the counteraction agent "reloads" the component and sets the load value to 0.

2.3 User Agent

User agents use the components sending requests that need to be processed, and thus simulate the process of internal activities of the CN (Fig. 4).

The request occurs with a certain probability, which is set as the parameter "Request probability" for each instance of the agent.

2.4 Intruder Agent

Intruder agents are a team of attacking agents (Fig. 5). They refer to the components with requests that need to be processed, and thus simulate the process of external appeals to the CN.

Because protection agents need some time to learn (gathering the information needed to calculate the deviation factor), attacking agents start their work with a delay, which is set by the relevant parameter "Delay". The value of the delay depends on the parameter "Minimal delay time" and takes a random value in the range [Minimum_delay; 2 × Minimum_delay].

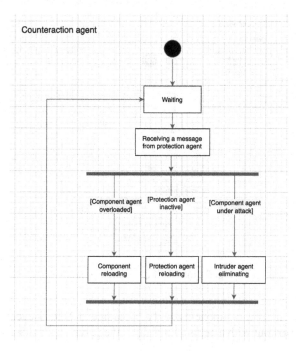

Fig. 3. Counteraction agent state diagram

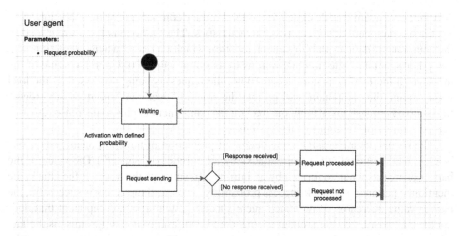

Fig. 4. User agent state diagram

During the delay, the attacking agent randomly selects the component defined by the "Target" parameter and simulates the attack by sending a corresponding request. After the delay, the actions of the intruder agent go into the state of "Waiting" for their processing by the protection agent. The logic of the probability of success or failure of

120   A. Hrebennyk et al.

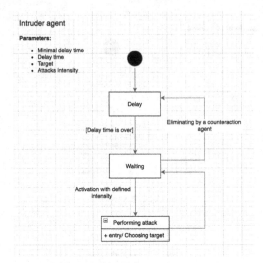

Fig. 5. Intruder agent state diagram

the attack is passed to the component agent as a parameter "Attack success probability". Re-attack is carried out with a certain intensity – the parameter "Attacks intensity".

2.5 Component Agent

A component agent was designed to model arbitrary components of the CN (Fig. 6).

Each component agent has two characteristics. The first one is the current load of the component (data availability characteristic), which increases when interacting with any other agent and after a while returns to its initial value – 0. Upon receiving of the message, if the load does not exceed 100%, the request is being processed. If the load is maximum, the component will go into the state of "overload" and does not process the received request. Over time, the load on the component begins to decrease (due to a certain number of iterations of the system).

The second characteristic is the degree of protection of the component (characteristic of data confidentiality) from attacks by an intruder – "Barrier". The value of the barrier decreases when requested by an intruder. To simulate the result of the attack, the mentioned parameter "Attack success probability" is used. If the attack is successful, the barrier value decreases. If an attack agent successfully attacks a component that does not have a barrier, that component is considered compromised. Compromise is the fact that an outsider has access to protected information. That is, the intruder captures the component, receives valuable data and can use them for their own purposes. If a zero-barrier component is attacked again, it sends an attack message to the related components involved in processing of the requests.

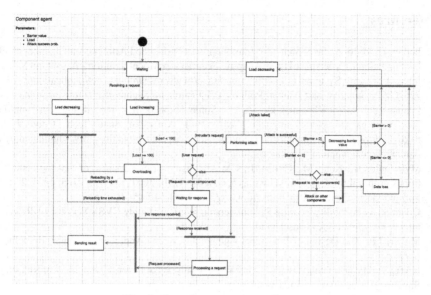

Fig. 6. Component agent state diagram

3 Conclusion

Implementation of the simulated multi-agent system of corporate network protection using one of the high-level programming languages would allow quantify C_{dev} and determinate the vulnerabilities of system, identify conditions, that make successful attacks by the intruder agent possible.

This approach has many advantages:

1. The components of a typical CN are distributed across several nodes, so agents of MAS will operate on different nodes as well. That ensures economy and mobility of computing resources;
2. Using MAS would allow to adapt easily to changes in the network architecture, because its composition can change depending on requirements of corporation in the current moment of time;
3. High flexibility and scalability of the solution due to ability to create new agents;
4. Distributed functioning of the agents increases the fault tolerance of the system: it is harder to attack and disable, than system with unified protection server;
5. Management of the whole corporate security system (CSS) can be performed in centralized way by associating the set of agents using an integration bus.

As an improvement to the system, the development of new protection agents with other approaches for defining C_{dev} may be proposed, for example, analysis of SQL queries to the CN database.

Acknowledgments. The work was carried out and funded under the NATO project CyRADARS (Cyber Rapid Analysis for Defense Awareness of Real-time Situation) – grant agreement number: G5286 [7].

References

1. Ferber, J.: Multi-Agent System: An Introduction to Distributed Artificial Intelligence (1999)
2. Getting Past the Cyberspace Hype: Adaptive Security – A Model Solution – A Solution Model, Internet Security Systems, (1997), 15 Jun. https://www.researchgate.net/publication/277714 726_Cyber-Security_and_Threat_Politics_US_Efforts_to_Secure_the_Information_Age
3. Landsberg, S.E., Khovanskikh A.A.: Some aspects of the design of multia-gent systems using the language UML. Bull. Voronezh State Tech. Univ. **9**, 4–8 (2012) https://cyberleninka.ru/article/n/nekotorye-aspekty-proektirovaniya-multiagentnyh-sistem-s-ispolzovaniem-yazyka-uml
4. Mylopoulos, J., Kolp, M., Castro, J.: UML for agent-oriented software development: the tropos proposal. In: Gogolla, M., Kobryn, C. (eds.) UML 2001. LN, vol. 2185, pp. 422–441. Springer, Heidelberg (2001). https://doi.org/10.1007/3-540-45441-1_31
5. Common Vulnerability Scoring System version 3.1: User Guide CVSS Version 3.1 Release. https://www.first.org/cvss/user-guide
6. Müller, J.P.: The Design of Intelligent Agents: A Layered Approach. Springer, Heidelberg (1996)
7. NATO SPS Project CyRADARS (Cyber Rapid Analysis for Defense Awareness of Real-time Situation). https://www.cyradars.net
8. Petrov, S.A.: Building adaptive security system based on multi-agent system, materials of the second international research and practice conference. Westwood (Canada) **2**, 196–201 (2013)
9. Shkarlet, S.M. (Ed.). Metody analizu ta modeliuvannia bezpeky rozpodilenykh informat-siinykh system [Methods of analysis and modeling of safety-related information systems]. Chernihiv: ChNTU [in Ukrainian] (2017)
10. Shoham, Y.: Multiagent Systems: Algorithmic, Game-Theoretic, and Logical Foundations. Cambridge University Press (2009). http://www.masfoundations.org/mas.pdf

Analysis of Workability of One-Way Functions Based on Cellular Automata in Diffie–Hellman Algorithm for Big Data Tasks

Volodymyr Shevchenko[1](✉) ⓘ, Georgi Dimitrov[2] ⓘ, Denys Berestov[1],
Pepa Petrova[2] ⓘ, Igor Sinitcyn[3] ⓘ, Eugenia Kovatcheva[2] ⓘ, Ivan Garvanov[2] ⓘ,
and Iva Kostadinova[2] ⓘ

[1] Taras Shevchenko National University of Kyiv, Kyiv, Ukraine
`vladimir_337@ukr.net`
[2] University of Library Studies and Information Technologies, Sofia, Bulgaria
[3] Institute of Software Systems, National Academy of Sciences of Ukraine, Kyiv, Ukraine

Abstract. The article deals with the peculiarities of using cellular automata as one-way functions in the Diffie-Hellman algorithm, which allows generating encryption keys for transmitting Big Data in conditions of information exchange via open communication channels. The authors improve the Diffie-Hellman algorithm by using a new type of one-way functions - cellular automats. The used automats have extended rules in the direction of determining the laws of birth rate, life continuation and death conditions, and control of the radius of intra-population interaction. The use of a multi-population cellular system is also considered as a separate extension of the cellular automata. Depending on user needs, the complexity of encryption can be adjusted (this will affect the time of algorithm execution and the reliability of a one-way function). A method has also been developed to test the performance of specific automats with configurable initial parameters, which allows testing the cellular automata before use. The new type of one-way functions allows using the Diffie-Hellman algorithm for frequent generation of encryption keys. The software was implemented in three programming languages: Python, MatLab and C#. This allows to compare results and implement the software required for the study in the languages most suitable for the tasks under consideration.

Keywords: Diffie-Hellman algorithm · Cellular automata · Mathematical statistics

1 Introduction

Actuality of the Work. Information exchange is an integral part of human society. The Internet makes it possible to exchange data faster, over greater distances and in greater volumes than it has been at any other stage of human development. According to Metcalfe's law, the larger the network, the greater its value. And where there is valuable information, there are abusers who want to illegally take advantage of the information stored on the network.

The number of attempts to maliciously obtain information from the information network is growing at least twice as fast as the global GDP growth rate [1–3], which is almost linearly related to the growth of the market for digital devices, mostly mobile. Among the main reasons for information security incidents are [4] targeted attacks - 36%, personnel errors, unpredictable actions - 29%, threats from third parties (suppliers, partners, etc.) - 26%. At the same time the success of cracking passwords amounts to 20–40% of passwords in the hacker's possession [5]. A highly skilled hacker [5] is able to break 38% of passwords in 4 h, 62% - in a week, 89% - in 5 weeks. These data refers to passwords that were created by humans. The logical steps to prevent password hacking are to use passwords which are generated without human intervention (random characters) and to change passwords as often as possible. The issue of secure data transfer is especially acute when it comes to the continuous transfer of large amounts of data, such as when transferring data between banks [6, 7] or other large companies. In this case, the transfer of data usually has to do in an open network environment. For this there are with Special and method and encryption of information. One such method is the **Diffie-Hellman** method [8, 9], the purpose of which is to generate joint private encryption keys using open channels. The basis for generating keys of this type is the use of **one-way arithmetic functions** [10] with the property of commutativity. An attacker can decrypt information without knowing the key only by finding an inverse function. Since the computational power of computers used for finding inverse functions increases rapidly every year, increasing the hack resistance of one-way functions is an **actual task**.

1.1 Analysis of Existing Developments and Problem Statement

Increasing computational power combined with social engineering techniques create the danger of finding inverse functions to known one-way functions [9, 10]. One way to overcome this situation is to introduce a new type of one-way functions and to extend parameters that diversify the behavior of such functions. Cellular automata have been chosen as a new class of functions. For example, in works [11], cellular automata are used to generate pseudorandom number sequences for cryptographic systems. This experience can be used, but firstly it does not directly concern one-way functions, and secondly the works use standard cellular automata, which were proposed already by von Neumann and are not diverse enough in the control parameters.

The problem is also that the vast majority of studies use the theory of cellular automata to model real-world processes, not for use in cryptography. In addition, existing examples of cellular automata are rather predictable in terms of their own behavior. They use a small number of parameters, which does not allow, on the one hand, to create diversity for choice of input parameters, and, on the other hand, creates models that cannot always exist for a long period of time without repetition of states of cell fields and statics. This generates contradictions between the need for diversity of one-way functions for the Diffie-Hellman algorithm and the one-way variety of rules, and the narrow set of control parameters of classical models of cellular automata such as John Conway's Game of Life.

Purpose of Work. To improve the quality of the process of generation of private encryption keys by open channels in the framework of the Diffie-Hellman algorithm by creating a one-way function based on the cellular automata with modified rules of behavior.

The notion of a cellular automaton was first proposed by John von Neumann to refer to models of self-replicating organisms. Most of the structures that he investigated were one- or two-dimensional. Automata received the most attention in the 60s and 70s, when scientists such as Gordon Moore, Edgar Codd, Stanislaw Ulam. John Conway invented the most famous cellular automaton, the "Game of Life," in 1970. He became interested in the problem proposed by Neumann, who was trying to create a hypothetical machine that could reproduce itself. Neumann managed to create a mathematical model of such a machine with very complex rules. Conway simplified Neumann's ideas and created the rules of the "Game of Life" [12]. The "Game of Life" model was popular among his colleagues as well as among ordinary amateurs. "Game of Life" and its modifications influenced (in some cases mutually) many sections of exact sciences such as mathematics, computer science, physics. This is evidenced by many different computer implementations of this game in various fields of knowledge. In particular, the model of increasing urban areas [13], studies of the dynamics of population growth in different living conditions, in particular in the model "predator-prey" [14, 15], the model of automobile traffic on one lane (one-dimensional cellular automaton) [16]. Rosana Motta Jafelice and Patricia Nunes da Silva [14] used an approach similar to the predator-prey model in their model of demographic dynamics. Such a model represents a two-dimensional cellular automaton, in which the neighbors of a cell are calculated according to von Neumann rules [14]. This model can be useful for creating a more complex model of cell behavior, but the disadvantage of this approach is that it does not take into account the ability of creatures to move in any direction, so the 4 diagonal neighbors are lost.

In his research John Conway considers one of 2025 possible variants of cellular automata of this type. This variant of initial conditions creates a persistent automaton compared to its counterparts, i.e. complete extinction or complete filling of the field is unlikely. Anyway, after some period of time the automaton arrives at a state where either static or cyclic sets of figures remain. This makes the classical "Game of Life" automaton incapable of creating sufficiently unpredictable cell structures. Therefore, it can be used only as a basis for a more complex model of cell interaction and development. Another disadvantage is that in the cellular automaton "Game of Life", as in most other automata, the radius of interaction is always $R = 1$. This imposes restrictions on the possible number of combinations of initial parameters of cell behavior.

In our work, the rules of the "Game of Life" are supplemented by the rules of cell interaction, which will be the tools for the subsequent creation of an unpredictable one-way function for the Diffie-Hellman algorithm.

1.2 The Classic Diffie-Hellman Algorithm

The need to develop an algorithm arose when two agents who need to exchange secret messages have only an open channel to exchange. It is possible to encrypt their messages, but the agents met (or had access to a closed channel) only once. At the same time, passwords must be changed regularly. In this case, the algorithm looks like this:

1. During the first covert meeting (or covert channel communication session), agents agree upon the use of a particular message conversion function $f(x)$ and its main properties and parameters. In this case, the covert may be the function, or its parameters and properties, or both.

   Properties of the function: unilateralism, commutativity.

   Agents communicate exclusively through an open channel, because the need to change passwords may arise daily or even more often.
2. When the need to change the password arises, agent 1 generates a secret word and applies it to find intermediate values of the function

$$y1 = f(x1).$$

   The function uses parameters, some of which can be called initial values of the function $y0$, which were agreed upon in the first (secret) step. In other words, it would be more correct to write the transformation as follows:

$$y1 = f(y0, x1).$$

   Agent 1 sends the value $y1$ to agent 2 via an open channel.
3. Agent 2 does not know the secret word $x1$, but sees the result $y1$. It forms its own secret word $x2$ and also uses the function:

$$y12 = f(y1, x2).$$

   Agent 2 now knows the password $y12$ and its secret word $x2$.
4. Agent 2 once again uses the function to find its intermediate value of the function

$$y2 = f(y0, x2)$$

   and sends it to agent 2 through the open channel.
5. Agent 1 does not know the secret word $x2$, but sees the result $y2$. He takes his secret word $x1$ and also uses the function

$$y21 = f(y2, x1).$$

Since according to the algorithms adopted in item 1, the function has a commutative property, then

$$y21 = f(y2, x1) = f(y1, x2) = y12.$$

That is, agent 1 and agent 2 now both know the password $y21$, although they have no idea about the secret words of their colleagues $x1$ and $x2$.

At the same time, probable intruders that eavesdrop on the open channel know intermediate values of the function $y1$, $y2$ from agent 1 and agent 2, but at the same time they know neither the password $y21$, nor secret words $x1$ and $x2$.

1.3 Classic One-Way Functions

One of the common variants of the one-way function is the discrete logarithm [9, 10]. Consider its use for the Diffie-Hellman algorithm discussed above. First, the agents form some numbers g and p that are not secret and possibly known to the attacker. Then agent 1 and agent 2 separately form secret words - very large numbers $x1$, $x2$ - and each use them to form intermediate values of the one-way function.

$$y1 = g^{x1} mod\ p$$

$$y2 = g^{x2} mod\ p$$

$y1$ and $y2$ agents send each other via open channel and repeat the same procedure with what they have received from their counterpart

$$y1^{x2} = g^{x1x2} mod\ p = y3,$$

$$y2^{x1} = g^{x2x1} mod\ p = y3.$$

As in the general algorithm considered above, both agents received information via an open channel, which allowed them to form a common secret code. It is as if the reverse function does not exist, but all the efforts of cryptanalysts today are thrown at solving this problem, which is at least well formalized. And it gives cryptanalysts hope that increasing computing power will make it possible to find the inverse discrete logarithm. Therefore, one of the ways to create irreducible one-way functions is to use algorithmic functions instead of arithmetic (algebraic) functions, which have mathematical formalization for separate elements, but have almost no mathematical formalization for the whole function, for example algorithmic functions based on cellular automata on the example of "Game of Life".

1.4 Classic Rules of «Game of Life»

The classic rules of John Conway's "Game of Life":

1) The game takes place on an infinite two-dimensional cell field, each cell of which can take one of two states: alive, dead.
2) Each cell has eight adjacent cells.
3) If a cell is alive and has 2 or 3 living neighboring cells, it remains alive at the next iteration. Otherwise it dies.
4) If an empty (dead) cell has 3 living neighbors, it becomes alive at the next iteration. Otherwise it remains dead.

The game ends if:
No "living" creature remains on the field.
The configuration in the next step exactly reproduces itself in the previous steps.
In the next step none of the cells changes its state.

In what follows, in order to illustrate the work of cellular automata "Game of Life" and its variations with improvements, two steps from the model will be shown (Fig. 1). The disadvantage of the given picture of "Game of Life" on creation of one-sided function is that already in the beginning the cells are assembled into static and cyclic figures.

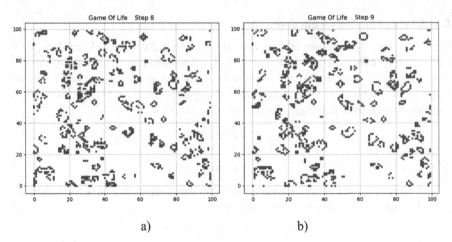

a)   b)

Fig. 1. Steps of the classic "Game of Life". a) First step, b) second step.

1.5 Task Statement

General Conditions

1. It is necessary to create a method by which encryption keys can be generated as often as the user needs and only by means of open channels of information exchange.
2. At least one covert exchange of information regarding properties, type, parameters of the one-way function and the sequence of agents when defining new encryption keys must take place before using the method.
3. The number of agents generating a shared encryption key must be arbitrary and limited only by the available number of covert information exchanges between agents.
4. The Diffie-Hellman algorithm and its modifications, if necessary, should be used as a reasonable basic algorithm for generating encryption keys.

The stage of refining the sequence of agents in determining new encryption keys should be concerned with determining the peculiarities of the algorithm at different numbers of agents in the open information exchange network.

Determination of the Operating Procedure of the One-Way Function Based on Cellular Automata

Let first divide the problem into two components:

1. Creating methods to transform the results of a cellular automata to something that can be used as a result of the standard one-way function in the Diffie-Hellman algorithm.
2. Modification of rules of behavior of cellular automata for increase of variants of behavior of one-way function.

Required Properties of the Function

Unilateralism. That is, it is possible to obtain the value of a function based on information about the arguments of the function $y = f(x)$ and at the same time it is impossible to obtain the value of the arguments based on the value of the function, that is, there is no inverse function that would provide for finding an argument for a given value of the function $x = f^{-1}(y)$.

Commutativity. If we denote the action of a function by «×», then the commutativity property of group operations means:

$$x1 \times x2 = x2 \times x1.$$

On the example of a function this might be:

$$f(x1 \times x2) = f(x2 \times x1),$$

$$f(x1 + x2) = f(x2 + x1),$$

$$f(x1, x2) = f(x2, x1).$$

The variety of parameters and variants of the behavior of a one-way function based on cellular automata should be held by extending the set of rules of the classical "Game of Life" automata.

2   Improvement of the Diffie-Hellman Algorithm

2.1   Modification of the Procedure for n Agents

Suppose we need to generate a single password for n agents. The algorithm in this case is similar to the classical algorithm, but we note certain differences:

1. During the first secret meeting (or secret channel communication session), the agents agree on the transformation function $f(x)$ and its parameters in the same way as in the case of two agents. The agents then communicate through an open channel.
2. When the need arises to change the password, all agents i form secret words xi, $i = \overline{1, n}$ and find the intermediate value of the level function

$$yi^{(1)} = f(y0, xi), i = \overline{1, n}.$$

The value $yi^{(1)}$ each agent open channel cyclically sends to the agent $i+1$. Cyclicity means that the agent sends intermediate level values 1 to agent 1. To generalize, the number of the next agent is equal to the remainder of the division $i + 1$ modulo n.

$$r = (i + 1)mod\ n.$$

3. Now each agent r at each new step k processes the information from the previous agents $yi^{(k-1)}$. To do this it uses its secret word xr each time. Only the intermediate value of the function $yi^{(k-1)}$ changes each time. The new intermediate value is equal to

$$yr^{(k)} = f\left(yi^{(k-1)}, xr\right), i = \overline{1, n}.$$

4. At step n each agent will receive an intermediate function value which it will use its secret word to turn into a new shared password.

$$yr^{(n)} = f\left(yi^{(n-1)}, xr\right), i = \overline{1, n}.$$

At the same time, each of the agents dealt only with two other agents: it sends information to one, it receives information from the other. And of the other agents he may not even know who they are or what their number is.

Likely attackers, as in the case of the two agents, listen to the open channel, know the intermediate values of the function from all agents, but know neither the password nor the secret words from individual agents.

Hiding (confusing) information about the number of agents.

To keep the number of agents in secret, it is suggested that one agent "play" instead of several agents. This will give the impression that there are more agents than there really are.

2.2 Formalization of Parameters and Properties of a One-Way Function Based on Cellular Automata

The initial picture of the cellular automaton can be sent out in coded form to the agents during the first covert communication or can be sent out by steganographic method. For example, a certain site on the Internet may contain a certain set of regular pixel graphic images. During the covert encounter it is determined that a certain area of the graphic image, which is located at some order number in the gallery of the site, is selected as the primary cellular field of the automata. After that pixel values of the chosen area can be transformed into certain binary or numerical characteristics of individual cells. In some cases, it is not even possible to hide which picture is used as a source picture because inverse function from results of intermediate functions in this case will also be almost impossible to determine.

The result of a cellular automaton is some picture of cell distribution, which can take one of two states: 1 (life) or 0 (no life). As a consequence of improving the rules of the classical cellular automaton "Game of Life" it is expected that each cell can contain not only binary information, but also code numbers describing the state of the cell, in a wider range of values. But this does not fundamentally change anything regarding the further use of these results. The intermediate cellular fields are sent by the agents to each other as they are. The final result in the form of an automata cell field can be used for generating a common password either directly as a sequence of state values of all cells in the field, or as a hash function.

In a case if it was decided to use a hash-function, then on the basis of values in separate cells it is offered to find a certain hash-function which transforms a cellular field into the standard set of figures, that it is offered to receive by means of arithmetic and (or) logic operations executed by certain rules for the numbers stored

- in separate rows or columns,
- in separate cells, which are chosen according to a pattern in a pseudorandom order,
- in certain areas of the cell field that may or may not overlap.

More strictly hash function can be created on the basis of the current standards of Ukraine [17, 18]. In our case the hash function is not the main element of the study, so the sum of values in the columns of the matrix reflecting the result were used as a test hash function for transparency of the results. But in numerical testing even such simple hash function for a 100×100 picture matrix did not give any coincidence of values for 100000 iterations of the cellular automata. Undoubtedly this result is obtained because of variety of behavior of the modified cellular automaton, which was chosen as a test one.

3 Increasing the Diversity of One-Way Functions by Improving the Rules for Implementing a Single Population Model

3.1 Improving the Rule of Birth and Continuation of Life

As the basis, John Conway's two-dimensional cellular automata "Game of Life" was chosen, in which the rules of fertility and mortality of cells are set by static values, which cannot be changed. Let us improve these rules so that fertility and mortality parameters can be set independently before starting to calculate iterations of the cellular automaton. To calculate the number of living neighboring cells we use Moore's rule [19], that is, we will consider 8 cells around the desired cell as neighboring cells.

Consider that all cells of the field can be in two states: alive (1), dead (0). This implies the following: the state of a cell at iteration $t + 1$, which depends on the number of living surrounding cells and its own state at iteration t, can be calculated using a Boolean function of nine variables, where the first parameter corresponds to the state of the cell at step t, and the other eight correspond to the state of neighboring cells. A cell becomes alive if the value of the expression is 1:

$$s_{t+1} = \bar{s}_t \bigwedge \left(d_l \leq n \right) \bigwedge \left(n \leq d_r \right) \bigvee s_t \bigwedge \left(a_l \leq n \right) \bigwedge \left(n \leq a_r \right) \qquad (1)$$

where n – the number of neighbors of the cell,
  s_t – the state of the cell at the stage t,
  d_l – minimum number of neighbors for transition to the state of a living cell,
  d_r – maximal number of neighbors for transition to the living cell state,
  a_l – minimum number of neighbors to store the state of a living cell,
  a_r – maximum number of neighbors to store the state of a living cell.

If the minimum number of living neighboring cells for the transition of the desired cell to the living state is equal to the minimum number of neighboring cells to keep the living state and the maximum number of living neighboring cells for the transition of the desired cell to the living state is equal to the maximum number of neighboring cells to keep the living state ($d_l = a_l$ and $d_r = a_r$), the formula (1) can be simplified to the following:

$$s_{t+1} = (d_l \leq n) \bigwedge (n \leq d_r) \tag{2}$$

When writing the program code for introducing the birth and continuation of life rule into the algorithm for calculating the states of the cellular automaton field, unexpectedly we found additional advantages of simulation (computer modeling). Thus, in MatLab and Python notations expression (1) can be presented more succinctly than the proposed Boolean function:

$$s_{t+1} = !s_t * (d_l \leq n \leq d_r) + s_t * (a_l \leq n \leq a_r) \tag{3}$$

Now the classic rules for the "Game of Life" can be presented as follows:

$$s_{t+1} = !s_t * (3 \leq n \leq 3) + s_t * (2 \leq n \leq 3) \tag{4}$$

The workability of dependencies (1) was tested by simulating the "Game of Life", in which the parameters were changed $d_l = 1$, $d_r = 7$, $a_l = 1$, $a_r = 8$ (Fig. 2):

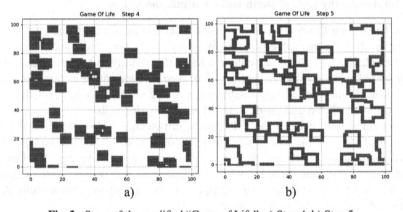

a)   b)

Fig. 2. Steps of the modified "Game of Life". a) Step 4, b) Step 5.

The initial location of live cells on the field is chosen at random using a pseudorandom number generator, or, as stated above, the initial field can be a piece of the originally chosen picture.

3.2 Introduction of the Closed Space Rule

In the classic Game of Life, the game takes place on a boundless field. In the case of modeling the behavior of a real population, the field must be either something bounded or closed. In the case of our model, the second option was chosen, because then there is no need to introduce special rules for the cells at the edges of the field. Closure occurs by joining opposite sides and corners. This situation would have been possible if the living space had been placed on a torus. On the programmatic level, closure is realized by creating, around the array that makes up the main field for the model, additional parts of the field corresponding to the opposite edges of the main field. Such modification increases the possibilities of survival.

3.3 Introduction of the Intrapopulation Radius Rule

In John Conway's classic cellular automaton "Game of Life", the state of each cell depends on the states of the surrounding cells within a radius of one cell ($R = 1$). This imposes restrictions on the number of combinations of possible values of the parameters of formula (1) for the fertility and continuation of cell life rule, such that an attacker in theory could simply pick possible input rules from a limited set (simply by analyzing the intermediate cell fields exchanged by the agents over open communication lines) and come close to obtaining the encryption key. This is unacceptable, so it was proposed to introduce an intra-population interaction radius rule, which allows agents to set the interaction radius around the desired cell. For example, the radius $R = 2$ (allows to have 24 neighboring cells), or $R = 3$ (maximum 48 neighboring cells). To find the number of neighboring cells at an arbitrary radius, we derive a formula:

$$n = (2R + 1)^2 - 1 = 4R * (R + 1)$$

where R – intra-population interaction radius.

The workability of the model with modified interaction radius was tested in the MatLab programming language on the example of simulation of previously used model with parameters $d_l = 1$, $d_r = 7$, $a_l = 1$, $a_r = 8$ and with interaction radius R = 2 (Fig. 3). The introduced rule solves the problem of counteraction of direct enumeration of values of parameters of the cellular automata, makes the one-way function reliable.

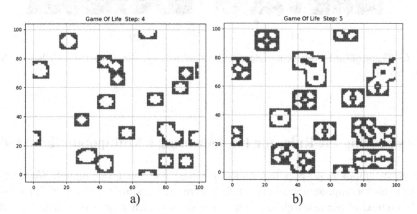

Fig. 3. "Game of Life" with modified radius R = 2. a) Step 4, b) step 5.

3.4   Introduction of the Rule of Death by Age

In the investigated automata used by other authors for modeling processes of the real world, formation of static cell structures on the field is possible, which in this case can lead to unsatisfactory work of the algorithm, namely to formation of collisions of cell fields (complete overlap of cell fields). In particular, very often static or cyclic cell structures are formed in the classical "Game of Life" automaton, on which we were based when developing our own cellular automata.

To correct this flaw, we introduced an age-death rule, which reads as follows:

with each iteration, the age of a living cell increases by one
if the age of a cell and exceeds the set maximum value of age *max_age*, it dies

The rule of death by age on the cellular field can be clearly seen with the help of the developed model (Fig. 4), in which the color of the cell indicates the age of the cell: the lighter the cells, the greater their age. For the contrast of the cell field the background color was made black.

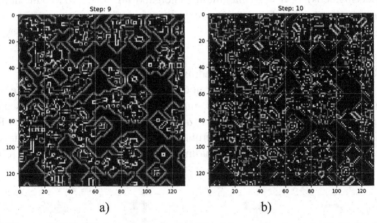

Fig. 4. "Game of Life" with the introduced rule of death by age (implemented in Python). a) Step 9, b) step 10.

4   Improving the Rules for Implementing a Multipopulation Model

The most famous multi-population model is the "predator-prey" model. We referred above to multicomponent models [14], they were used to simulate real-world processes. In the context of our research, the meaning is not so much what was modeled, but that these models complicate the behavior of populations (corresponding cellular automata of the model), which makes the behavior of automata more difficult to predict. That is why it was decided to introduce a multipopulation model by introducing additional rules for multiple populations.

To introduce a multi-population model, we first split the model into two: the first is responsible for the "victim" population and the other for the "predator" population. Each population has its own individual survival parameters independent of the other: the radius of intrapopulation interaction R, parameters of birth conditions d_l, d_r and life extension a_l, a_r. This allows a more flexible management of the model.

The model also has rules for the interaction of the two populations themselves:

Rule 1. "Predators eat victims".

If the predator and the victim are in the same cell, only the predator remains in that cell (the victim disappears - it has been eaten). Let's assume that the victims have a radius of interaction $R = 1$, and the predator $R = 3$, although these parameters can change by any value depending on the user's needs or other circumstances. This is necessary to adjust the model (Fig. 5).

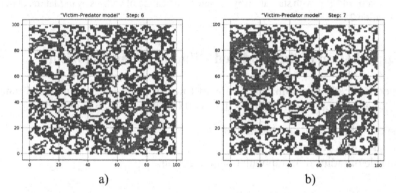

a)   b)

Fig. 5. Cellular automaton with the introduced rule of eating victims by predators (implemented in Python). a) Iteration 6, b) iteration 7, c) iteration 8.

Rule 2. "Hungry Predator".

Let's introduce an additional parameter for the predator population, namely the parameter $food_{min}$, denoting the minimum required number of victims within the predator's interaction radius necessary for continuation of existence. That is, we will assume that if there are not enough victims within the predator's interaction radius, the predator dies of "Hunger". This rule was introduced in order to equalize the chances of populations to survive and thus increase the unpredictability of the model.

A similar rule could be introduced for the victim population, but it is not feasible, because then there is a chance of complete population extinction, which would make the one-way function dysfunctional (because the fields would start repeating, producing an empty field). An implementation of a model with two rules (predator eating and predator starvation) to compare with an implementation with only the first rule will work with the same population parameters as before (Fig. 6). In the model with the introduced victim-eating rule, the field on which the model is implemented is white, with red indicating cells of the predator population and blue indicating cells of the victim population.

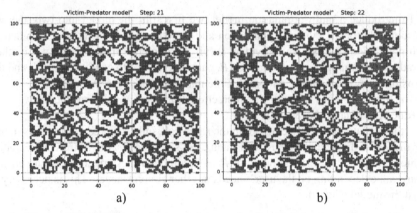

Fig. 6. "Game of Life" with starvation by predators and eating of victims by predators. a) Iteration 21 b) iteration 22

5   Approbation of the Modified Diffie-Hellman Algorithm

The modified cellular automaton "Game of Life" was chosen as a one-sided function. The cellular field of the automaton is 100×100 cells with such extended rules:

- The rule of birth and continuation of life.
- The rule of closed space.
- The rule of radius of intrapopulation interaction.

Approbation of Work with Large Cellular Fields

A common primary cellular field (Fig. 8) was generated with the first selected (through a secret communication channel) graphical image (Fig. 7), which will be used for further work of the cellular automata.

Fig. 7. Image for the generation of the primary cell field for the automata.

As soon as the primary cell field is generated, each agent chooses its own secret integer (in our case, 3728 and 5307). These secret numbers correspond to the number of iterations of the cellular automaton. The cellular automaton of each agent goes through the number of iterations specified by the agents, and then the agents receive intermediate cellular fields (Fig. 9a, b), which should be sent through open communication channels to each other. After receiving each other's cellular fields, the agents' cellular automata again go through the same number of iterations as chosen by the agents: the first agent's cellular

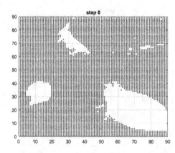

Fig. 8. The generated primary field of the 100 × 100 cellular automata.

automaton accordingly goes through $3728 + 5307 = 9035$ iterations, and the second agent's automaton goes through $5307 + 3728 = 9035$ iterations. Thus, both agents in different ways will get the same cellular fields (Fig. 9c), from which a common secret password or encryption key can be generated.

The final cellular fields obtained by the agents can be converted into passwords or encryption keys in the format desired by the agents, depending on the security requirements set. This can be either 10,000 characters in binary code or a more compact hash (Fig. 10).

Also have been tested the computational cost of computer time.

For the test I used a regular desktop notebook Dell Inspiron, Intel Core 3 Gen.8 processor, clock frequency MHz, 8 Gb RAM, 256 Gb SSD. Test results: 40000 steps of a cellular automaton for a field of 100 × 100 cells was counted in 6 s.

Simultaneously with the time cost testing, the cellular fields were tested for repeatability. Since each cell field had to be compared to each of the other 40,000-1 other fields, to save memory and test time, the comparison of the cell fields was replaced with a comparison of the hashes of the indicated cell fields. In this case there is a danger that some different pictures will have the same hash. But this can be corrected by additional checking of cell fields with the same hash. That said, in several implementations among the 40,000 fields no two had the same hash, at the same time no two cell fields were the same. In fact, the number of iterations of the cellular automaton was limited by the memory capacity of the computer, but by optimizing the algorithm of cell fields comparison and rewriting it in a less resource-dependent programming language than Python (like C#), the maximum number of iterations available for checking may increase. Also, if you reduce the size of the cell field, the memory limit will not be as tight. True, this will increase the risk of field repetition. Additional testing was done to test this hypothesis.

Approbation of Work with Small Pictures

The cellular automaton "Game of Life" on the 16 × 16 field with the same extended rules as in the previous approbation was used as a one-sided function.

Based on a random image from the open regular graphical images (Fig. 7), the agents formed a one-for-all primary "Game of Life" field for themselves (Fig. 11).

138   V. Shevchenko et al.

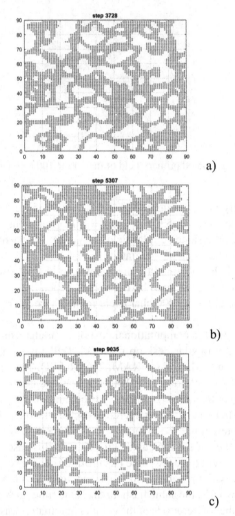

Fig. 9. Pictures "Game of Life" 100 × 00 in the process of applying the secret words. a) Intermediate picture of agent 1, b) intermediate picture of agent 2, c) the final picture of both agents.

6664665349464746485154605966635751504442455152535866665856626868
6049505050545766798177827572626062707876656064676260616873797061
5466727267554950504645485665747671685959556670664

Fig. 10. Encryption key generated from the cellular field as a hash.

After that the procedure would have been repeated as it was before, but unfortunately at step 102 the cellular automaton went into a static state (Fig. 12), which made it impossible to use such a cellular automaton as a one-way function in the future. This

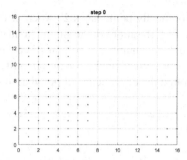

Fig. 11. A primary cell field of size 16 × 16 was generated.

leads to the conclusion that the size of the picture essentially influences on its life cycle and it is necessary to take it into account when choosing the picture size.

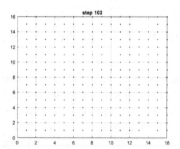

Fig. 12. Static state of the cell field of size 16 × 16.

In general, testing of the algorithm has shown that the use of cellular automata with modified rules allows to create one-way functions for the Diffie-Hellman algorithm when the rules of the cellular automaton and the size of the cellular field are chosen correctly.

6   Checking the Workability of the One-Way Function Based on the Cellular Automata

One of the problems in selecting a cellular automaton to use as a one-way function was the uncertainty of the reliability of a particular cellular automaton. This is due to the fact that the random setting of cellular automata parameters does not provide its unambiguous survival stability: in some cases, the field population died out legally, in some cases the field overflowed due to too high survival rate, in some cases the life path of cells looped. These cases are unacceptable, because an intruder must have as little information about the cellular automaton under study as possible, and looping is a peculiar pattern. Therefore, it is necessary for the one-way function to be hard-to-predict, that is, no iteration of the cellular automaton should repeat the states of the cellular field that have already been in the previous iterations.

Each cell field can theoretically be in states 2^k where k is the number of cells per field. And since to compare 2^{n*m} iterations of the automata (in our case 2^{10000}), where n - number of rows of the cell field, m - number of columns, is not effective it was decided to use statistical methods for approximate prediction of reliability of the cellular automata.

For this purpose we plotted the dependence of population size on time (Fig. 13).

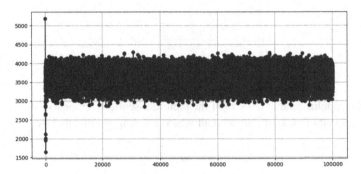

Fig. 13. The graph of population size vs. time.

In the graph of the dependence of the population number on time, we can see that in the first iterations of the cellular automaton a stabilization stage occurs, during which the value gradually reaches values that are between 2850 and 3350. After that comes the stability stage, in which the value fluctuates chaotically between 2850 and 3350 cells per field. Thus, the range of possible values is limited to a range of 500 values. The larger this interval is, the better in theory a cellular automaton, and correspondingly a one-way function, will be.

But the size of the interval in which the population values should be located is not the only indicator needed when evaluating a cellular automaton, what is also important is how often specific values occur. In order to obtain this information, a graph of the population size distribution was constructed (Fig. 14). On this graph, we can see that the value occurring most often is approximately in the middle of the previously mentioned interval. A cellular automaton can be considered better than another if, for the same interval of possible values, the values are distributed more evenly.

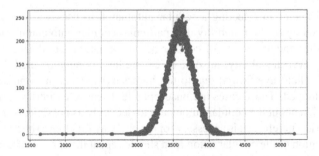

Fig. 14. The graph of the frequency distribution of the population size.

The graph of probability distribution of population number was also plotted (Fig. 15). From this graph we can also draw additional conclusions, but already in terms of the probability of meeting a particular value during the operation of the cellular automata.

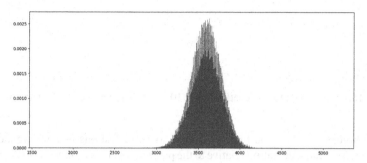

Fig. 15. Graph of the probability distribution of the population size.

To analyze a cellular automaton, it is also appropriate to search for patterns in its behavior, in particular, to search for the dependence of the population number on the automaton iteration number. Ideally, the automaton should be able to output as close as possible to 2^{10000} unique cell fields, but the choice should be unpredictable for the attacker. To check the dependence of the population number on the iteration number, it was decided to use the Pearson correlation coefficient, which is calculated by the formula:

$$r_{xy} = \frac{\sum_{i=1}^{m}(x_i - \overline{x})(y_i - \overline{y})}{\sqrt{\sum_{i=1}^{m}(x_i - \overline{x})^2 \sum_{i=1}^{m}(y_i - \overline{y})^2}}$$

where x_i – i-th element of the sample x^m,

y_i – i-th element of the sample y^m,

$\overline{x}$ – mean of the sample x^m,

$\overline{y}$ – mean of the sample y^m.

Thus, it was obtained that the Pearson correlation coefficient for the whole sample of cell field population values: $r = 0.00032$. This corresponds to a very weak correlation between the cell iteration number and its population size. The lack of correlation was also tested for intervals of different lengths, namely individual intervals of 10 (Fig. 19), 100 (Fig. 18), 1000 (Fig. 17), and 10000 (Fig. 16) iterations.

In the case where the correlation was calculated for intervals of 10,000 (Fig. 16) iterations, it was determined that the correlation is quite weak, at some intervals (for example for the interval between 10,000 and 20,000 iterations) even less than for the entire sample. But there are also deviations exceeding the correlation values of the whole sample by a factor of two. This suggests that the local correlation may be greater than for the whole sample.

In the case where the correlation is calculated for intervals of 1000 (Fig. 17) iterations, the correlation at local intervals, although increased by two orders of magnitude, still changes from interval to interval quite sharply. It should also be noted that the Pearson

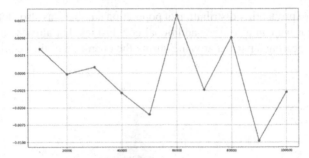

Fig. 16. Pearson correlation coefficient for 10 intervals (1 interval - 10000 iterations).

correlation coefficient for the interval from 1 to 100 iterations is approximately $r = 0.114$, which is a large deviation relative to the past values. This is only due to the fact that at the beginning of the cellular automaton there is a stabilization stage, during which the population size steadily increases until the stabilization. Therefore, it does not make sense to take it into account when estimating the work of the cellular automata. This is only due to the fact that at the beginning of the cellular automaton there is a stabilization stage, during which the population size steadily increases until the stabilization. Therefore, it does not make sense to take it into account when estimating the work of the cellular automaton.

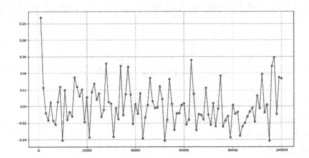

Fig. 17. Pearson correlation coefficient for 100 intervals (1 interval - 1000 iterations).

For the case where the correlation was calculated for intervals of 100 (Fig. 18) iterations, we continue to observe an increase in the scatter of correlation values in the local intervals. We do not observe any regularity in the distribution of values.

In the case where the correlation was calculated for intervals of 10 (Fig. 19) iterations, the correlation value fluctuates in even larger intervals.

To make a conclusion about the quality of the cellular automaton we plotted the values of minimum, mean and maximum values of Pearson correlation coefficient for intervals of 10, 100, 1000 and 10000 iterations (Fig. 20). Red indicates the maximum values of Pearson correlation for the intervals of the corresponding length, blue indicates the mean values, and green indicates the minimum values. Thus, we can conclude that although locally the population size of the cell field can correlate with the automata

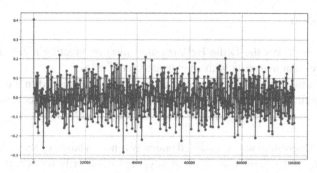

Fig. 18. Pearson correlation coefficient for 1000 intervals (1 interval - 100 iterations).

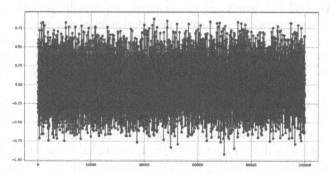

Fig. 19. Pearson correlation coefficient for 10000 intervals (1 interval - 10 iterations).

iteration number, these variables are not globally correlated. Based on this, we can assume that the cellular automata under study is workable and can be used as a one-way function of the modified Diffie-Hellman algorithm.

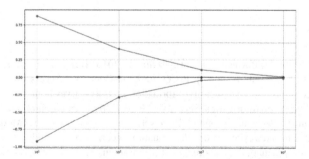

Fig. 20. Graph of the minimum, average, and maximum values of the Pearson correlation coefficient for intervals of different lengths. (Color figure online)

7 Conclusion

1. The study improves the Diffie-Hellman algorithm by creating a one-way function based on cellular automata with an extended set of rules.
2. For the first time the rules of the cellular automata are extended in the directions of universal definition of the rules of fertility and continuation of life, control of radius of intrapopulation interaction, rules of death from age of cells, multicomponent system of cells.
3. The created algorithm with a modified one-way function based on the cellular automaton can be used to create encryption keys and passwords for secure information transfer.
4. Depending on the users' needs, the password complexity can be increased by varying the cellular field parameters and cell behavior, which will also adjust the rate of encryption key generation in particular and encryption in general.
5. The software is implemented in three algorithmic programming languages C#, Python and MatLab, which allows the comparative analysis of results and consciously choose the programming language of individual parts of the software to optimize the process of encryption key generation.
6. Since hash function development is not the purpose of the study, but only one of the tools, we used the sums of the values in the columns of the matrix of the result field as a hash function for transparency of the results. But even such a simple hash function in numerical testing did not yield a single repeat of the values on 40,000 iterations of the modified cellular automaton, which is a consequence of the modification of the rules of the cellular automata.
7. A method for statistical verification of one-way functions based on cellular automata has been developed to select the optimal one-way function depending on the needs of the user.
8. Directions for further research - expansion of rules of created cellular automata for a variety of variants of behavior of one-way function.

References

1. The Global State of Information Security® Survey 2016. Turnaround and transformation in cybersecurity [electronic resource]. PricewaterhouseCoopers - Access Mode. https://www.pwc.com/gx/en/issues/cyber-security/information-security-survey.html
2. The Global State of Information Security® Survey 2018. Turnaround and transformation in cybersecurity [electronic resource]. PricewaterhouseCoopers - Access Mode https://www.pwc.com/gx/en/issues/cyber-security/information-security-survey.html
3. Viktor, S., Shevchenko, A., Fedorenko, R., Shmorhun, Y., Hrebennikov, A.: Designing of functionally stable information systems optimal for a minimum of losses. In: Proceedings of the 15th International Conference on the Experience of Designing and Application of CAD Systems (CADSM), February 26–March 2, 2019 (CADSM 2019), pp. 36–40. IEEE Ukraine Section, IEEE Ukraine Section (West), Polyana-Svalyava (Zakarpattya), Ukraine (2019). MTT/ED/AP/EP/SSC Societies Joint Chapter Part Number: CFP19508-USB. ISBN: 978-1-7281-0053-1

4. Cybercrime in the World. State of cybercrime in different regions of the world [electronic resource]. Tadviser - Access Mode http://www.tadviser.ru/index.php
5. Matt Weir. DEFCON 17. Hacking 400,000 passwords, or explaining to a roommate why your electricity bill went up. Part 1 [electronic resource]. Habr - Access Mode https://habr.com/ru/company/ua-hosting/blog/422731/
6. Petrov, P., Dimitrov, G., Ivanov, S.: A comparative study on Web Security Technologies used in Irish and Finnish Banks. In: Proceedings of the 18th International Multidisciplinary Scientific Geoconference SGEM 2018: Conference Proceedings, 2–8 July 2018, Albena, Bulgaria. Informatics, Geoinformatics A. RemoteSensing Informatics, vol. 18, no. 2.1, pp. 3–10. STEF92 Technology Ltd., Sofia (2018)
7. Petrov, P., Krumovich, S., Nikolov, N., Dimitrov, G., Sulov, V.: Web technologies used in the commercial banks in Finland. In: Rachev, B., Smrikarov, A. (eds.) Proceedings of the 19th International Conference on Computer Systems and Technologies (CompSysTech 2018), pp. 94–98. ACM, New York (2018). https://doi.org/10.1145/3274005.3274018. ISBN: 978-1-4503-6425-6
8. Diffie, W., Hellman, M.E.: IEEE Transaction on Information Theory, vol. IT-22, no. 6, pp. 644–654 (1976)
9. Diffie-Hellman Protocol. [electronic resource]. Wikipedia - Access Mode https://en.wikipedia.org/wiki/Diffie_-_Hellman_Protocol
10. Mukhachev, V.A., Khoroshko, V.A.: Methods of Practical Cryptography, 215p. K.: Polygraph-Consulting LLC (2005)
11. Bilan, S.: Formation Methods, Models, and Hardware Implementation of Pseudorandom Number Generators: Emerging Research and Opportunities, 301p. IGI Global (2017). https://www.igi-global.com/book/formation-methods-models-hardware-implementation/178719
12. Hawking, S., Mlodinow, L.: The Grand Design, ст. 187–196. Bantam Books, New York (2010)
13. Heppenstall, A., See, L., Al-Ahmadi, K., Kim, B.: CA City: simulating urban growth through the application of cellular automata. In: Salcido, A. (ed.) Cellular Automata - Simplicity Behind Complexity, pp. 87–104 (2011)
14. Jafelice, R.M., da Silva, P.N.: Studies on population dynamics using cellular automata. In: Salcido, A. (ed.) Cellular Automata - Simplicity Behind Complexity, pp. 105–130 (2011)
15. Astaf'ev, G.B., Koronovsky, A.A., Khramov, A.E.: Cellular Automaton: A Manual, pp. 10–11. State University Publishing House "College", Saratov (2003)
16. Salcido, A.: Equilibrium properties of the cellular automata models for traffic flow in a single lane. In: Salcido, A. (ed.) Cellular Automata - Simplicity Behind Complexity, pp. 159–192 (2011)
17. Oliinnikov, R.V.: Kupin's hashing function is the new national standard of Ukraine. In: Oliynykov, R.V. (eds.) Radio Engineering, no. 181, pp. 23–30 (2015)
18. DSTU 7564: 2014. Information technology. Cryptographic Protection of Information. Hashing Function. - Intro. 01-04-2015. - K.: Ministry of Economic Development of Ukraine, 39p (2015)
19. Cellular Automata - Simplicity Behind Complexity. Salcido, A. (ed.) 165p

Advanced ICT Security Solutions

Cipher Attack Against the Assymetric Cipher RSA

Peter Antonov[(✉)] and Nikoleta Georgieva

Vaptsarov Naval Academy, Varna, Bulgaria
`antonovp@nawal-acad.bg`

Abstract. After the analysis of the possible cipher attacks against the popular asymmetric cipher RSA, a new method is proposed. This method uses the factorization of large numbers and is successful against RSA only when the two prime numbers used to generate the keys for the cipher have close values.

Keywords: RSA · cipher attack · factorization of large numbers

The most common asymmetric cipher currently used is RSA (Rivest-Shamir-Adleman). RSA is one of the few algorithms that is unique and his uniqueness is the fact that it has universal usage. It is used for encrypting messages, digital signatures and the exchange of private keys in hybrid cryptographic schemes.

The algorithm for RSA encryption is very simple [1, 3, and 5]. The first step is to choose two prime numbers "a" and "b" and calculate these formulas:

$$\mathbf{n = ab} \quad \text{and} \quad \mathbf{\Phi(n) = (a - 1)(b - 1)}.$$

Then, the public key K_P and the private key K_S form the pair "public/private" keys have to be calculated based on these relations:

$$\mathbf{GCD[\kappa_P, \Phi(n)] = 1} \quad \text{and} \quad \mathbf{(\kappa_S.K_P) \bmod \Phi(n) = 1},$$

where GCD – greatest common denominator of K_P and $\Phi(n)$.

Later, in encrypting and decrypting operations, the pairs (K_P, n) and (K_S, n) are used. The first pair is made public knowledge, the second one is kept private and the two prime numbers "a" and "b" are destroyed.

In order to send an encrypted message, the sender encrypts the plain text M with the public key of the receiver K_P and then the cipher text E is generated and send. Only the receiver can decrypt the plain text M with his own private key K_S.

If, for example, an attacker somehow has gotten the cipher text E, he also knows K_P and n. In order to retrieve plain text M, the attacker must find the common denominators of n and find a and b (this is also known as factorization of n). Afterwards the attacker must calculate $\Phi(n)$ и K_S. This whole operation is very difficult and time consuming when the two prime numbers a and b are large as well as with the capability of technology and hardware.

T. Tagarev and N. Stoianov (Eds.): DIGILIENCE 2020, CCIS 1790, pp. 149–153, 2024.
https://doi.org/10.1007/978-3-031-44440-1_20

Another way to find out M is to directly find $\Phi(n)$, without the factorization of n, however this is even more difficult.

The third option is to directly calculate K_S, without the factorization of n and calculating $\Phi(n)$. However, if K_P и K_S are large enough, as it is recommended, it is again too difficult and time consuming.

The three attacks mentioned above are brute force attacks. The only attack that could be realized against RSA cipher is for the factorization of n.

There are a lot of methods in solving the task of finding the factors of n [2, 3, 4, etc.] and the only difference between them is their complication. In this paper, we are going to show you a different method of finding a and b that is easier compared to the already known ones.

If there is a successful factorization of n and later on the numbers a and b are found, $\Phi(n)$ can be calculated and then the secret key K_s, based on this relation:

$$(\kappa_S.K_P)\,\text{mod}\,\Phi(n) = 1.$$

$$a = 13, b = 29, n = 377, \lfloor \sqrt{n} \rfloor = 19$$

The method this reports suggest could be explained by this simple example:

Afterwards we are going to write down in two rows the numbers from $(1 \div \lfloor n^{0.5} \rfloor)$ and $(\lfloor n^{0.5} \rfloor \div 37)$ in a way that the sum of numbers between each other is going to be equal to 2. $\lfloor n^{0.5} \rfloor = 2.19 = 38$:

```
 1  2  3  4  5  6  7  8  9  10 11 12 13 14 15 16 17 18 19
37 36 35 34 33 32 31 30 29 28 27 26 25 24 23 22 21 20 19
```

It is known that a < b, and in the first row the number a = 13 is located closer to 19 $= \lfloor n^{0.5} \rfloor$ then b = 29 on the second one. The distance from a to $\lfloor n^{0.5} \rfloor$ in this case is $L_a = \lfloor n^{0.5} \rfloor - a = 19-13 = 6$ and from b to $\lfloor n^{0.5} \rfloor - L_b = b - \lfloor n^{0.5} \rfloor = 29-19 = 10$. If we increase $\lfloor n^{0.5} \rfloor = 19$ with one or two, then the next consecutive numbers written in two rows would look like this:

```
 1  2  3 ............... 11 12 13 14 ................. 19 20
39 38 37 ............... 29 28 27 26 ................. 21 20
```

```
 1  2  3 ................ 11 12 13 14 ................ 19 20 21
41 40 39 ............... 31 30 29 28 ................ 23 22 21
```

In the second variation the numbers a = 13 and b = 29 are located one under the other. Their sum in equal to 42 = 2.21 and their multiplication n = 377. In this case, the solution is made with just with two iterations.

If we say that the needed rotations of finding n is V, then we can prove the validity in this relation:

$$V = \frac{1}{2}(L_b - L_a) = \frac{a + b - 2\lfloor \sqrt{n} \rfloor}{2}.$$

$$a = \lfloor \sqrt{n} \rfloor + V - x \quad b = \lfloor \sqrt{n} \rfloor + V + x,$$

Based on this formula, the prime number a and b could be generated from this relation:

$$a + b = 2\left(V + \lfloor\sqrt{n}\rfloor\right)$$

where

In the example above $V = 2$ and $x = 8$, and $a = 19 + 2\text{-}8 = 13$ and $b = 19 + 2 + 8 = 29$. X is the distance between a and b as well as the distance of the right most column of the rows in the last iteration. After the second iteration the numbers a and b appear above each other and they are at the same distance from the beginning of the rows, where the number for the example is $(\lfloor n^{0.5}\rfloor + V) = 21$.

$$a + n/a = 2\left(V + \lfloor\sqrt{n}\rfloor\right)$$

Since $ab = n$, then b also equal to $b = n/a$ and then:

$$a^2 - 2\left(V + \lfloor\sqrt{n}\rfloor\right)a + n = 0.$$

From the above quadratic equation we see that:

$$a = V + \lfloor\sqrt{n}\rfloor - \sqrt{\left(V + \lfloor\sqrt{n}\rfloor\right)^2 - n},\ b = V + \lfloor\sqrt{n}\rfloor + \sqrt{\left(V + \lfloor\sqrt{n}\rfloor\right)^2 - n}\cdot$$

These two equations can be used in order to factorize n. In order to solve them, we must set two consecutive values of V and start from the number 1. For every value of V, we must calculate this statement and compare the result of a square root of an integer.

$$\sqrt{\left(V + \lfloor\sqrt{n}\rfloor\right)^2 - n}$$

If the comparison is not equal, then V gets the next value and so on. The correct solution of a and b is the one that the statement bellow gets an integer.

If in the formula for V we substitute b with αa, then

$$V = \frac{a + \alpha a - 2\lfloor\sqrt{\alpha a^2}\rfloor}{2} = \left\lfloor a\frac{1 + \alpha - 2\sqrt{\alpha}}{2} + 1\right\rfloor.$$

In order to calculate how many iterations are needed, we can use the following formula:

$$V^* = a\frac{1 + \alpha - 2\sqrt{\alpha}}{2},$$

Or a simplified version of it:

$$\left(\frac{V^*}{a}\right) = 0.5\left(1 + \alpha - 2\sqrt{\alpha}\right).$$

The graphic of variation of (V^*/a) in relation to α is shown below.

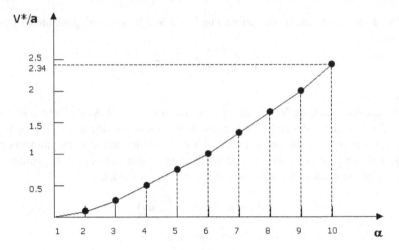

If the prime digits a and b have equal decimal values, then

$$a_{min} = 1000\ldots.$$
$$b_{max} = 9999\ldots.$$
$$\text{and} \quad a_{max} = 9,999\ldots. \approx 10.$$

In the worst case scenario of factorization of n, $V^* = 2,34.a = 2,34.10^h$, where h is the decimal value of a and b. This is the reason why, we can say that this method of n factorization requires fewer iterations when the values of a and b are close to each other. Also, the method is useful when a and b aren't prime but odd or even numbers.

When a comparison is made against other methods, the iteration needed for ours gives different results. For example, for a factorization of n = 22317 we would need only two iterations. In comparison with [4] the required iterations, Dixon's algorithm would need are:

$$e^{\sqrt{\log n . \log(\log n)}} \cong 6 \quad \text{итерации,}$$

and for the Quadratic Sieve Algorithm:

$$e^{\sqrt{\ln n . \ln(\ln n)}} \cong 122 \quad \text{итерации.}$$

In conclusion we can state, that the method that we propose could be seen as a development of the factorization problem. By using it, a quicker cipher attack can be achieved against the popular RSA algorithm, when a and b have close values. This is the reason why, with the generation of the key pairs in RSA, the chosen values of a and b have to be significantly different, since we have proved that it creates a general security threat.

References

1. Antonov, P., Malchev,: Cripthography in computer communications. Varna, p. 315. National Library: COBISS.BG-ID – 1289332452л (2000)

2. Knut, D.: The Art of Programming EVM, vol. 2. Mir, Moskow (1977)
3. Schneier, B.: Applied Cryptography. Protocols, Algorithms and Source Code. John Wiley & Sons Inc., Hoboken (1996)
4. Goldwasser, S., Belare, M.: Lecture Notes on Cryptography. Massachusetts Institute of Technology, Cambridge (1997)
5. Antonov, P., Antonova, V.: Development of the attack against RSA with low public exponent and related messages. In: Proceedings of the International Conference ComSysTech 2007, Rousse, 14–15 June 2007, pp. IIIB3.1–IIIB3.8. ACM (2007). ISBN 978–954–9641–50–9

Securing and Analyzing Media Signal Transfer over LoRaWAN Networks

Maksym Brazhenenko[1]([✉]) [iD], Viktor Shevchenko[1] [iD], Oleksii Bychkov[1] [iD],
Pepa Vl. Petrova[2] [iD], Bojan Jekov[2] [iD], and Eugenia Kovatcheva[2] [iD]

[1] Taras Shevchenko National University of Kyiv, Kyiv, Ukraine
office.chief@univ.net.ua
[2] University of Library Studies and Information Technologies, Sofia, Bulgaria

Abstract. Low-power wide-area networks became truly popular just recently and nowadays is a subject of active research. Network coverage and cost efficiency unlock hidden power and technology capabilities. Nevertheless, there are still many concerns raised. Reliability and quality of service that can be delivered are hard to control. CIA Triade in connection to IoT networks have complications and adopting face challenges. Processing large batches of data over LPWAN complex and has bandwidth limitations on both physical and regulation layers. In this paper, we adopt an algorithm controlling the quality of service for huge batches of data transmission (based on media file examples) over LPWAN networks. We propose an approach that enables institutionalization based on Semtech LoRa controllers with well defined-predictable outputs of the system. Research various configurations and discover possible capacity limits. Proposed algorithms and practices allow the system to self-configure and optimize the amount of traffic sent over the network based on the application needs, which eventually provide the desired level of control over data integrity and availability within given technology boundaries.

Keywords: IoT · Security · Cloud · LoRa · Image

1 Introduction

The world around us is becoming a whole lot smarter. We hear lots of predictions about how the Internet of Things (IoT), cloud computing, and other exciting technologies will change our lives in the next decades. IoT is enriching and transforming applications throughout our daily lives in industries from home and healthcare to smart cities, retail, and industrial. The application space is diverse with hundreds of sub-segments and thousands of applications. These applications generate a lot of data, but the data itself is not the important thing, it is the value we can extract from it. We cannot rely on the common approach of sending all the data back to servers in the cloud. As the data increases, this cannot scale. We need a different solution.

Transferring data from endpoints to the cloud introduces costs including longer latency, data transmission energy, bandwidth, and server capacity which in the end can

T. Tagarev and N. Stoianov (Eds.): DIGILIENCE 2020, CCIS 1790, pp. 154–168, 2024.
https://doi.org/10.1007/978-3-031-44440-1_22

make or break the value of a use case. This occurs especially in IoT, many applications rely on data analytics and decision making in real-time and at the lowest latency possible. Sometimes, endpoints might only have limited (if any) connectivity. As a result, intelligence must be distributed across the network to make the right processing capabilities available in the right place, all the way to the endpoint at the source of the data. Increasing the on-device compute capabilities combined with machine learning techniques, has the potential to unleash real-time data analytics in the IoT endpoints – this convergence is also known as "Endpoint AI".[1].

1.1 IoT Information Security

Modern LPWAN networks were actively analyzed recently and still lack appropriate information security solutions. One of the first complete analyses of threats and vulnerabilities in our opinion was published just recently [2]. Within a paper, authors figured out that LoRa devices have coexisting problems with other LoRa networks and devices. Devices using lower spreading factors can corrupt signals from devices using higher spreading factors in the same network. Furthermore, most LoRaWAN security measures such as the key management and frame counters need to be implemented and taken care of by developers or manufacturers. The poor implementation may put end-devices and gateways at risk. A series of articles on key management for LoRa based networks [3, 4] was published later advocating for the implementation of proper key-management solutions. Another research proposed approach to secure communication for the healthcare monitoring system [5]. Within another research were described IoT technology interference vulnerability [6].

IoT solutions data flow Information Security due diligence and Threat modeling should be performed for many aspects including, but not limiting data collection by sensors, data transmission, capturing, and analysis. All the above should be considered as sensitive and a source of risk. Any risk and threat that is captured during review assigned with severity and probability marks, which is quite a common industry-wide approach. As usual, we can use STRIDE to help ourselves get closer to the root source of the problem. However, there is one more way to look at the issue – the very basic concept CIA (Confidentiality, Integrity, and Availability) giving us a different understanding of a threat in the IoT environment.

Integrity and Availability threats within IoT in many use-cases are technology-related issues and limitations. Confidentiality threats in difference to the previous ones mostly can be considered as human-based and our understanding that end-users will fail to follow strict instructions to maintain the security of sensitive information. Rather do something easy to follow and so put their data at risk. Worth to mention that the data interface level is under question as well - data integrity and data delivery guarantee are other big challenges.

In this paper, we propose a new way to define data integrity for IoT solutions, discover and classify existing security threats and limitations. We propose an adoption for image transfer via the LPWAN network, with an example of LoRa as hardware, that can self-configure quality of output data and provide reliable input for Machine Learning algorithms.

1.2 Methodology

One of the major differences between IoT and other applications, that even if they are not worldwide enterprise solutions security perimeter for them remains unclear. The end-node devices can be located anywhere. That means that given the size of the battery is enough system maintainers may not visit nodes unless there is a need to replace/recharge the battery or the node stop responding. Given that threat of physical attack is given, and solution /methodology used should acknowledge that.

We decide to start our work by reviewing existing security profiles. Those for sure cannot be used in the way they build and with constraints/rules they are following. As part of our review we perform an investigation on each specific rule and requirement and understand to which degree we can apply them in an IoT environment: fully, partially, or mostly unreachable. Once we figured out requirements that partially, or at most impossible to secure, we review what we really can do with that, so it will start working in IoT and to which extend we can solve an issue. By exploring problematic points, we were able to propose an amendment to security practices, that can be used for IoT applications.

We have used image compression/decompression methodologies and algorithms such as JPEG/JP2000, SSIM, PSNR for our practical example with image transfer over LPWAN networks. We take advantage of having some statistical and experimental results captured to build our assumptions and projections for the real-life scenarios of image transfer in LoRa networks.

1.3 Baseline paper

Initial research for this issue was made [7] and published in ISIJ, this article is an extension focusing on building further review of security profiles and IoT solutions classification. We explore the security needs of sensor-based applications and constraints that must be followed to match security profile limits. Propose how to overcome some of these requirements.

2 Security Profiles

IoT software like traditional computer systems is passing multiple stages in its evolution. Those stages might include, but not limited to, building prototypes with limited functionality, system improvement, and adding new features, system scaling by adding more end-nodes, and improving coverage. Both hardware and software components might evolve as part of this process. Together with system security controls expected to evolve and improve. However, missing security requirements for future security profiles during the initial system design might have a consequence of inability or complexity to implement them in the future. Now we can move on to defining security criteria for IoT solutions based on LPWAN technology as a transport.

Based on [8] we can define security criteria for security profiles. Criteria can be functional and each of them will describe requirements for services that would develop protection from 1 out of 4 major types. The document also defines one non-functional criterion allowing to measure the guarantee level of protection.

1. Confidentiality – threats related to unauthorized access to information.
2. Integrity – threats related to unauthorized data modifications or can break data integrity.
3. Availability – threats related to loss of ability to use system or data.
4. Audit – identification and control of user activity or system administration related threats.
5. Guarantee of Service – are criteria defining that implemented in software system services can guarantee protection from specific types of threats. Also, this includes an assessment that the security system is capable of providing all necessary controls. These criteria are defined as non-functional and their levels are pre-requisite for functional requirements so will be analyzed after possible security profiles will be elaborated.

2.1 Confidentiality

Confidentiality is expected to provide protection services allowing to prevent unauthorized data access and modification and consists of the following types:

- Trusted confidentiality (TR) – this service allows a user to administrate information streams from secured objects that belong to his domain, to another user. Levels are defined based on requirement coverage.
- Administrative confidentiality (AR) – this service allows admin or special users to administrate information streams from secured, to another user. Levels are defined based on requirement coverage.
- Objects reuse (OR) – this service guarantee that in the scenario object copy being provided to a new user or process it will not contain data from a previous user or process.
- Analysis of hidden channels (AHC) – this service is continuously monitoring the system and attempts to identify uncontrolled by other services activity.
- Exchange confidentiality (EC) – this service allows secure access to objects when they are transferred over an unsecured channel.

Within a majority of IoT solutions TR, AR, AHC, and EC barely can be achieved on an end-node device. This is because the end-node cannot be trusted and usually placed in an unsafe location with the ability of physical access to it and possible reconfiguration or duplicating/capturing data packages in another location.

Possible mitigation here is not to store or transfer any sensitive data from end-node in unsecured locations. Privacy can be warranted by data-masking or pseudo-anonymization so the potential attacker cannot take any benefit from data that we could not protect. However, no data-masking will prevent end-user from sharing any sensitive information within a message body, and as we mention earlier approach will have a huge dependency on the user will support privacy rules. No storage on end-node devices reduces risk and the need to protect end-node physical storage from unauthorized access. However, with a server-side of IoT solutions, all the above criteria still can be met (Table 1).

Table 1. Confidentiality requirements in IoT

Requirement	IoT end-node	IoT Server-side
TR	Level 3 for LoRa (device authorize and represent himself within a network)	Yes
AR	Level 3 for LoRa (admin can send a message and request node configuration update)	Yes
AHC	No – Physical access threat	Yes
OR	N/A – Level 1(Given no data saved on end-node)	Yes
EC	No – interference vulnerability	Yes

2.2 Integrity

Integrity provides protection services allowing to prevent unauthorized data modification.

- Trusted integrity (TI) – this service allows users to administrate information streams from secured objects that belong to his domain, to another user. Levels are defined based on requirement coverage.
- Administrative integrity (AI) – this service allows admin or special users to administrate information streams from secured, to another user. Levels are defined based on requirement coverage.
- Rollback (R) – this service allows to rollback operation or set of activities and gets an object in its previous state.
- Exchange integrity (EI) – this service allows secure access to objects when they are transferred over an unsecured channel.

Integrity has very similar concerns to Confidentiality with physical access to end-node and inability to trust location. End-nodes do not need to rollback data because of all it does – stream values to the server. Configuration of end-node can be safely stored on a server and then restored when necessary. The exchange channel cannot be fully trusted due to physical access and the possibility of the attacker get access to encryption keys and perform traffic sniffing. Worth to mention that the LoRa community made a great step forward in securing data payloads from end-nodes and ensuring that executing man in the middle attack is not that trivial (Table 2).

2.3 Availability

Availability provides protection services allowing the use of the system in general, it is functions and data during a given point in time, guarantees that the system will keep working in the event of components failure, and consists of:

- Resource usage (RU) – service allows users to administrate the usage of services and resources.
- Failure Persistence (FP) – the ability of the system to stay online after components failure.

Table 2. Integrity requirements in IoT

Requirement	IoT end-node	IoT Server-side
TI	Level 3 for LoRa (device authorize and represent himself within a network)	Yes
AI	Level 3 for LoRa (device authorize and represent himself within a network)	Yes
R	Level 1 Configuration can be picked from the server	Yes
EI	No – interference vulnerability. Physical access threat	Yes

- Hot Replacement (HR) – the ability to replace any component of the system without the whole system restart.
- Restore after Failure (FR) – the ability of the system to restore after failure to its previously secured state.

Hot Replacement in the IoT world is much better compared to traditional applications of the past, but not that good as modern cloud services. This function still requires physical access to installation location and in some use-cases might be not that quick or hard to achieve. Restore after failure can be always done by provisioning configuration to end-nodes from the server and so do not carry threat itself. IoT systems due to their decentralization architecture and design are quite good at persisting failures. However, loss of end-node capturing the specific critical types of data can be mitigated only by using redundant node of the same type within the same location, that stay offline unless needed. Resource usage is performed on the server-side of IoT solutions and so has no difference from traditional apps (Table 3).

Table 3. Availability requirements in IoT

Requirement	IoT end-node	IoT Server-side
RU	N/A – out of scope for end-node	Yes
FP	Level 1 for LoRa– depends on redundant nodes availability and environment	Yes
HR	Level 1 for LoRa – depends on end-node location. (can be Level 3 under certain condition)	Yes
FR	Level 2 for LoRa – via configuration sharing by the server	Yes

2.4 Audit

The audit provides protection services allowing to control dangerous activity for the system. Levels depend on the selectivity of control; the complexity of system journal review and the ability to identify suspicious activity.

- Registration (RG) – registration of users and nodes in the system

- Authentication and Authorization (AAA) – authentication and authorization of user/end-node and its permissions.
- Trusted channel (TC) – can be one-way or two-way, ability to trust transport layer.
- Permissions split (PT) – ensuring that all users in the system hold a bare minimum of necessary
- Integrity of security system (ISS) – ensure that a security system cannot protect itself and manage the object's security.
- Self-testing (ST) – ensuring that the security system able to self-check its state.
- Authentication and Authorization on Exchange (AAAE) – the ability of data consumers to confirm the identity of the data sender.
- Authentication of a caller (AC) – the ability to ensure the identity of the caller and fact that he is sending data.
- Authentication or receiver (AV) – the ability to ensure the identity of the sender and fact that he is receiving data (Table 4).

Table 4. Audit requirements in IoT

Requirement	IoT end-node	IoT Server-side
RG	Level 5 for LoRa (device authorize and represent himself within a gateway)	Yes
AAA	Level 2 for LoRa (no MFA)	Yes
TC	Level 2 for LoRa (encrypted channel)	Yes
PT	Level 3 for LoRa (data streaming only)	Yes
ISS	Level 2 for LoRa – Physical access cannot be controlled and so access to end-node streaming data is possible	Yes
ST	Level 3 for LoRa (self-check and identity verification possible in real-time)	Yes
AAAE	Level 2 – node level and data source authorization and authentication	Yes
AC	Level 1 – acknowledgment payload is expensive for LoRa	Yes
AV	Level 1 – acknowledgment payload is expensive for LoRa	Yes

3   Security Profile Classes

Security profile class is giving a set of requirements to be met to get security controls in place for the desired type of system. Since IoT solutions are distributed systems and their users can have different levels of permissions we choose class 2 standard profiles. [9].

Class 2 profiles that can satisfy all 3 CIA concerns propose the following baseline profiles:

CIA1 = {
>   TC-2, OR-1,
>   TI-1, R-1,
>   RU-1, FR-1,
>   RG-2, AAA-2, TC-1, PT-2, IIS-2, ST-2}

CIA2 = {
>   TC-2, OR-1, AR-2
>   TI-1, R-1, AI-2
>   RU-1, FR-1,
>   RG-2, AAA-2, TC-1, PT-2, IIS-2, ST-2}

CIA3 = {
>   TC-2, OR-1, AR-2, AHC-1
>   TI-1, R-2, AI-3
>   RU-2, FP-1, HR-1, FR-2
>   RG-3, AAA-2, TC-1, PT-2, IIS-3, ST-2}

CIA1 can be considered as a baseline profile for the IoT system, it provides the very basic security controls, that are reasonably possible to achieve. [10] Unless end-node devices are not working with personal user data security controls should be able to lock the security perimeter on all 3 aspects and allow them to evolve when necessary. This kind of profile solves the needs of IoT solutions for farms, eco-sensors, etc. One important thing to note that we should not mix security profiles for different parts of integrations, since even if those represent parts of bigger solutions, they still have a difference in concerns just because of a threat nature and source Fig. 1.

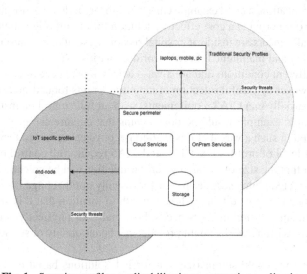

Fig. 1. Security profiles applicability in an enterprise application.

CIA2 has some improved capabilities to control security but in general, provide not that much difference to CIA1 profile. This can be considered as an operational profile for the majority of IoT applications as they mature.

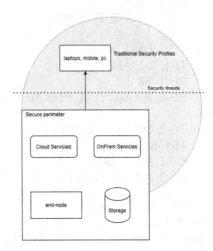

Fig. 2. End-nodes within a physically secured perimeter

CIA3 introduce a couple of features that can be achieved only under certain conditions, one of them is AHC-1and IIS-3 (Fig. 2) which require control on end-node physical access, so this profile can be used only for applications that can safely put their end-nodes within a secure location, a good example can be healthcare industry – hospitals. LPWAN technologies would provide a cost-effective solution for monitoring patient health state and given that all sensors are inside of hospital risk of physical intervention in their work can be controlled and maintained. In real-world scenarios IoT networks might be used under many different conditions and not always achieving the necessary security profile is possible, however by careful selection of mounting points for end-node installation it is possible to partially met CIA3 requirements, without full control on installation location. One possible example would be police cams that capture car speed on the roads and are mounted in such a way that it is hard to get physical access to them.

The higher level of profiles like CIA4 and CIA5 require full control on installation location, given that the size of the area where installation can be potentially performed (physically protected with a security perimeter) usually not that huge LPWAN technology might not be the most efficient choice, worth to mention that this still can match healthcare or manufacturing industry needs. For smaller or physically controlled areas cable ethernet or wi-fi networks might provide way better quality of service and expose less risk.

Given above we could summarize that for IoT solutions based on LPWAN technology applicable security profiles Fig. 3 can be built and provide the necessary level of protection under certain conditions and limitations. Overcoming any of them would mostly require a change of transport layer – LPWAN and so is the subject of another research and analysis. First, the end-node device should not store any data on its physical

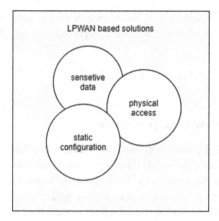

Fig. 3. LPWAN based solutions applicability

storage. This would allow to minimize exposure on a physical connection to the device and exploring data that was captured. Secondary there should be a way to restore the end-node configuration from the server. That eventually means that end-nodes should be passing registration in the system with a third-party identity provider and ensure that any security-related configurations are continuously compared with server backup copy and restored if they were corrupted. Thirdly sensitive data should not be transferred via LPWAN unless sensors and transmitters are not within a physically controlled security perimeter. It might sound a reasonably good idea to use LPWAN as an alternative for short message exchange for example SMS. However, in the long-term, this introduces a huge risk to end-user privacy. There is no way to effectively mitigate potential man in the middle attack for CIA1-CIA2 profiles above and so sending any sensitive data can be considered as unsecured.

4   Data Integrity and IoT

We define data integrity as the maintenance of, and assurance of the accuracy and consistency of data over its life cycle within a traditional application. IoT-based solutions are expected to follow the same. However, a closer look at the meaning of integrity might allow us to understand that the meaning can be slightly different and require adjustment. By maintenance, we usually mean the ability of the systems to maintain data over a certain period, which works perfectly fine for IoT-based solutions if data captured by a sensor is stored on a remote server. Assurance of accuracy and consistency is different. Usually, if we insert a record in DB, we expect to retrieve the same record from the database, but for IoT sensors, it is not the same. When a sensor captures the current temperature in a freezer every 5 min, we know for sure that even if we fail to deliver a couple of measurement results in a row, we still can understand the lowest and highest possible temperature for the period, average, etc. Sporadic data loss in IoT is expected and in most cases does not prevent algorithms and humans made the right decisions and interpretations. Based on the above we propose to extend our definition of data integrity for signal (sensor) based payloads as the assurance of the accuracy and consistency of data interpretation by the systems or humans comparing with an interpretation of original signal (1).

$$f(x) = f(x)' \qquad (1)$$

4.1 Practical example with image transfer

Interpretation of data in the same way made by humans can't demonstrate effectiveness or quality of the approach, so we decided that unless output signal coming from the sensor is interpreted in the same way as original by some machinery algorithm like Machine Learning (for example image recognition and classification neural networks), we can conclude that data loss happens in transit is not affecting data integrity.

The transport layer has a significant influence on the Quality of Service for data transmission. The latest research in this area demonstrates that [11] TCP (Transmission Control Protocol) is slightly better than UDP (User Datagram Protocol) even in a constraint environment. Another research shows that DCCP (Datagram Congestion Control Protocol) is the optimal one for media transfer [12]. Latter research shows that there is no reason to send lost packages again because it will not add any value for the end-user. We advocate that this behavior is applicable for IoT applications as well.

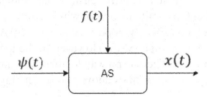

Fig. 4. Automated continuous system

The process of data transmission in the IoT environment can be represented as a mathematical model of a continuous system (Fig. 4). One of the obvious conclusions lay in a physical behavior of $f(t)$ representing a variety of environment influence and package loss during data transmission. It does not matter what was the root cause of package damaged or loss, your data receiver will be able to read and store it or not, so effectively $f(t)$ will produce either 0 for lost package or 1 for delivered. We propose to take the Heaviside step function [13] for $f(t)$ modeling, where $t \geq 0$ representing successful packet delivery (2):

$$f(t) = \begin{cases} 0, t < 0 \\ 1, t \geq 0 \end{cases} \qquad (2)$$

The above formula allows us to formulate transformation function $\phi(t)$ (3) and its domain $D(\phi)$ (4) for the automated system:

$$\phi(t) = \frac{x(t)}{\psi(t)} = \frac{\psi(t)f(t)}{\psi(t)} + a_t f(t)^{-1} = f(t) + a_t f(t)^{-1} \qquad (3)$$

where a_t is a fallback value when $t < 0$

$$D(\phi) = (-\infty, 0) \cup (0, +\infty) \tag{4}$$

Payloads transferred by sensors are different in nature, frequency of sending, and quality of measurement. Nevertheless, we still can classify them to some extend and generalize the approach to measure.

- Streaming data – like temperature sensors, GSM (Global System of Mobile Communications). Taking priority for the most recent data over lost packets, make huge sense for this group.
- Packet data – like image, but in a raw format: TIFF (Tagged Image File Format)
- Dynamic streaming data – accelerometer is an example. Losing the packet might cause false-positive results in the data analysis stage.
- Compressed or Encrypted data – any application-level data, which is encrypted or compressed.

We have chosen the following scenarios of interaction and $f(t)$ behavior for experimental modeling:

1. Loosing 5% of data (message sequence is not controlled) (5)

$$\phi(t) = f(t) + a_t f(t)^{-1}, a_t = 0 \tag{5}$$

2. Loosing and mixing 5% of data (message sequence is not controlled) (6)

$$\phi(t) = g(t) \tag{6}$$

3. Loosing 5% of data and replacing it with defaults (message sequence is controlled) (7)

$$\phi(t) = f(t) + a_t f(t)^{-1}, a_t \in \mathbb{R}, a_t \neq 0 \tag{7}$$

Each packet sent over LPWAN due to well-known constraints will not represent an image [14]. To compare images, we should first aggregate a series of packets into a package that can be compared to the original signal [15] (8).

$$im = \sum_{t=0}^{n} x(t) \tag{8}$$

$$\xi = Q(im_{in}, im_{out}) \tag{9}$$

To complete the analysis, we must compare signals from both sources (9), with algorithms that demonstrate similarities and allow us to conclude output image quality. This exercise may be done with many different algorithms, including those used for image recognition and classification. However, the latter will require extensive computational resources and so cannot be used on regular basis. The most widely used and common way to compare images is PSNR [16]. And SSIM [17] (11), (12) indexes, where MSSIM - Mean Structural Similarity Index Method:

$$PSNR = 10log\frac{s^2}{MSE} \tag{10}$$

$$SSIM(x, y) = \frac{(2\mu_x\mu_y + c_1)(2\sigma_{xy} + c_2)}{(\mu_x^2 + \mu_y^2 + c_1)(\sigma_x^2 + \sigma_y^2 + c_2)} \quad (11)$$

$$MSSIM = \frac{1}{p}\sum\nolimits_{j=1}^{p} SSIM_j \quad (12)$$

4.2 Experimental results

For an initial review of image transfer quality and capabilities, JPEG and TIFF images were chosen to represent Compressed or Encrypted data type.

After processing images through basic scenarios, we were able to identify that JPEG being visually identically might be useless for processing engines, TIFF images within scenario A, B cannot be opened because image rectangle cannot be constructed without lost packages. Scenario C show much better results, the image looks like the original one and is a good candidate for the next processing steps. Another finding made is that raw images like TIFF show better performance, but the worst file size. Encrypted (compressed) images like JPEG have better file size but cannot tackle the package loss issue. Also, it is clear enough that the absence of packet sequence control makes things even worse. [7].

Previous research shows that compressing with JPEG2000 has much better outputs compared to other algorithms [17]. However, compression with this algorithm expects data loss and requires more computational time, which negatively influences power consumption. In case the amount of loss will be too huge machine learning algorithms will not be able to recognize objects on a final image processing stage and it became useless. JP2000 algorithms use PSNR as an input value, so eventually, when we do compression, we choose a degree of data loss. Worth to mention that valuable comparisons can be done for the image of the same size only. After detailed review [7] we were able to conclude that setting up optimal PSNR value input should be an iterative self-configuration process (13), where k_{min} is either machinery regulated value or human input

$$\begin{cases} y_{i+h} = y_i + h, h \in [0, 100], h \in N \\ \overrightarrow{x}_{y+h} = \frac{\xi_{y+h}}{\lambda_{y_0}}, x_{y+h} \geq k_{min} \end{cases} \quad (13)$$

4.3 Adopting security profile

One of the major requirements for IoT security profile is the ability of the system to restore its configuration to the working state. That eventually means for our practical example several things that end-node should be able to do:

- register again in the system after connection loss.
- acquire security-specific configurations.
- acquire renewed addresses of services to post data.
- acquire configuration to compress images to a degree that match LoRa standards on traffic and allow to keep interpretation similarity [7]

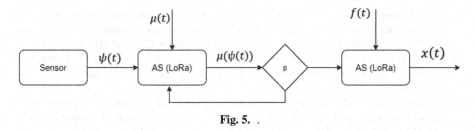

Fig. 5. .

Out of the above requirements self-configuration and adoption to changing needs more elaboration. We propose to add the self-configuration algorithm using the following generalized schema (Fig. 5).

In simple words, before the processing can be started LoRa acquire QoS numeric value that it should reach, based on the value standard compression is performed iteratively unless data loss is not lower than the value provided (14). Once initial computation and practice are completed LoRa can estimate the number of messages sent per day, the notify server, and start processing [7].

$$x(t) = \mu((f(t) + a_t f(t)^{-1})\,\mu(\psi(t)))^{-1} = f(t)\,\mu(\psi(t))^{-1} + (f(t)\mu(a_t))^{-1} \quad (14)$$

, where a_t should be an appropriate representation of absent value and decompression function should be able to consume those.

5 Conclusion

In this paper, we discover security profiles for sensor-based solutions and propose to differentiate them from any other type. We build classification criteria allowing us to estimate security measurements for sensor-based solutions separately in a less restrictive and practical manner. We propose a mathematical model able to adopt a security profile to our practical reference implementation. We evaluated the definition of data integrity for IoT applications and the definition of data loss. We believe that for IoT solutions data integrity could not be achieved within its traditional meaning and so we should apply less restrictive requirements and rely on data similarity – the ability of the system to interpret input and modified signal in the same way.

References

1. T. Lourensen. https://community.arm.com/iot/b/internet-of-things/posts/endpoint-ai-the-road-to-a-trillion-intelligent-endpoints
2. Aras, E., Ramachandran, G.S., Lawrence, P., Hughes, D.: Exploring the security vulnerabilities of LoRa. In: 2017 3rd IEEE International Conference on Cybernetics (CYBCONF), pp. 1–6. IEEE (2017). https://doi.org/10.1109/CYBConf.2017.7985777
3. Xu, W., Jha, S., Hu, W.: LoRa-key: secure key generation system for lora-based network. IEEE Internet Things J. **6**(4), 6404–6416 (2019). https://doi.org/10.1109/JIOT.2018.2888553

4. Xing, J., Hou, L., Zhang, K., Zheng, K.: An improved secure key management scheme for LoRa system. In: 2019 IEEE 19th International Conference on Communication Technology (ICCT), pp. 296–301. IEEE (2019). https://doi.org/10.1109/ICCT46805.2019.8947215
5. Manoharan, A.M., Rathinasabapathy, V.: Secured communication for remote biomedical monitoring system using LoRa. Sens. Lett. **17**(11), 888–897 (2019). https://doi.org/10.1166/sl.2019.4146
6. Wiklundh, K.C.: Understanding the IoT technology LoRa and its interference vulnerability. In: 2019 International Symposium on Electromagnetic Compatibility - EMC Europe, pp. 533–538. IEEE (2019).https://doi.org/10.1109/EMCEurope.2019.887196
7. Brazhenenko, M., Shevchenko, V., Bychkov, O., Jekov, B., Petrova, P., Kovatcheva, E.: Adopting machine learning for images transferred with LoRaWAN. Inf. Secur. Int. J. **47**(2), 172–186 (2020). https://doi.org/10.11610/isij.4712
8. НД ТЗІ 2.5–004–99. Критерії оцінки захищеності інформації в комп'ютерних системах від несанкціонованого доступу. Затверджено нак. Департаменту спеціальних телекомунікаційних систем та захисту інформації СБ України від " 28 " квітня 1999 р. № 22 із змінами
9. НД ТЗІ 2.5–005 -99. Класифікація автоматизованих систем і стандартні функціональні профілі захищеності оброблюваної інформації від несанкціонованого доступу. Затверджено нак. Департаменту спеціальних телекомунікаційних систем та захисту інформації СБ Укра
10. Tolubko, V., Kurchenko, O., Shevchenko, A.: Stabilization of the functional stability of the information system by controlling the dynamics of security profiles. Mod. Inf. Secur. **3**, 51–57 (2018). https://doi.org/10.31673/2409-7292.2018.035157
11. Fahad Taha AL-Dhief and Naseer Sabri and N. M. Abdul Latiff and Nik Noordini Nik Abd. Malik and Musatafa Abbas Abbood Albader and Mazin Abed Mohammed and Rami Noori AL-Haddad and Yasir Dawood Salman and Mohd Khanapi Abd Ghani and Omar Ibrahim Obaid. Performance Comparison between TCP and UDP Protocols in Different Simulation Scenarios. Int J Eng Technol. 2018;7(4.36):172--176.]
12. Awang Nor, S., Alubady, R., Abduladeem, K.W.: Simulated performance of TCP, SCTP, DCCP and UDP protocols over 4G network. Proc. Comput. Sci. **111**, 27 (2017). https://doi.org/10.1016/j.procs.2017.06.002
13. Baowan, D., Cox, B.J., Hilder, T.A., Hill, J.M., Thamwattana, N.: Mathematical preliminaries. In: Modelling and Mechanics of Carbon-Based Nanostructured Materials, pp. 35–58. Elsevier (2017). https://doi.org/10.1016/B978-0-12-812463-5.00002-9
14. TheThingsNetwork. The Things Network 2016 Update (2016). https://speakerdeck.com/wienke/the-things-network-2016-update.
15. Jebril, A., Sali, A., Ismail, A., Rasid, M.: Overcoming limitations of LoRa physical layer in image transmission. Sensors. **18**(10), 3257 (2018). https://doi.org/10.3390/s18103257
16. PSNR. https://en.wikipedia.org/wiki/Peak_signal-to-noise_ratio
17. Wang, Z., Bovik, A.C., Sheikh, H.R., Simoncelli, E.P.: Image quality assessment: from error visibility to structural similarity. IEEE Trans. Image Process. **13**(4), 600–612 (2004). https://doi.org/10.1109/TIP.2003.819861
18. Kirichek, R., Pham, V.D., Kolechkin, A, Al-Bahri, M., Paramonov, A.: Transfer of multimedia data via LoRa. In: Galinina, O., Andreev, S., Balandin, S., Koucheryavy, Y. (eds.) Internet of Things, Smart Spaces, and Next Generation Networks and Systems. ruSMART NsCC NEW2AN 2017 2017 2017. Lecture Notes in Computer Science, vol. 10531, pp. 708–720. Springer, Cham (2017). https://doi.org/10.1007/978-3-319-67380-6_67

K Band Radar Drone Signatures

Nikolai Kolev[✉], Jordan Sivkov, and Ekaterinoslav Sirakov

Nikola Vaptsarov Naval Academy, 9002 Varna, Bulgaria
n.kolev@naval-acad.bg

Abstract. An experimental K-band radar setup has been developed using industrial radar board IVS-465 and NI MyRIO for control and data acquisition. Experimental drone K band signatures have been recorded and analyzed. It has been confirmed by analysis of recorded spectrograms that drone K band radar signatures are influenced mainly by the drone frame motion. The signals from the rotation of the propellers are of lower intensity with characteristic spectral lines. A phenomenological model of a drone radar Doppler signature is proposed, based on experimental data, representing a reflected signal from a scattering point with harmonic motion. The comparison of the measured and modeled signals shows similarity in the parameters. Electromagnetic FEM model of drone propeller has been investigated for radar cross section estimation and scattering points visualization in K band.

Keywords: Radar · Micro-Doppler · Drone · Signature · Signal · Model

1 Introduction

1.1 Micro-Doppler Signature Definition

In recent years, the use of sensors with coherent signals for detecting moving objects has been increased. They use the changes of the reflected signal due to the Doppler Effect to identify the signatures of moving objects: machines, people, animals.

The signature can be defined as a characteristic reflected signal - voltage, function of time and space, formed at the output of a receiving module generated by a radiating sensor: radar, laser, sonar. One advantage of coherent systems is the use of phase information of the reflected signal. In these systems, even a small vibration or rotation of the object causes a significant phase change. The term "micro-Doppler", first introduced in coherent laser systems, has become popular in the literature. The micro-Doppler effect was first studied systematically by Victor Chen using a radar sensor [1]. The micro-Doppler effect appears as Doppler frequency modulations in coherent laser or microwave radar systems induced by mechanical vibrations or rotations of a target or any part on the target. These Doppler modulations become a distinctive signature of a target that incorporates vibrating or rotating structures and provides evidence of the identity of the target with movement. The source of micro-motion depends on the subject and can be a rotating propeller on a fixed-wing aircraft, the multiple spinning rotor blades of a helicopter, or

T. Tagarev and N. Stoianov (Eds.): DIGILIENCE 2020, CCIS 1790, pp. 169–186, 2024.
https://doi.org/10.1007/978-3-031-44440-1_25

an unmanned aerial vehicle; the vibrations of an engine shaking a vehicle; an antenna rotating on a ship; the flapping wings of birds; the swinging arms and legs of a walking person; and many other sources [2].

Doppler radar was developed for moving target indication and ground clutter suppression. It detects targets moving at certain speed with respect to the radar. If the target has only translational motion, the spectrum of the signal in the receiver will consist of only one spectral line with frequency $F_d = 2V_r/\lambda$, where V_r is the radial velocity of the target and λ is the transmitted wavelength. The aircraft however has moving parts such as propellers with their own motion. Because the target has a finite size and irregular geometry, it represents a distribution of scattering points over its surface. During the flight, the target will roll, pitch, yaw, and vibrate, causing changes in the intensity and position of these scattering points over time. The movement of the propellers of the target aircraft, in addition to causing modulation of the airframe Doppler signal, produces Doppler signals of its own [3]. If this is a two-bladed propeller, the pattern will be repeated every 180° of rotation, and Vr therefore will be a continuous sinusoidal function with a frequency of $2\Omega t$.

$$Vr = A\,(\vec{r},\,\vec{n}) \cdot \Omega R \cdot \sin(2\Omega t) \qquad (1)$$

where $A\,(\vec{r},\,\vec{n})$ - amplitude constant depending on direction from radar to propeller and propeller rotation plane; R – radius of the propeller blade; Ω – angular speed of propeller rotation; $Vt = \Omega R$ - tangential speed of a scattering point on the tip of a rotating propeller

The aim of the present investigation is to study the effectiveness of consumer drone doppler detection radars, to develop a radar experimental setup in K band for drone detection, analyze drone scattered signal and to propose an adequate signal model.

1.2 Automotive Doppler Radars for Drone Detection and Signal Analysis

Lately, the technology of Doppler radars for industrial applications and in the automotive field has been developed. There is a growing interest in the use of Doppler radars for drone detection and signal identification. It is known that in Doppler radars the carrier frequency is compensated in the quadrature detector-multiplier, because part of the transmitted RF signal is fed to one of its inputs as a reference signal, just as the received reflected RF signal from an object is fed to the other input. At the output of the quadrature detector the baseband signal is with Doppler change in frequency caused by the movement of the drone. It can be considered that parts of the drone that move at a higher speed cause reflected signal. These parts are the drone propellers.

Experimental measurements and simulation of the RCS of consumer drones in an anechoic chamber are investigated in [4]. These investigations show that the drone frame creates prevailing scattering signal. During the simulations RCS signatures of different drone parts are estimated: motor with propeller, drone frame only, the full model. It can be observed that the impact of the drone frame is the largest so that the RCS of the full drone model is very close to that of the frame only. The simulated spectral level of the drone propellers signal with motors is 10–20 dB below the signal of the full drone model.

Experimental investigation of UHF doppler radar scattered signals from rotating propellers is carried out in [5]. There a harmonic amplitude modulated model of the scattered signal in time domain is proposed. Harmonic frequencies to the main rotation frequency of propeller are experimentally measured in scattered signal spectrum in confirmation of the proposed model.

Method of moments is used for the modeling of electromagnetic scattering from a rotating propeller blade with length half a wavelength in [6]. The harmonics of the frequency of rotation are seen in the spectrogram of the output signal.

Drone RF spectrograms analyzed in [7] have shown that signal of the rotating propellers is at least 20–25 dB weaker than the signal of the drone frame.

It is interesting to mention that there is similarity in micro-Doppler signatures in electromagnetics and acoustics. The noise signatures of rotating drone propellers create dominating acoustic tonal signal related to rotational motion [8]. The characteristics of the Phantom quadcopter acoustic noise are tested in an anechoic chamber at 3840 RPM rotation speed of the propellers. It was observed that tonal noise dominated at propeller shaft rate, 64 Hz and the blade passing frequency, 128 Hz, as well as their harmonics.

Radar micro-Doppler signatures of flying Phantom type drone are presented in [9]. There signal except from the main body of the drone but also flashes from the blades were observed at much higher Doppler frequencies. If the drone was moving in open space at speeds 2–4 m/s, blade flashes were observed in short time Furrier transforms at 10–20 m/s. The micro-Doppler spread from the propellers was clearly visible with levels around 30 dB lower than the bulk Doppler caused by the larger main body. The used K band radar was built on evaluation board from Analog Devices EV-RADAR-MMIC2 with added power amplifier giving +25 dBm RF power at the output. Additional EIRP was increased with 24.5 dBi with high gain horn antennas. The drone was clearly seen at distances 70–120 m [10].

Drone Micro-Doppler signatures are analyzed in [11]. There the authors experimentally investigated radar drone propellers reflected signals with two types of pulse doppler radars. They analyze the signal created by the rotation of the drone blades in terms of the tangential velocity of a scattering point on the surface of the blade. The analysis in confirmation of (1) shows the presence of a high-frequency periodic part in the spectrum of the scattered signal caused by the change of the radial velocity component. Using so-called rotor spectral lines – helicopter rotor modulation lines (HERM), they try to determine the number of blades of a rotating propeller in a similar way as is done in underwater and aero acoustics. The low-frequency spectral lines allow to determine the speed of rotation of the propeller, if the number of blades is known as experimentally observed by the authors in the articles [5, 6]. For example, if the propeller rotates with some frequency and there are two blades, the spectral lines frequency will be two times higher. However, the high-frequency components in the spectrum that are also caused by the rotation of the propeller are caused by conditions (1).

2   K Band Radar Experimental Setup

One of the possibilities for realization of a coherent radar setup is the use of a widespread low-power radar module with industrial application. One of the conventional radar low power front ends - IVS-465 is used in 24 GHz K band [11]. This board has no preamplifier and custom conditioning board is used in the application. National Instruments data acquisition board MyRIO is used in the experiments [12] (Figs. 1 and 2).

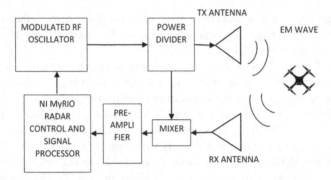

Fig. 1. Block diagram of K band radar experimental setup.

Fig. 2. Photos of drone and radar experimental setup.

The experiments were carried out in an enclosed space with drone motion in front of the radar antenna. MyRIO is the basic control and data storage unit of the radar system. It is a multiprocessor system characterized with:

- Xilinx Z-7010 processor 667 MHz (ARM Cortex A9 × 2 cores 28 nm process)
- Memory: NV: 256 MB, DDR3 512 MB, 533 MHz, 16 bits
- FPGA type same as processor

The control and data recording are done with designed host main application software on ARM processors together with FPGA application software. A LabVIEW virtual instruments were designed for FPGA signal generation for voltage-controlled oscillator frequency control and I/Q data read and recording on internal MyRIO flash system. After that the recorded data files were processed with Matlab (Fig. 3).

The radar experimental setup has the following parameters:

- Operational frequency bandwidth from f1 = 24.00 GHz to f2 = 24.54 GHz;
- EIRP = 16 dbm;
- Polarizations VV, HH with mechanical rotation of the antenna module.

Parameters of MyRIO data acquisition board:

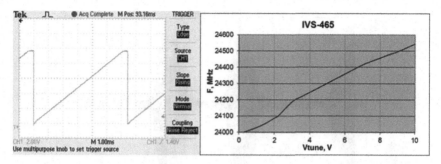

Fig. 3. MyRIO FPGA saw tooth control voltage and radar VCO output frequency.

- Parallel sampling 12-bit ADC for I/Q baseband signals;
- Two channel I/Q signal sampling with Fs = 158760 Hz, 12-bit;
- Capacity of raw I/Q recorded signal - 41 191 kB.

  Software:

- NI LabView built virtual instruments for data acquisition and IVS-465 board control.

3   Drone Scattered K Band Radar CW Signatures Analysis

Careful examination of the recorded scattered signals from the drone, considering the conditions of the experiment, allows us to draw some important conclusions. Analysis of recorded time domain reflected signals on Fig. 4 and Fig. 5 show that the signals have significant non-stationary changes in amplitude in the low-frequency domain, caused by the observed movement of the drone main frame in thrusts - with stopping and running including change of the motion direction. At the same time, the propellers continue to rotate, but since their signal is assumed to be much weaker, the signal is observed only from the main body motion.

The movement of thrusts is most likely due to the enclosed space in which the drone's anti-collision sensors send control signals to the electric motors.

The analysis of the spectrogram of the continuous signal – Fig. 6 shows the presence of tonal spectral components at frequencies 2.883 kHz, 5.796 kHz, eventually caused by the rotation of the drone propellers. The level of the 2.883 kHz harmonic is lower by 35 dB than the value of the low-frequency signal caused by the movement of the drone frame.

Using expression (1) in reverse order, the angular velocity of rotation of the propeller can be calculated by first estimating the tangential velocity Vt, with regard that we are measuring twice as high doppler frequency with a propeller with two blades.

$$Vr = \frac{Fd\lambda}{4} = \frac{2883 * 0.0125}{4} = 9 \text{ m/s} \tag{2}$$

It can be assumed in the limit case that the radial velocity is equal to the tangential velocity $Vr = Vt = 9$ m/s. Knowing that $Vt = \Omega R$ it follows that the angular frequency is:

$$\Omega = \frac{Vt}{R} = \frac{9}{0.075} = 120 \text{ rad/s} \tag{3}$$

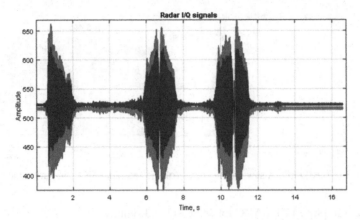

Fig. 4. Recorded radar I/Q signals reflected from drone in motion.

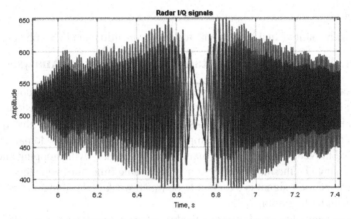

Fig. 5. Low frequency amplitude and LF modulation of the reflected from drone main frame signal with superimposed signal from drone propellers

where R = 0.075 m is Phantom-4 propeller radius.

From the last expression the frequency of propellers rotation could be estimated as $19\ s^{-1}$. This frequency multiplied by two is hardly observed in the low-frequency part of the spectrum in Fig. 7. There is however a low frequency dominating line $72\ s^{-1}$ in the signal of the drone in the approaching to the radar phase, which could have been derivative of the number of blades of two propellers – see Fig. 7.

Significant information can also be obtained from the levels, nature and values of the low-frequency spectrum of the signal obtained from the translational motion of the drone frame. Figure 7 shows linear frequency modulation at low frequency caused by a variable drone frame speed during trust back and forth. The frequency bandwidth and the values of the complex spectrum of the linearly modulated signal allow to estimate the change of the speed and the direction of motion of the drone frame.

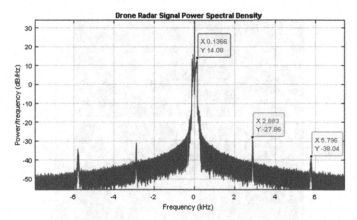

Fig. 6. Power spectral density of drone reflected CW signal.

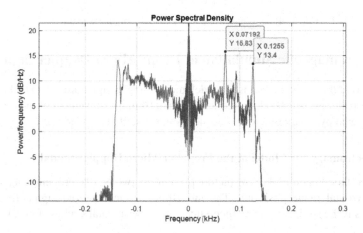

Fig. 7. Power spectral density with LFM of drone frame reflected CW signal.

On Fig. 7 the low frequency part of spectrum is presented. Here also low frequency tonal spectral lines are observed connected with propeller rotation and/or drone frame motion. Stronger tonal components should be expressed in this part of the spectrum corresponding to the approach of the drone to the radar. In the figure, this is in the positive part of the complex spectrum.

On Fig. 8 micro-doppler drone signature in time domain is constructed with STFT. Unfortunately only the low frequency spectrum is seen on this image caused by drone frame motion/vibration and/or propellers rotation alone or combined.

The ambiguity and uncertainty of the analysis of drone micro-Doppler signatures requires the improvement of radar experimental setup and providing a higher signal-to-noise ratio. Development of adequate models of the EM physical process is also required.

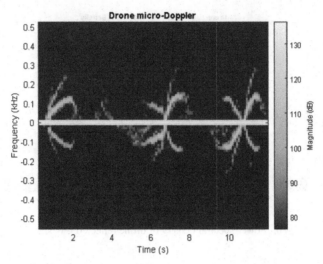

Fig. 8. Phantom-4 drone STFT micro-Doppler signatures.

4 Electromagnetic Simulation of Drone Micro-Doppler Signatures

In this part of the study the aim is to model micro Doppler signatures of a DJI Phantom 4 drone propeller as well as a low frequency signal from the movement of the drone body approximated by a harmonic one axis mechanical oscillator - pendulum.

4.1 Electromagnetic Model of the Propeller Micro Doppler Signal

On Fig. 8 static Phantom-4 drone picture presents its two by two propellers axis orthogonal horizontal plane positions. The modelling of the scattered signal from drone propellers is the subject of many theoretical and experimental studies (Fig. 9).

Fig. 9. DJI Phantom 4 drone [14].

In modern drones, propellers are made of composite materials based on carbon fibers. To a large extent, the surfaces of propellers made of composite carbon materials can be considered conductive for the K band of radio waves [15]. There will be a small error if we accept that the surface is PEC.

Two by two the propellers rotate opposite directions. Two of the drone propellers are rotating CCW and the other two are rotating CW but they are turned upside down to have the same lifting power and total zero angular momentum. Besides two by two propellers are in the horizontal plane with an angle between them of 90°. If the orientation remains the same during rotation this means that the peak signals of the radar cross section may be considered coinciding if we neglect the spatial displacement of the phase centers of rotation of the individual propellers.

To model the micro-Doppler signature of the drone propeller, a known approach is applied in which the scattered electric field in the far zone is calculated as a function of the angle of rotation of the propeller in the horizontal plane. Subsequently, the reflected complex electrical signal can be used as a base in the simulation of the micro Doppler signature. Depending on the speed of rotation of the propeller, a digital complex signal sequence is formed, which can be resampled in time domain at different speeds of rotation. This approach is also used in the formation of radar images of objects by the method of inverse synthetic aperture in the so-called start stop approximation [16]. The modeling of the electromagnetic scattered field by the propellers was performed with the program for electromagnetic analysis FEKO [17]. A three-dimensional model of the propeller is imported in the CADFEKO system. A three-dimensional mesh is applied to the surface with finite elements. Subsequently, the scattered field in the far zone is calculated a specific type of polarization. The calculation for all possible propeller plane orientations is difficult to achieve. Symmetry is observed in the calculated fields, and even when the propellers rotate in the opposite direction, it can be assumed that the maxima of the fields are equally oriented. It is possible to form a sum of the fields of four propellers as the corresponding complex signals are modified with a phase multiplier corresponding to the mutual difference in the location of the propellers on the drone frame. However, this is difficult to achieve because the orientation of the drone relative to the radar is not known and changing all the time. Figures 10 and 11 show the propeller models and the calculated radar cross section RCS. The figures show that the absolute value of the scattered field changes elliptically as a function of the angle of rotation of the propeller.

We assume that the signals from the four propellers have the same orientation of the rotational maxima if we consider that the propellers are arranged two by two mutually perpendicular. The signals are also assumed to be mutually in-phase. If the assumption of the orientation of the maxima and the in-phase condition is not fulfilled, this will lead to an increase in the beating frequency in the output signal and a shift of the main spectral lines to higher frequencies.

In Fig. 12, the signal is resampled, and a complete rotation of the propeller is performed in 21.5 ms, which corresponds to a propeller rotational frequency of 46.5 Hz.

With this complex signal, the micro Doppler signal of the propeller with short-term fast Fourier transform in Matlab was calculated. The micro Doppler signature is shown in Fig. 13.

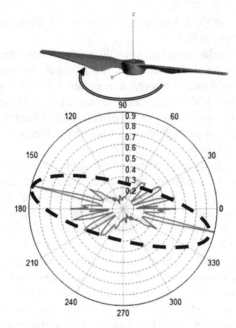

Fig. 10. Radar cross section of Phantom-4 drone propeller rotating CW.

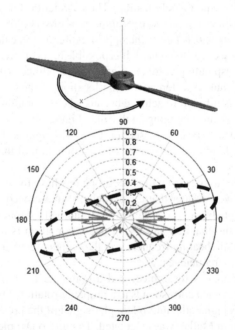

Fig. 11. Radar cross section of Phantom-4 drone propeller rotating CCW.

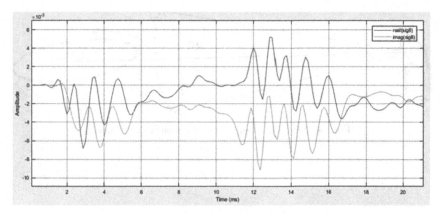

Fig. 12. Complex electric scattered signal of Phantom-4 drone propeller.

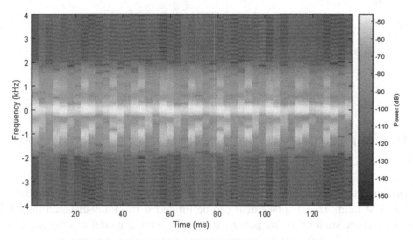

Fig. 13. Micro Doppler signal of the rotating propeller.

5 Simplified Model of Drone Micro-Doppler Signature

5.1 Simplification of the Complex Phenomena of EM Scattering from a Distributed Target in Motion with a Point Model

A simplification of the complex phenomena of EM scattering from a distributed radar object in motion could be simplified with a point model preserving the type of motion. In this case, the movement of this point target must resemble the movement of the real radar target.

In physics and electromagnetism, it is known that extreme values of the induced alternating currents and potentials, which are sources of the electromagnetic field, are observed at the edges and at a sharp change or interruption of the geometry of objects. On Fig. 15 such case is the surface current on the blade of a drone propeller. When the propeller rotates, the bright spot moves on the surface depending on the instantaneous

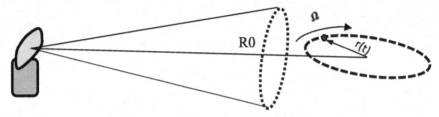

Fig. 14. Model of a point target with harmonic motion.

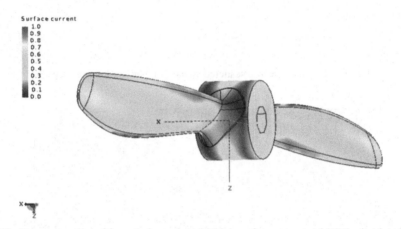

Fig. 15. Drone propeller with scattering point with high surface current at 24 GHz simulated with FEKO.

orientation of the propeller relative to the radar and the direction of the potential of the incident EM field. This displacement can be limited if from a distributed model with a complex shape such as the propeller we perceive a point model located at a distance from the center of rotation of the propeller equal to its radius or in general the center of motion of the object if it is not a drone propeller but a drone frame. The simplification of the electromagnetic physical process is justified if the results from the model simulating the process are corresponding to the results of the experimental measurements.

One way to limit the movement of current in the horizontal plane when rotating in this plane is to place a vertical wire conductor rotating in a circle of a certain radius and look for the reflected vertical potential in the far zone for the radar. The projection of this motion in the horizontal plane is a rotating point. The wire conductor is not directed in the horizontal plane. Figure 4 shows the complex value of the reflected vertical electric field in the far zone of a rotating vertical conductor with a length of 1 m in a circle with a radius of 0.5 m. The frequency is 300 MHz. The calculation was performed by the method of moments (Fig. 16).

Micro-Doppler signal of the rotating wire is presented on Fig. 17. Change in the frequency of rotation is done with resampling.

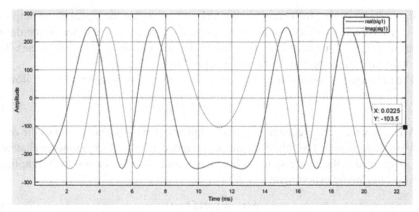

Fig. 16. Real and Imaginary part of the scattered electric field from a rotating wire with speed 44.4 Hz or 2667 rpm. The distance between the wire and rotation centrum is 0.5 m. The frequency is 300 MHz.

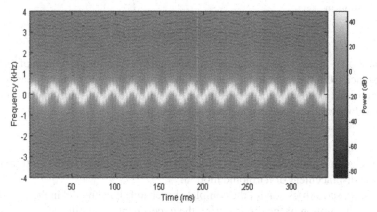

Fig. 17. Micro Doppler signal of a rotating wire.

5.2   Micro Doppler Signal of a Point with One Axis Harmonic Motion

In continuation of what has been said so far, a model of the scattered field of a point with harmonic motion has been adapted in this part, which resembles the scattered signal during the movement of the drone in the described experiment.

The aim of the development is to make a signal model that resembles the signal at the output of the coherent Doppler radar receiver mixer. In the mixer, due to its quadratic volt ampere characteristic, a part of the transmitted signal is multiplied by the received signal. At two high-frequency voltages, the output low-frequency current has a different frequency or Doppler frequency with a moving radar target. The quadrature signals I, Q are available at the output of the receiver mixer. These analog low frequency Doppler signals are sampled and recorded. After a Fourier time-to-frequency transformation, the target's micro Doppler signature is presented. In the application we are proposing signal model in the time domain.

It was found during the experiment in a closed space that the signal at the output of the radar receiver is formed mainly by the signal scattered by the drone frame during its harmonic oscillating motion with a change in amplitude and frequency (phase). This motion resembles the harmonic motion of a pendulum – Fig. 14.

The radar output signal during the harmonic motion, can be described as follows.

$$S(t) = A(t) * cos((\varphi)t) \tag{4}$$

A(t) characterizes the change in signal amplitude due to the movement of the drone relative to the antenna. The following simplified model of amplitude harmonic change in time is accepted in the application as a function of time, which is closest to the amplitude signal change in the experiment:

$$A(t) = cos(\Omega * t) \tag{5}$$

The phase angle $\varphi(t)$ in radians of the reflected signal as a function of time is determined by multiplying the doubled phase change per unit wavelength of the EM (wave constant) by the variable one-way distance from the radar to the scattering point during harmonic motion.

$$\varphi(t) = \left(4 * \frac{\pi}{\lambda}\right) * (R_0 + r(t)) \tag{6}$$

Where $\varphi(t)$ - characterizes the phase change due to the harmonic motion of the drone; R_0 – distance from the radar to the center of the target harmonic motion (constant); $r(t)$ – instantaneous position of a vector (point) along the axis of harmonic motion with angular velocity Ω; λ – electromagnetic wavelength.

$$r(t) = a * cos(\varphi_0 + \Omega * t) \tag{7}$$

Where φ_0 - an angle constant and determines the initial phase of the motion; a is the maximum displacement of harmonic motion.

The proposed expression for the complete baseband signal model in the time domain describing the motion of the drone during the experiment is as follows:

$$\dot{S}(t) = cos(\Omega * t) * \exp(-j\left(\left(4 * \frac{\pi}{\lambda}\right) * (R_0 + a * cos(\varphi_0 + \Omega * t))\right) \tag{8}$$

After the quadrature detector we have the following I(t), Q(t) signals (Figs. 18 and 19):

$$I(t) = Re\{\dot{S}(t)\} = A(t) * cos\left(\left(4 * \frac{\pi}{\lambda}\right) * (R_0 + r(t))\right) \tag{9}$$

$$Q(t) = Im\{\dot{S}(t)\} = A(t) * sin\left(\left(4 * \frac{\pi}{\lambda}\right) * (R_0 + r(t))\right) \tag{10}$$

A periodic signal in time domain with duration 8 s is generated with the proposed model with constants $R_0 = 3$ m, $a = 0.5$ m. The signal and its spectrogram is shown on Fig. 20 and 21. Spectrum estimation of the signal is shown on Fig. 22. Spectrum estimation of the signal shown on Fig. 22 follows the spectrum estimation of the recorded signal during the experiment – Fig. 7. Maximum doppler frequency of 120 Hz corresponds according (2) to maximum drone frame radial speed of 0.75 m/s.

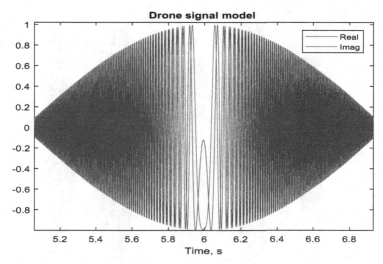

Fig. 18. One oscillation of I, Q signals in time domain.

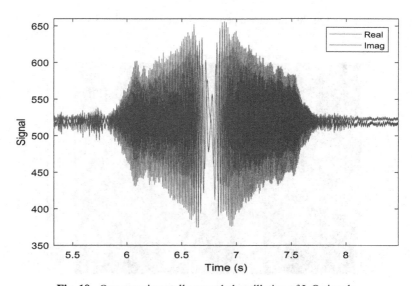

Fig. 19. One experimentally recorded oscillation of I, Q signals.

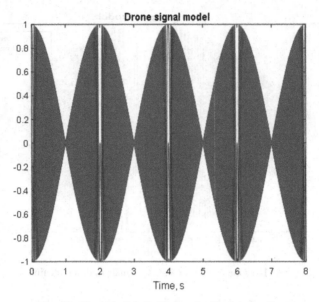

Fig. 20. Simulated periodic signal with duration 8 s.

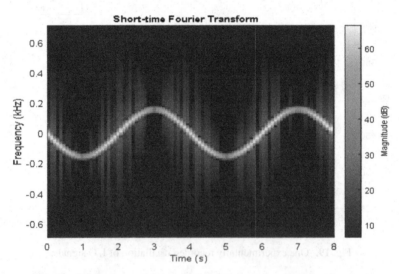

Fig. 21. Spectrogram of the simulated signal – micro Doppler signature.

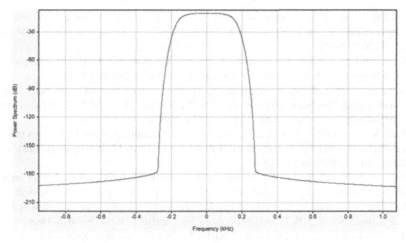

Fig. 22. Spectrum estimation of the signal.

6 Conclusion

An assessment of the current state of radar systems for experimental measurement of the radar cross section and Doppler signatures of drones has been made. Methods for modeling of Doppler signatures are analyzed.

An experimental K band radar experimental setup has been developed with a low-cost industrial module. Radar drone reflected signals are recorded in CW mode. The recorded signal reflected by the drone during its movement was analyzed. The spectrograms of the drone signal allow assessment of its motion parameters - speed and direction. Electromagnetic modeling of signals reflected by a drone propeller by the finite element method with the FEKO system was performed. A simplified model of the Doppler signal from a scattering point with harmonically motion is proposed, which simulates the drone motion during the experiment. The signal model is to greater extent adequate to the experimental data from the drone motion. The proposed simple model can be used to model the harmonic motion not only of the drone frame, but also the signal from the rotating drone propeller. Obviously, more experiments are needed to obtain reliable statistics on the harmonic frequencies of a drone in motion and in statics with rotating propellers.

References

1. Chen, V., Tahmoush, D., Miceli, W.: Radar Micro-Doppler Signatures Processing and Applications. The Institution of Engineering and Technology (2014). ISBN 978-1-84919-717-5 (PDF)
2. Tahmoush, D.: Review of micro-Doppler signatures. IET Radar Sonar Navig. **9**(9), 1140–1146 (2015). ISSN 1751-8784
3. Gardner R.: Doppler Spectral Characteristics of Aircraft Radar Targets at S-Band. U. S. Naval Research Laboratory, Washington D.C. (1961). https://apps.dtic.mil/dtic/tr/fulltext/u2/263478.pdf

4. Semkin, V., et al.: Analyzing radar cross section signatures of diverse drone models at mmWave frequencies. IEEE Access **8**, 48958–48969 (2020). https://doi.org/10.1109/ACC ESS.2020.2979339
5. Peto, T., Bilicz, S., Szucs, L., Gyimóthy, S., Pavo, J.: The radar cross section of small propellers on unmanned aerial vehicles. https://doi.org/10.1109/EuCAP.2016.7481645
6. Marák, K., Pető, T., Bilicz, S., Gyimóthy, S., Pávó, J.: Electromagnetic simulation of rotating propeller blades for radar detection purposes. IEEE Trans. Magn. **54**(3), 1–4 (2018). Art no. 7203504. https://doi.org/10.1109/TMAG.2017.2752904
7. Patel, S., Fioranelli, F., Anderson, D.: Review of radar classification and RCS characterisation techniques for small UAVs or drones. IET Radar Sonar Navig. **12**(9), 911–919 (2018). https://doi.org/10.1049/iet-rsn.2018.0020
8. Nanyaporn, N., Alexander, W., Devenport, W.: Experimental study of quadcopter acoustics and performance at static thrust conditions (2016). https://doi.org/10.2514/6.2016-2873
9. Rahman, S., Robertson, D.: Radar micro-Doppler signatures of drones and birds at K-band and W-band. Sci. Rep. **8**, 17396 (2018). https://doi.org/10.1038/s41598-018-35880-9
10. Rahman, S., Robertson, D.: Coherent 24 GHz FMCW radar system for micro-Doppler studies. In: Radar Sensor Technology XXII [106330I] (Proceedings of SPIE; vol. 10633), 4 May 2018 (2018). https://doi.org/10.1117/12.2304368
11. Klaer, P., et al.: An investigation of rotary drone HERM line spectrum under manoeuvering conditions. Sensors **20**, 5940 (2020)
12. IVS-465. Technical data. Innosent DE
13. NI My RIO 1900 Technical data. National Instruments
14. https://www.dji.com/bg/phantom-4/info
15. Gradoni, G., et al.: Determination of the electrical conductivity of carbon/carbon at high microwave frequencies. Carbon **54**, 76–85 (2013)
16. Kolev, N.Z.: Computer simulation of ISAR images of PEC models of complicated objects. In: Proceedings of EUSAR 2000 Conference, Munich, 23–25 May 2000, pp. 475–478. VDE Verlag, Berlin (2000). https://www.researchgate.net/publication/284651840Computer_Sim ulation_of_ISAR_Images_of_PEC_Models_of_Complicated_Objects
17. https://altairuniversity.com/feko-student-edition/

Education and Training for Cyber Resilience

Leadership Playbook for the Digital Age: Preparing the Western Balkan Leadership for the Digital Transformation

Mitko Bogdanoski[✉] and Metodi Hadji-Janev

Military Academy, Vasko Karangelevski bb, 1000 Skopje, Republic of North Macedonia
mitko.bogdanoski@ugd.edu.com

Abstract. The ongoing digital transformation caused by emerging technologies poses novel challenges but also opportunities. Western Balkan (WB) leaders are lagging behind the ongoing processes of this transformation. The article argues that WB leaders need to comprehend digital transformation and use this process to improve governance, boost the economy and address existing social challenges.

Keywords: Digital transformation · Western Balkan leadership · Disruptive technologies · Governance

1 Introduction

Emerging technologies such as information and communication technologies (ICT), artificial intelligence (AI) applications and systems (particularly in terms of machine learning and robotics), nanotechnology, space technology, biotechnology, quantum computing, etc. are driving the ongoing digital transformation. This process affects the way individuals and groups across society live, work and interact. Political leadership, academia, and experts in different fields and disciplines argue for new principles, protocols, rules and policies to accelerate the positive and inclusive impacts of these technologies while mitigating their negative impacts. Unfortunately, WB leadership is way behind the current trends in digital transformation (including EU members and NATO allies).

Instead of being passive observers and suffer the negative impacts of disruptive nature of digital technologies, WB leaders should seize the initiative and comprehend these technologies as a key driver of economic growth and improving overall governance.

The article begins with elaborating how and in what ways emerging technologies provide novel challenges to effective governance as an important element for WB leadership. The second part of the article analyses why WB leaders need to close the existing gap in the ongoing digital transformation and provides some incentives for the EU's role in supporting the digital transformation of the WB. This part concludes that WB leaders should capitalize on the transformative dynamics that emerging technologies are introducing and address existing economic, political and social challenges. The last part of the article provides a recommendation for WB leadership as valuable incentives in their playbook during the digital transformation.

T. Tagarev and N. Stoianov (Eds.): DIGILIENCE 2020, CCIS 1790, pp. 189–201, 2024.
https://doi.org/10.1007/978-3-031-44440-1_26

2   From the Opportunity to Disruptions: The Emerging Challenges for the WB Leadership in the Digital Age

2.1   A Subsection Sample

Modern technology and technological advances are entering WB's societies faster that these countries' leadership thinks. Market liberalization and chasing opportunities by the many start-ups or creative corporate management from the region, along with the ability of global communication and liberalized transport, have put them in the globalized network of technology advancement projects spurred by the digital revolution. As a result, the advancement of ICT and AI applications (and to some extent systems) are conquering a range of fields across the WB societies. While some of these connections and engagements have a pure economic goal, there are those with malicious intent that serve as a side safe havens in other actors' political ambitions. Hence, while the promise of significant social and economic benefits, increased efficiency, and enhanced productivity across a host of sectors of the society are proudly recognized by the WB leadership the disruptive effects of these technologies are rather neglected.

Mounting concerns ranging from negative effects on labour force dislocations, including other market disruptions and exacerbated inequalities, to the new risks to public safety and national security dominate experts, academics and national security pundits' forums across the world. In the interconnected and interdepended world, the chances to isolate cascade effects and consequences of technological advances are minimal.

In its latest report on the issue titled "The changing nature of work and skills in the digital age", the Joint Research Centre (JRC), the European Commission's science and knowledge service offers an evidence-based analysis of the impact of technology on labour markets and the need to adapt education policies to boost digital skills [1]. Many businesses around the world (which to a certain degree is being replicated in the region of WB) follow the so-called digital transformation trend. Internet of Things (IoT), digital platforms, social media, AI, Machine Learning (ML), and Big Data as an integral part of this transformation have already been employed by the majority of firms in the region [2]. The transformative effects of this process (the digital transformation) on the market are setting the agenda for new mechanisms of competition, structures, work organizations, and relations. What is more important for WB countries, however, is that the digitalization has already affected the business dynamics, processes, routines, and skills [3]. Across different sectors and regardless of organization size, the number of companies in the WB are converting their workplaces into digital workplaces [4]. Many jobs already involve extensive use of technology with a requirement of having a workforce capable to exploit it at a fast pace [5]. At the same time, however, according to a KPMG LLP (KPMG) and Forbes Insights tech risk management survey, increased focus on emerging technologies to help transform businesses, has not been matched by a parallel focus on the risks that come with their adoption [6]. Hence, as the report concluded, disruption became a new norm [6].

The disruptive nature of modern technologies is evident in legal and regulatory terms as well. Many reports emphasize the ability of these technologies to "disturb the deep values upon which the legitimacy of existing social orders rests and on which accepted legal and regulatory frameworks draw" [7]. The challenge is even more concerning that these technologies are entering the fields where already regulatory regimes are under certain strains and disagreements. Simple example for this is cyberspace. Frameworks that govern cyberspace are complex and dynamic [8]. The current regulations are a mix of existing international law, collection of political agreements, technical standards and protocols, trade, business, and human rights standards up to the regulation of the use of force and the laws of armed conflict. Leading countries in this area also dictate and the rest follow research principles, national regulations, and self-regulatory frameworks from the private sector. The complexity stems from the fact that these conglomerates of regulations are shaped not just vertically (top-down by governments) but also horizontally by actors who usually have different agendas and step-up in stimulating regulations shaped by their needs and objectives. Giving that these interests usually are market-based or profit-driven, they usually fell short of social responsibility or governance driven objectives. Moreover, as a Harvard professor Joseph Nye observed important elements of national security-related regimes that derive from a growing body of confidence and capacity-building measures and efforts aimed at enhancing security and resilience are contested [9]. In this line, the dual-use nature of these technologies (such as the IoT or AI applications and systems even the cyberspace itself) poses concerns beyond the market or regulatory regimes.

The dual-use nature of these technologies has already attracted crafters of the geopolitical interplay [10]. State and non-state actors have already exploit modern technologies in a non-traditional context in achieving strategic ends. The ability of global reach of many emerging technologies and do a harm without accountability have consequently reflected in national security prioritization. Using modern technologies some authoritarian regimes have emerged as peer competitors and challengers to undisputed dominance of the democratic leading states. The disruptive nature of modern technologies provides leverage to diverge from international principles and standards and blend the lines of officially recognized forms of use of force. While technological innovation in democratic societies is largely taking place beyond the governments' oversight authoritarian regimes have a rigorous focus on strategic national-security based investment, development and research [11].

On several occasions, NATO military leaders have concluded that modern technologies (precisely AI) will profoundly change the warfighting and using the military as an instrument of national power in achieving strategic ends [12]. That these technologies will change military organizational planning and coordination has already been confirmed on several occasions [13]. Some have even warned that the use of modern technologies in achieving strategic ends is driving the world to a "hyper war" [14]. Disruptive technologies have already proved capable of affecting decision-making processes by the enormous speed of development and the ability of machine learning. NATO missions and operations, which involve a high number of different countries and military organizations, are already heavily dependent on data and information exchange. Adversarial employment of modern technologies could influence, and even alter, information and communication amongst NATO allies while an operation is ongoing, creating confusion and distrust [15].

These and similar disruptive trends pose impending dilemmas on the governance of emerging technologies. The ability to increase velocity and the volume of processing data and causing radical shifts in the decision making require greater attention on fixing the governance in the digital age. Emerging technologies unequivocally urge transformation in traditional WB governance structures and policy-making models and adapt more "agile" methods of governance [16]. The new reality shaped by the disruptive technologies challenges states' ability to ketch-up with the latest technological developments and their potential societal impacts. Unlike traditional construct, to which, most of the WB states are used to govern and craft policies and regulations the digital transformation imposes more comprehensive forums and consensuses involving a variety of actors in drafting technical and normative solutions. The problem even for Western societies (that are the way to experience in governing under liberal market-based rules, i.e. to comprehend horizontal, not just top down-centralized governing solutions) is that the impacts of modern technologies require new approaches to multilateral governance that are much more difficult to agree on.

Existing debate on the issue of governing emerging technologies indicates that the challenge is beyond the question of how these technologies are designed, evolve, and function. In fact, the debate is substantial and touches the core of the existing construct upon which liberal democracies function. Moreover, as these technologies mature, they converge and combine, creating ever stronger and impactful ecosystems, which can become self-governing by algorithms, coding rules and internal dynamics independently of human action and decision [16]. Therefore, governments are urged to pay greater attention to mitigating risks on human conditions, reconsider socio-economic, legal and ethical impacts while incorporating the benefits of these technologies from stimulating innovation through e-governance up to national security. As the EU commission in their Collaborative Doctoral Partnerships – Call 2020 put it, *"This raised expectations for governments to play a more prevalent role in the digital society and to ensure that the potential of technology is harnessed, while negative effects are controlled and possibly avoided"* [17].

These and other relevant sources unequivocally confirm that governance "with and of" digital technologies is crucial for the future of WB societies. WB leadership must understand that modern technologies are of strategic importance and a key driver of economic growth, as it can radically improve the functioning of government and even change the way in which institutions are designed. Regardless of these trends, WB leadership is way behind the western EU and NATO partners.

3   Catching the Last Train: Where Do the WB Leadership Stand in Terms of Digital Transformation and Governance of Modern Technologies and the Role of the EU

The focus of enhancing structural changes in the WB societies has largely been driven by the EU and to certain degree NATO initiatives. While NATO has generally designed these transformations through the defence focused MAP action plan processes [18] the EU efforts were largely focused on civil sector reforms and enhancing infrastructure in the Western Balkans to improve economy and wellbeing as a form of stabilizing the region [19]. The focus on digital transformation has in general been relatively limited. This trend, however, has changed in 2018 when the European Commission launched Digital

Agenda for the Western Balkans [20]. The Commission together with Ministers from six Western Balkan partners - Albania, Bosnia and Herzegovina, Kosovo, Montenegro, Republic of North Macedonia – commit to investing in broadband connectivity, increase cybersecurity, trust and digitalization of industry, strengthen the digital economy and society and to boost research and innovation [20]. Presented on 6 February 2018 as one of the six flagship initiatives of engagement objectives in the Communication on a credible enlargement perspective for and enhanced EU engagement with the Western Balkans, the Agenda has lunched in-depth researches in order to enhance the ambition to help these countries leadership.

Many studies since then have pointed out that digital transformation will be an important pillar in improving the overall WB societies and converging with the EU standards [21]. It is well estimated that closing the digital gap in the Western Balkans provides for opportunities in terms of growth, job creation, as well as promoting good governance and addressing social inequalities, as well as regional cooperation. However, common conclusion in almost all of these studies is that WB's state of digitization is lagging behind the EU in all measures [21].

The danger of this gap, as we have already pointed above, and the reason why the EU needs to pay greater attention to the issue is two-folded. First, the outcomes of digital transformations are unclear. Some estimates are already challenging to the well-developed liberal democracies themselves. Disruptive nature of these technologies' impact on the WB societies thus holds the potential to further complicate challenging stability in the EU neighbourhood and endanger the EU itself. Geopolitical interplay is the other reason why the EU needs to be more serious about boosting the WB on a fast train transformative venture [22]. Emerging peer state actors such as Russia [23], China, or the UAE [24] and the Kingdom of Saudi Arabia (KSA) [25] have challenged the EU integration (including Euro-Atlantic integration) in many sectors [26]. Meddling through the ill-governed markets across the WB these actors undermine EU and to some extent NATO efforts in the region and strengths corrupt governance behind the quasi liberal market-based dynamics. Using trolls via cyberspace and state-sponsored market proxies Russia has already proved how dangerously at almost no cost can deny years of comprehensive and expensive efforts to support stability and integrate WB into the EU and NATO [27]. Denying arms trade regulations and EU strict test criteria of these practices [28] both the UAE and Kingdom of Saudi Arabia have sneaked under the carpet of foreign investment and provoked chaos across the WB arms industry [29]. Put in disruptive technologies context the WB current political leadership set-up is a force amplifier to the dark side of the political-based concerns of emerging technologies.

In this context, while liberal democracies (NATO and EU countries) pay greater attention to the political nature of advanced technologies, the emerging challengers already present in the WB are free to employ these challenges into their advancement. Political incentives of governing emerging technologies and aligning them to the liberal based principles (for example equal opportunities etc.) is an important avenue for the EU because building economies, societies and world views through these technologies shape how we interpret the world and the possibilities we envision [30].

Put differently, the danger of leaving digital transformation unintended stems from the fact that the ideas going into them, the ideologies, the norms and values in the context within which they are developed and deployed reflect the developers' views, believes and intentions. The above-mentioned practice of other state actors interplay in the region so far indicate that emerging states actors' agenda in the region could either have direct (such as Russian in disrupting Euro Atlantic integrations) or indirect (to serve the pure market and interest ambitions such as in the case of the UAE and KSA practice) political context. Both ways will do damage that is beyond the pure economic challenges. Nevertheless, this should not be interpreted in a way that all burden should crash on the EU arms.

Quite the opposite, the role and duty of the WB leadership to close these gaps is crucial. The WB needs a strong commitment to their leadership and readiness to pay greater attention to catch-up with the fast-paced changing nature of digital transformation that is ongoing. In doing so, the WB leadership needs to fix old well-identified structural challenges and adapt contemporary trends in governing emerging technologies. The role of the EU at the same time is essential in enhancing this process of fixing the structural (already identified) impediments by avoiding old mistakes entrenched under the so-called "stabilocracy" based behaviour and by explicitly encouraging clear merit-based leadership and results [31].

The change must be led by the WB governments. Their focus should be toward encouraging decisive administrative transformation free of any partisan relations and based on professional already prescribed EU based standards. Only by doing so, the WB leadership will be able to start fixing the non-functional market economy and can start coping with the competitive pressure and market forces in the union [32]. This substantial transformation in the public administration will enhance the implementation of other relevant policies and will encourage professional region-based solutions in many important sectors such as cybersecurity, critical infrastructure protection, etc., all of which are crucial in the context of digital transformation and disruptive technology context. To catch the last train toward converging with the EU trends in digital transformation the WB leadership needs new policies, acts of governance, and new collaborative mechanisms between public-private partnerships including Civil Society Organisation/Non-Governmental Organisations (CSO/NGO) and academia. These mechanisms again need to be free of partisan connection, based on professional and competitive merits and free of corruption. By following this approach, the promise for the WB leadership lays in their ability to design adaptive governance in line with the EU and NATO leadership. Though given in a different context, the former US Secretary of Defence statement, that the "success does not go to the country that develops a new technology first, but rather, to the one that better integrates it and more swiftly adapts its way of fighting" remains relevant for the WB leadership [33]. WB countries need willingness, ability, and means to implement digital transformation and deploy cutting-edge technologies if they are about to catch-up with the last leaving train.

Failing to do so, common wisdom is that there will not be adequate reform in the design and management of technology platforms. WB governments will worsen the practice of not responding in the best interests of its citizens. The speed, scope and impact of modern technologies will work in favour of actors with different than the Euro-Atlantic agenda. Consequently, the darkest predictions about how emerging technologies could hamper democracy could become a playbook in the WB [34].

Established powerful elites could use these technologies to maintain their power by building systems that serve them, not the masses. Recent examples of abusing technologies (such as the case in North Macedonia [35], Serbia [36], or Croatia [37]) leads one to believe that current WB elites are prone to practices of employing disruptive technologies tools and tactics to enhance their power. Disruptive technologies could augment the growing imbalance in the WB and thus further erode individuals' belief in the authorities. Moreover, poorly governed disruptive technologies could enhance misinformation and disinformation campaign that are on large in the region and usually sponsored from abroad [38]. Instead of lessening the negative impacts of disruptive technologies on societies' education and the market these technologies could be exploited for lucrative and damaging scenarios nested under suspicious agendas serving others instead of the WB citizens' interests. Eventually, this will persist public's institutional trust erosion, thus further lowering incentives to reform and rebuild fragile institutions.

4 Way Forward for the WB Leadership in Embracing Modern Technologies: From Challenges to Opportunity

The structural change in WB leadership is imminent. The digital era that these countries have already entered urges WB leadership to embrace a transformative model of governance based on the liberal market's platform. This requires enforcement of explicit (EU harmonized rules) backed by the power to reward or impose sanctions exclusively on the merit-based criteria. The WB leadership should encourage a smart way to ease explicit social norms, produce clear guidelines, best practices based designed policies, and bolster professionally defined command structures. Although producing legislative or executive acts in line with their political contexts will continue to drive WB leadership digital transformation requires that leaders adapt to the contemporary trend of multi-stakeholder-based governance incorporating businesses, civil society, including regional cooperation and the EU guidance. As Apoorve Dubey, founder and CEO of Kreyon Systems Pvt, asserted "Digital leadership is about empowering others to lead and creating self-organized teams that optimize their day-to-day operations. Leadership is no longer hierarchical – it needs participation, involvement and contribution from everyone" [39]. Furthermore, this shift in WB governance is necessary, because governments and policymakers are finding themselves increasingly constrained to just being reactive to the speed of technological innovation.

Aligning to the EU efforts entrenched in the 2018 EU Strategy for the Western Balkans' digital transformation, the WB leadership can turn the challenges into opportunity and use the EU project as a crosscutting boost to transform the region. Culturally the WB societies are prone to have strong leadership and guidance. Therefore, the WB leadership has an obligation to lead the way forward amid transitions, disruptions, chaos and ambiguity.

The WB leadership should be the driving force in broadening engagement. Rapid ongoing dynamics shape the digital economy. WB leadership needs to understand that the Government cannot take ownership of everything. Though the former socialist regimes embedded a centralized approach in governing which has been largely inherited across the WB [40] the digital transformation is clearly at odds with a top-down approach that is no longer sustainable. This should be enhanced by building on existing or initiating new regional platforms. Multi-stake holder approach in this direction involving EU and relevant actors (academia, business and CSO) as necessary should be crucial in sharing best practices and independent advice on issues of digital transformation and expertise that will facilitate and enhance the process. This approach will help the WB leadership to engage stakeholders effectively and implement smart innovative solutions tailored in accordance with the regional dynamics and EU best practices.

Based on such platform, WB leadership should craft tailored regulations that will anchor WB administration to enhance transparency, oversight, and accountability. Emerging disruptive technologies require an innovative and cautious approach in crafting policies and regulations. While debates about advances in ICT, AI, machine learning, bio- and nanotechnology occupy EU and most of the world's forums, these themes are sporadical if not, not present at all among the WB forums. In doing so the WB leadership should ensure that is careful in avoiding past mistakes, ready to adjust market regulations to fit the digital transformation, ensure regional synchronized regulatory approach and instead of being pushed (either by EU or NATO or another relevant initiative) to adopt strategies, legislation and regulations WB leadership need to step forward and take the initiative.

Past experience in similar novel transformative periods (such for example development of cybersecurity strategies or transitioning from civil-defence robust defence systems to a crisis management concepts, etc.) dictate that lagging behind will result in ineffective, copy-past solutions suitable for democratic societies with different cultures, perspectives and traditions. Even though some regulations can provide effective solutions for specific regions due to the different dynamics (education, economic development, culture, tradition, perspective, etc.), the same regulations in other regions could be hardly applicable. For example, if in some EU countries preventive measures are enough in crafting the regulation to address specific behaviour, a combination of preventive and punishment (reactive) based regulations might be necessary to address the same issue. A clear example of such practice represents the issue of dealing with the foreign fighters' phenomenon where unlike most of the EU countries, the WB countries were bolster in criminalizing the participation in foreign armed groups [41]. Similarly, seizing the initiative the WB leadership could prosper around whether to choose for hard regulation, soft law initiatives (such as guidelines, certification procedures, and labelling schemes) or pre-empt trends of self-governance shaped by private entities (some of whom with suspicious legacy).

In a line with previous recommendations, the regulatory solutions should be adjusted to the cross-border nature and effects that emerging technologies have, allow the economies to scale and ensure cross-country interoperability where synergies from cooperation and cross-border access would be enabled and avoid uncoordinated national rules and policies to be ineffective. Moreover, WB leadership should ensure that national regulatory barriers are removed as a way of facilitating faster digital transformation and boosting investment incentives. Particularly, great attention needs to be paid to synchronizing labour contracts with digital market dynamics and national priorities.

Crafting regulations by the WB leadership must ensure greater investment in transparency, oversight, and accountability mechanisms. Despite the lack of a political mandate, technology pioneers are increasingly developing private rules, certification schemes, standards, social norms or policies that end up, by default, governing the way societies live, work and interact and often without being restricted by national borders or limited to a single jurisdiction [16]. The WB leadership should assess the nature of national regulatory oversight bodies and decide if they should be public, private, or mixed composition [42]. Giving the negative experience with questionable and "morally flexible" investors [43], the WB leaders need to be careful in drafting regulations for oversight mechanisms (such as ethics councils and advisory boards) as these bodies are already identified as crucial for legitimacy into some of these processes [44].

To successfully comprehend the digital transformation the WB leadership needs to provide direction, clarity and purpose. This is an important task giving that the process of industrial mutation that continuously revolutionizes the economic structure from within, incessantly destroying the old one, incessantly creating a new one, in the digital transformation is affecting corporate survivability [45]. A 2018 Corporate Longevity forecast study run by Innosight, showed that "creative forces are accelerating the corporate destruction" [46]. According to these study findings, the average age of the stock market index that measures the stock performance in 1964 was 33 years. This was reduced to 24 years by 2016 and is expected to shrink to 12 years by 2027 [46]. Therefore, the WB leaders need to be on the top of their game to survive and thrive. Recognizing the paradox of leadership in staying focused on the present, while also visualizing the future and creating a roadmap to reach it, Apporve Dubey rightly asserted that "innovation is the way to remain immune to creative destruction and disruptions. Leaders need to drive innovation and experimentation, and to continuously evolve to meet dynamic needs" [39].

In this context, the WB leaders must encourage studies that will predict which sectors are endangered by digital transformation. Consequently, they need to establish programs allowing for transitioning to the digital markets labour demands. To sustain these programs leaders should create an environment to bridge the gap of disappointing records of using EU funding through the IPA and twinning program. In doing so leaders will enhance not just the digital transformation but also incorporating the best practices from digital frontrunners in the EU, as well as support mechanisms for small businesses and startups and other frameworks for digital transformation, such as shared workspaces with high-speed broadband and other incubators. Innovative approaches to introduce the digital dimension across the other fields of integration, (for example the state of e-governance and Rule of Law particularly chapters 23 and 24) are also necessary. In addition, WB leaders should not forget to merge digital transformation with education. Drafting a culture of learning, based on failures and experiments leads to inventions and innovations. Building human capacities capable to think digitally at all levels provides the leverage required for nations to iterate their way to success.

Last but not least, WB leadership must rethink safety and security. Disruptive technologies have already proved capable to compound the existing threats and vulnerabilities. As we have previously noted both EU and NATO have adequately recognized the converging and diverging nature of these technologies with the Euro-Atlantic values. WB leadership need to be serious about asserting the security conceptions and adequately consider an adjustment in normative and governance frameworks. The current state of play in a world of disruptive technologies is that the lines between human agency and "smart agent-like devices" become increasingly blurred [47]. Therefore, WB leaders must understand that the safety and security of related services and devices remain serious problems. Even though WB countries have not developed strategies for AI, new threats are rapidly migrating toward jeopardizing critical systems dependent on AI. The dual-use as well as the dual targeting of these technologies (already present in numerous sectors and industries, including decision-making processes), are making these technologies susceptible to manipulation for political and strategic effects. Advancing toward the digital transformation WB countries will in no time face these challenges and could be caught off guard.

5 Conclusions

Digital transformation induced by emerging technologies such as ICT, IoT, AI applications and systems etc. is ongoing and is impacting societies faster than WB leadership thinks. The WB leadership needs to take decisive steps to catch-up with the ongoing processes of digital transformation and craft new policies, approaches and social protection mechanisms to improve overall governance while mitigating existing challenges. To alter the challenges of the ongoing digital transformation to opportunity, the WB leadership needs to broaden engagement in the digital transformation process, craft regulations to enhance transparency, oversight, and accountability, provide direction, clarity and purpose, and rethink safety and security.

References

1. Joint Research Centre: The Changing Nature of Work, The European Union (2019). https://ec.europa.eu/jrc/en/publication/eur-scientific-and-technical-research-reports/changing-nature-work-and-skills-digital-age. Accessed 01 June 2020
2. Harvard Business Review Analytic Services: Operationalizing Digital Transformation: New Insights into Making Digital Work (2017). https://hbr.org/resources/pdfs/comm/xl/HBRASOperationalizingDigitalTransformation.pdf. Accessed 01 June 2020
3. Cascio, W.F., Montealegre, R.: How technology is changing work and organizations. Annu. Rev. Organ. Psych. Organ. Behav. **3**, 349–375 (2016)
4. Mondekar, D.: The digital economy in Southeast Europe, Friedrich Ebert Stiftung, Zagreb, pp.17–19 (2020)
5. Haddud, A., McAllen, D.: Digital workplace management: exploring aspects related to culture, innovation, and leadership. In: Proceedings of the Portland International Conference on Management of Engineering and Technology, PICMET, pp. 1–6. HI, Honolulu (2018)
6. KPMG. Disruption is the New Norm, Forbes insight (2017). https://advisory.kpmg.us/articles/2017/disruption-new-norm.html. Accessed 02 June 2020
7. Brownsword, R., Scotford, E., Yeung, K. (eds.): Oxford Handbook of Law, Regulation and Technology. Oxford Handbooks Online, Oxford (2017)
8. Olagbemiro, A.O.: Cyberspace as a complex adaptive system and the policy and operational implications for cyber warfare, school of advanced military studies United States army command and general staff college fort Leavenworth (2014)

9. Nye, J.S., Jr.: The regime complex for governing global cyber activities, global commission on internet governance, May 2014. https://www.cigionline.org/sites/default/files/gcig_p aper_no1.pdf. Accessed 02 June 2020
10. Harsh, P.V., Aarshi, T.: Emerging technologies and geopolitical contestation, observer research foundation (2019). https://www.orfonline.org/expert-speak/emerging-technologies-and-geopolitical-contestation-50562/. Accessed 02 June 2020
11. Meia, N., Helena, L.: China's pursuit of advanced dual-use technologies, the international institute for strategic studies (2018). https://www.iiss.org/blogs/research-paper/2018/12/eme rging-technology-dominance. Accessed 02 June 2020
12. ATC: artificial intelligence - a game changer for the military, NATO allied command transformation (2019). https://www.act.nato.int/articles/artificial-intelligence-game-changer-mil itary. Accessed 02 June 2020
13. The congressional research service: US. ground forces robotics and autonomous systems (RAS) and artificial intelligence (AI): considerations for congress, CSR reports (2018). https://www.everycrsreport.com/files/20181120_R45392_3498c78ccb2aa0e6a22c9 bf995d59aef90e08edc.pdf. Accessed 02 June 2020
14. John, A.R., Amir, H.: On hyper war, naval institute, vol. 143/7/1,373 (2017). https://www. usni.org/magazines/proceedings/2017/july/hyperwar. Accessed 02 June 2020
15. Tomáš, V.: How artificial intelligence could disrupt alliances, Carnegie Europe (2017). https:// carnegieeurope.eu/strategiceurope/72966. Accessed 02 June 2020
16. World economic Forum.: agile governance: reimagining policy making in the fourth industrial revolution (2018). http://www3.weforum.org/docs/WEF_Agile_Governance_Reimagi ning_Policy-making_4IR_report.pdf. Accessed 02 June 2020
17. European commission: collaborative doctoral partnerships – call 2020 (2020). https:// ec.europa.eu/jrc/sites/jrcsh/files/cdp.call_.2020_thematic.field-1_digital.governance.pdf. Accessed 02 June 2020
18. NATO: membership action plan (MAP) (2020). https://www.nato.int/cps/en/natolive/topics_ 37356.htm. Accessed 02 June 2020
19. The European commission: strategy for the Western Balkans: EU sets out new flagship initiatives and support for the reform-driven region (2018). https://ec.europa.eu/commission/pre sscorner/detail/en/IP_18_561. Accessed 02 June 2020
20. European commission: European commission launches digital Agenda for the Western Balkans (2018). https://ec.europa.eu/commission/presscorner/detail/en/IP_18_4242. Accessed 02 June 2020
21. Barbić, T., Bieber, F., et al.: The impact of digital transformation on the Western Balkans: tackling the challenges towards political stability and economic prosperity, the digital WB6+, (2018). https://wb6digital.files.wordpress.com/2018/01/wb6-study.pdf. Accessed 02 June 2020
22. Bieber, F., Tzifakis, N.: The western balkans as a geopolitical chessboard? Myths, realities and policy options, Balkans in Europe policy advisory group (2019). http://biepag.eu/wp-con tent/uploads/2019/08/The_Western_Balkans_as_a_Geopolitical_Chessboard.pdf. Accessed 02 June 2020
23. Kuczyński, G.: Russia's hybrid warfare in the Western Balkans, Warsaw Institute (2019). https://warsawinstitute.org/wp-content/uploads/2019/03/Russias-Hybrid-War fare-in-the-Western-Balkans-Warsaw-Institute-Special-Report.pdf. Accessed 02 June 2020
24. Dragojlo, S.: Serbian bilateral agreements: benefit unknown, detriment paid by the citizens, Insajder (2017). https://insajder.net/en/site/news/3541/Serbian-bilateral-agreements-Benefit-unknowndetriment-paid-by-the-citizens.htm. Accessed 02 June 2020
25. Gall C.: How Kosovo was turned into fertile ground for ISIS, New York Times (2016). https://www.nytimes.com/2016/05/22/world/europe/how-the-saudis-turnedkosovo-into-fertile-ground-for-isis.html. Accessed 02 June 2020

26. Lasheras, F.B., Tcherneva, V.: Is the EU losing the Western Balkans? What local experts think, European council on foreign relations (2015). https://www.ecfr.eu/article/is_the_eu_losing_the_western_balkans_what_local_experts_think3093. Accessed 04 June 2020
27. Stronski, A., Himes, A.: Russia's game in the Balkans, Carnegie (2019). https://carnegieendowment.org/2019/02/06/russia-s-game-in-balkans-pub-78235. Accessed 04 June 2020
28. Besch, S., Oppenheim, B.: Up in arms: warring over Europe's arms export regime, center for European Reform (2019). https://www.cer.eu/publications/archive/policy-brief/2019/arms-warring-over-europes-arms-export-regime. Accessed 04 June 2020
29. Chrzová, B., Grabovac, A., Hála, M., Lalić, J.: Western Balkans at the crossroads: assessing influences of non-western external actors, Prague security studies institute (2019). http://www.pssi.cz/download/docs/682_final-publication.pdf. Accessed 04 June 2020
30. The world economic forum: agile governance reimagining policy-making in the fourth industrial revolution, white paper, WEF (2017). http://www3.weforum.org/docs/WEF_Agile_Governance_Reimagining_Policy-making_4IR_report.pdf. Accessed 04 June 2020
31. Bieber, F.: The rise (and Fall) of Balkan stabilitocracies. Horizons; J. Int. Relat. Sustain. Dev. (10) (2018). https://www.cirsd.org/files/000/000/005/21/5401cb7afdd44a46f24311cb2e627154c75639a8.pdf. Accessed 04 June 2020
32. European Commission (EC): A credible enlargement perspective for and enhanced EU engagement with the Western Balkans, p. 13 (2018). https://ec.europa.eu/commission/sites/beta-political/files/communication-credible-enlargement-perspective-western-balkans_en.pdf. Accessed 04 June 2020
33. Mattis, N.J.: Remarks by secretary Mattis on the national Defense strategy, The US department of Defense (2018). (https://www.defense.gov/Newsroom/Transcripts/Transcript/Article/1420042/remarks-by-secretary-mattis-on-the-national-defense-strategy/. Accessed 04 June 2020
34. Anderson, J., Rainie, L.: Many tech experts say digital disruption will hurt democracy, pew research center (2020). https://www.pewresearch.org/internet/2020/02/21/many-tech-experts-say-digital-disruption-will-hurt-democracy/. Accessed 04 June 2020
35. Gardner, A.: Wire-tapping scandal hits Macedonia, Politico (2015). https://www.politico.eu/article/wire-tapping-scandal-hits-macedonia/. Accessed 04 June 2020
36. N1: Moscow daily says Russia pulled into Serbian surveillance scandal (2019). http://rs.n1info.com/English/NEWS/a505224/Moscow-daily-says-Russia-pulled-into-Serbian-surveillance-scandal.html. Accessed 04 June 2020
37. Budak, J., Rajh, E.: Citizens' online surveillance concerns in Croatia. Editor.: Surveill. Post-Commun. Perspect. **16**(3), 347–361 (2018)
38. European Western Balkans: GMF study: Western Balkans is a fertile ground for Russian disinformation, EWB (2019). https://europeanwesternbalkans.com/2019/06/19/gmf-study-western-balkans-is-a-fertile-ground-for-russian-disinformation/. Accessed 04 June 2020
39. Dubey, A.: This is what great leadership looks like in the digital age, world economic forum (2019). https://www.weforum.org/agenda/2019/04/leadership-digital-age-leader/. Accessed 06 June 2020
40. Jusić, M., Obradović, N.: Enlargement policy and social change in the Western Balkans, Friedrich Ebert Stiftung, Sarajevo (2019). https://library.fes.de/pdf-files/bueros/sarajevo/15801-20191120.pdf. Accessed 06 June 2020
41. The US library of congress: treatment of foreign fighters in selected jurisdictions: country surveys (2020). https://www.loc.gov/law/help/foreign-fighters/country-surveys.php#_ftn53. Accessed 06 June 2020
42. Benkler, Y.: Don't let industry write the rules for AI. Nature **569**(7755), 161 (2019)
43. Jirouš, F.: China in the Balkans: neutral business partner or a foreign power? European Western Balkans (2019). https://europeanwesternbalkans.com/2019/06/28/china-in-the-balkans-neutral-business-partner-or-a-foreign-power/. Accessed 06 June 2020

44. Floridi, L., Cowls, J.: A unified framework of five principles for AI in society, Harvard data science review (2019). https://doi.org/10.1162/99608f92.8cd550d1. Accessed 06 June 2020
45. Schumpeter, A.J.: Capitalism, Socialism and Democracy, pp. 82–83. Routledge, London (1994)
46. Anthony, D.S., Viguerie, S.P., Schwartz, I.E., Van Landeghem, J.: 2018 corporate longevity forecast: creative destruction is accelerating, Innosight (2018). https://www.innosight.com/wp-content/uploads/2017/11/Innosight-Corporate-Longevity-2018.pdf. Accessed 06 June 2020
47. Camino, K.: Stemming the exploitation of ICT threats and vulnerabilities: an overview of current trends, enabling dynamics and private sector responses, UNI-DIR (2019). http://www.unidir.org/files/publications/pdfs/stemming-the-exploitation-of-ict-threats-and-vulnerabilities-en-805.pdf. Accessed 06 June 2020

An Accessibility Heuristic Evaluation
of Bulgarian and Polish Academic Web Sites:
Visually Impaired Users' Perspective

Radka Nacheva[1]([✉]), Adam Stecyk[2], and Pavel Petrov[1]

[1] Department of Informatics, University of Economics –Varna, 9002 Varna, Bulgaria
{r.nacheva,petrov}@ue-varna.bg
[2] Faculty of Economics, Finance and Management, University of Szczecin,
71-454 Szczecin, Poland
adam.stecyk@usz.edu.pl

Abstract. Accessibility issues are actively involved in the field of information and communication technologies. To improve human-machine interfaces, it is necessary to study the specifics of the interactions of people with special needs, including to improve their security of access to various digital resources. Thanks to the state of the art, people with disabilities have wide access to the Internet, including educational resources. The aim of this paper is to propose an approach for the heuristics evaluation of web accessibility based on the analytic hierarchy process (AHP) method. As there are many groups of people with disabilities, to narrow the scope of this study, we turn our attention to the perspective of the visually impaired users. To approve the approach, the authoring team applies it using Bulgarian and Polish academic websites.

Keywords: web accessibility · digital access · accessibility evaluation · WCAG · Analytic Hierarchy Process (AHP) method

1 Introduction

The Web has become a major source of information for people around the world. For 2019, 4.48 billion users are reported to have Internet access, 4.07 billion of which use the Internet via mobile devices [31]. For 2017, [39] and [20] state that just over 49% of the world's population has an Internet connection. In two years, in 2019, there is a 4% increase - Internet users increased to 53.6% [20]. According to Eurostat, within the European Union (28 countries), users between the ages of 16 and 74 with Internet access are 85% [13]. People are increasingly using web services and products of a different kind, which in turn "have a high impact on building social and economic development" [1].

In comparison, data for 2023 shows that internet users have grown to 5.19 billion [31]. This is an increase of 31 million new users in 5 years. According to the data of [20] and [40], between 65% and 67% of the world's population uses the Internet, or this is a growth of 12%–14% in the last 5 years.

© The Author(s), under exclusive license to Springer Nature Switzerland AG 2024
T. Tagarev and N. Stoianov (Eds.): DIGILIENCE 2020, CCIS 1790, pp. 202–215, 2024.
https://doi.org/10.1007/978-3-031-44440-1_29

This expansion of the Internet among the world's population also leads to an increase in the dependence of businesses on online presence. "In the era of the growing role of the Internet in the development of individual economies, the use of this medium in social and economic life is gaining importance, translating into the level of development of the information society" [9]. As of January 2020, Internet Live Stats reports that there are 1.74 billion websites in the World Wide Web [37]. According to [3] they are approximately 1.72 billion and continue to increase every minute. On average, users spend more than 6 h a day for online activities [17], which confirms the active Internet penetration into people's lives. Among the most visited sites worldwide are search engines, social networks, video sharing sites, e-commerce sites, news sites, etc. [2]. For 2022, there was a 2% increase in the amount of time users spend online compared to 2019, or 6 hours and 37 minutes for the end of 2022.

People can use the Internet for a variety of purposes, including communication, education, entertainment, research, shopping, financial transactions and more. Its impact in the educational field is growing steadily, providing students, regardless of age, with easier access to such services. Teachers and students can communicate with each other regardless of distance. It is a common practice today for universities around the world to offer free online courses, thus attracting students from all over the world, and the best subsequently being able to be faculty or researchers.

The tools used to enhance digital learning services can range from electronic documents through bulletin boards and videos [12] to virtual and augmented reality. Interactive training methods can have different benefits for learners, such as increasing their engagement with the learning process, easier memorization of learning material, stimulating teamwork, and more [15, 29].

To achieve these goals, websites, as well as educational materials, must be designed and developed in accordance with the principles of user-oriented design, one of which focuses on creating affordable designs. Human-machine interfaces should reduce complexity of software systems. They have to create trust and openness in networked information and network-based interactions, including the people with special needs. Human-machine interfaces should be accessible, to include wide range of people. Accessibility issues are increasingly taking up the field of information and communication technologies. Thanks to assistive technologies (hardware, software, or peripherals), people with disabilities have access to digital resources through which they can compete in the labor market. "These technologies also affect the traditional processes of information exchange, teaching, learning, social utility to connect people, research, and business, which are profoundly modifying the patterns of behavior, family, and social relationships" [1].

The purpose of this article is to propose an approach for the heuristics evaluation of web accessibility based on the analytic hierarchy process (AHP) method. As there are many groups of people with disabilities, to narrow the scope of this study, we turn our attention to the perspective of the visually impaired users. To approve the approach, the authoring team applies it using Bulgarian and Polish academic websites.

2   The Concept of Universal Design

First of all, in order to create accessible and usable human-machine interfaces (HMIs), the principles of so-called "design for all" (DfA) or "universal design" must be studied, in which the environment, including buildings and objects, shall be designed to be accessible to all persons, regardless of age, disabilities or other prerequisites requiring special attention. At the core of this concept is the removal of barriers to humans and the provision of an aesthetic, usable and accessible way of interacting with the environment. The DfA is also transferred in the field of software design providing an equal opportunity for people with disabilities to access modern technologies.

The Center for Universal Design at North Carolina State University suggests the following universal design principles [33]:

- Equitable use – the HMI is useful and marketable to people with diverse abilities;
- Flexibility in use – the HMI accommodates a wide range of individual preferences and abilities;
- Simple and intuitive - the HMI is easy to understand, regardless of the user's experience, knowledge, language skills, or current concentration level;
- Perceptible information - the HMI communicates necessary information effectively to the user, regardless of ambient conditions or the user's sensory abilities;
- Tolerance for error - the HMI minimizes hazards and the adverse consequences of accidental or unintended actions;
- Low physical effort – the HMI can be used efficiently and comfortably and with a minimum of fatigue;
- Size and space for approach and use – they are provided for approach, reach, manipulation, and use regardless of user's body size, posture, or mobility.

Each of the principles of the Center for Universal Design includes guidelines for their implementation, which make them practical and make it easier for developers of both everyday "stuff" and software products.

On the other hand, the Center for Inclusive Design and Environmental Access at The University at Buffalo develops the principles of universal design by offering them the following goals: Body Fit; Comfort; Awareness; Understanding; Wellness; Social Integration; Personalization and Cultural Appropriateness [8].

The first four are related to human performance when interacting with the environment. They impose knowledge of the human body associated with [32]:

- Body fit is related to Anthropometry that objects are characteristics and abilities of the human body at rest and in motion;
- Comfort makes a reference to Biomechanics – the forces on the body in rest and in motion;
- Awareness is related to Perception that is the reception and interpretation of information from the world around the body;
- Understanding is related to the Cognition – learning process and mental representations which we form when we interact with the environment.

According to Design for All Foundation the criteria for universal design are the following [11]:

- Respectful: it should respect the diversity of users. Users should not feel marginalized and have to be able to access the environment;
- Safe: it should be free of risks to all users that means all elements of the environment have to be designed in a safe way;
- Healthy: there should not exist health risk or cause problems to those who suffer from certain illnesses. It should promote the healthy use of spaces and products;
- Functional: it should be designed to carry out the function for which it was intended without any problems or difficulties;
- Comprehensible: all users should be able to orient themselves without difficulty within a given space, including:

  - Clear information: usage of icons that are common to different countries, avoiding the use of words or abbreviations from the local language which may lead to confusion;
  - Spatial distribution: this should be coherent and functional, avoiding disorientation and confusion;

- Sustainable: there should be avoided natural resources which guarantee that future generations will have the same opportunities as us to preserve the planet;
- Affordable: anyone should have the opportunity to enjoy what is provided;
- Appealing: the result should be emotional and socially acceptable.

In our view, universal design goals, principles, and criteria can be used as a basis for making expert assessments for the accessibility of human-machine interfaces, in particular web accessibility. However, they are not sufficient in themselves to carry out such assessments because they are not bound by a formal method. Therefore, it is necessary to examine methods applied in the field of user-oriented design. Those methods will be applied in the particular case of web accessibility assessment.

3   Comparison of Evaluation Methods

The process of creating user-oriented products is inevitably related to evaluating their human-machine interfaces. It can be said that, in general, expert assessments cannot cover the full range of design problems. It is because they are conducted by highly qualified specialists whose mental models for the operation of software applications are based on their experience in the field of information and communication technologies. These specialists have certain structured expectations for how the software works, and for this reason, they would be able to handle much more quickly than non-specialists when learning a new interface. On the other hand, the result of applying such methods at the beginning of the development process is the identification of potential problems with the usability and accessibility of software products. This identification saves the cost of a possible redesign in subsequent phases.

In the field of user-oriented design, some basic methods have been imposed to evaluate the usability of the user interface. We argue that they can also be successfully applied to web accessibility evaluation, and of course, some minor changes may be required. The methods used mostly are described in Table 1.

Table 1. Comparison of the evaluation methods

Method	Participants[a]	Tools
Heuristic Evaluation	1–6 + 0 + 0	Automated Testing software
Cognitive Walkthrough	1–4 + 1–2 + 0	Prototype
Pluralistic Walkthrough	1 + 1 + 2	Prototype
Feature Inspection	1 + 0 + 0	Prototype
Compliance with Standards	1 + 0 + 0	Prototype/Developed system

We use data published on www.usabilityhome.com, www.useit.com/alertbox/20000319.html and www.useit.com/alertbox/quantitative_testing.html (30.04.2020). We present the minimum number required by the following scheme: E + D + U, where E - experts, D – developers, U – users.

The methods discussed in Table 1 are not subject to automation. Also, none of them receives quantitative data. A prototype of the software product or system developed can be used to investigate the problems of user-oriented design. The number of participants and their specialization are different for different methods.

The Heuristic Evaluation method is based on Jacob Nielsen's heuristics (principles) [26]:

- Visibility of system status;
- Match between system and the real world;
- User control and freedom;
- Consistency and standards;
- Error prevention;
- Recognition rather than recall;
- Flexibility and efficiency of use;
- Aesthetic and minimalist design;
- Help users recognize, diagnose, and recover from errors;
- Help and documentation.

The advantage of this method is that it is carried out quickly since only usability specialists participate in its implementation. The users do not participate in it. The downside is that a maximum of 75% of usability problems could be detected, as Jacob Nielsen summarizes in his study [26]. The method could not be fully used for web accessibility evaluation because it does not take into account the ergonomic features of the HMIs, but rather emphasizes the cognitive part when users interact with the interfaces.

Another commonly used method is Cognitive Walkthrough. A group of specialists simulate the behavior of potential users by performing a scenario with standard tasks. The evaluators want to achieve expected consumer behavior when performing each task. They try to succeed at every step of the process. But if they cannot do it, they evaluate why the user may not complete the task with the HMI. In the context of simulating visually impaired cognitive walkthrough, the evaluators have to use a specialized software such as speech synthesizer and screen reader. They are important for finding the specific problems of HMI.

On the other hand, the Pluralistic Walkthrough method consists in discussing and evaluating the design if a prototype is available. Its advantage is the involvement of a different representatives of the developing team They discuss user-centered design issues at a faster rate. There are involved users who are expressing their points of view of the design which would be different from that of the experts. To detect web accessibility issues, it is advisable to include people with special needs.

Another method is Feature Inspection. The focus of evaluators is on analyzing the availability, readability, and other aspects of user-centered design for each feature. This is usually involved in the execution of a specific product scenario. The experts only establish the correspondence between the requirements set out in the project contract and their implementation. No users are involved.

Compliance with Standards is related to the examine the standards in the field of user-oriented design and the comparison of the software interface with the recommendations and guidelines in these standards. In terms of web accessibility, the main international standard is Web Content Accessibility Guidelines (WCAG) of WWW International Consortium (W3C). Its last version is 2.1. Since June 2018. It encompasses four principles (perceivable, operable, understandable, and robust) that unite 13 guidelines. Each guideline provides "the basic goals that authors should work toward in order to make content more accessible to users with different disabilities" (W3C 2018). The guidelines cover a framework and overall objectives to help authors understand the success criteria and better implement the techniques (W3C 2018). In this paper, we focus on guidelines that are useful from the perspective of visually impaired people.

The methods listed in Table 1 are generally applied on their own. The disadvantage may be the lack of user satisfaction reporting, as well as the lack of quantitative data, on which to base in-depth conclusions about software design. As a result of their implementation, a major expert opinion is obtained, including designers, ergonomics specialists and others involved in the development of the evaluated software.

It can be said that the execution of certain task scenarios would be useful in the early stages of the development lifecycle to address most of the accessibility issues. In the later stages, it is advisable to apply testing methods as well, since it is imperative to obtain consumer feedback. Testing sessions with users will certainly highlight some additional issues that may not be identified by experts. This applies especially to the development of innovative products which functionality is new to consumers and gives rise to the need for optimization methods of the web code and all web-based information systems [18, 28].

4 An Approach to Web Accessibility Heuristic Evaluation

In the current paper, we propose a modification of the Heuristic Evaluation method adapted to the principles, goals, and criteria of DfA discussed above, combined with the method Compliance with Standards. The authors suggest the following universal design heuristics:

- Flexibility in use – it is associated with the provision of user control and freedom. Users can adjust the environment to their needs, such as increasing the text size, switching from one design version to another, etc.;

- Aesthetic design – we can express the opinion that the beauty of the design lies in its simplicity. Excessive accumulation of ornaments and colors leads to discomfort at work, and from there to user dissatisfaction. On the other hand, fewer cognitive resources are used when handling the interface, which increases user speed. A simple design does not mean an unfriendly design. Choosing the right colors, fonts and graphics are essential, especially for users who have an affinity for the visual. Aesthetic design is a prerequisite for creating user satisfaction;
- Comfort in use – it is related to the perception of pictures and sounds, i.e. with the human senses - vision, hearing, and touch. Touch is more important for hardware product development. In terms of software development, visual and auditory perceptions of the person are essential. Some of the actions that can be taken to provide visual comfort are: choosing the right, matching colors, ensuring the readability of buttons and texts (messages, settings, etc.), color differentiation of important functions. The accessibility standards imposed on the environment should be respected for the people with disabilities;
- Perceptible information – it is advisable to allow certain options to be turned off and on again, i.e. design should be adaptable to the temporary needs of the audience;
- Tolerance for error – to enable users to perform the same task in different ways so that, in the event of errors, they can find a "way out" of the situation. At the same time, they should not be allowed to perform activities that are not specific to them;
- Cognitive resources – the extent to which users have to invest additional cognitive resources in the performance of their tasks. As it is written in [4], "visual complexity is known to affect both website users' cognitive load and overall affective impressions". The software product should minimize the thought processes and hence the involvement of working memory[1]. Card, Moran, and Newell studies of the Human Processor Model[2] can be used to determine the cognitive load of users. Another widely known rule is that one cannot hold more than 7 ± 2 elements (words, numbers, numbers) in his short-term memory. This necessitates the gradual completion of some tasks; it is not advisable for the user to remember more than 7 ± 2 steps/actions and to assist them in the execution process;
- Alternatives – we connect with providing a multivariate approach to achieving the goals. In order to reduce the cognitive input from users, it is necessary to limit the ways to achieve the goals. This will avoid situations of uncertainty from taking a decision when choosing an approach. On the other hand, it is necessary to provide alternative content of multimedia for people who cannot read it without interruption. For example, images should be provided with alternative text and video content should be subtitled.
- Help information – including tips in new features, maintaining documentation (if necessary).

---

[1] The ability of the human brain to store a limited amount of information as long as it is used. It can be said that this type of memory combines short-term memory with knowledge extracted from long-term memory to support processes such as decision-making or calculations.

[2] The full name is "The Human Processor Model: An Engineering Model of Human Performance" since 1983. It describes the cognitive processes that people perform between the process of perception and the actions they take. Finds application in determining the performance of users when working with computer interfaces.

Similarly, to [24], we propose to link these heuristics with the guidelines from the WCAG 2.1. In this way, we combine the methods of Heuristic Evaluation and Compliance with Standards. Our goal is to maximize web accessibility issues. In Table 2, we summarize the universal design heuristics proposed in this study and the corresponding WCAG 2.1 success criteria.

Table 2. Overlap between universal design heuristics and WCAG 2.1 guidelines

	Universal Design Heuristic	WCAG 2.0 Success Criteria
1	Flexibility in use	1.4.2; 1.4.4; 1.4.8; 2.2.2; 2.2.4
2	Aesthetic design	
3	Comfort in use	1.3.3; 1.4.1.; 1.4.3; 1.4.6; 1.4.11; 5.2.1
4	Perceptible information	1.4.7; 2.1.4.; 2.2.1.; 3.2.5
5	Tolerance for error	3.3.1; 3.3.2; 3.3.3; 3.3.4; 3.3.6
6	Cognitive resources	1.3.1; 2.4.2; 2.4.6; 2.4.10
7	Alternatives	1.1.1.; 1.2.1.; 1.2.2; 1.2.3; 1.2.5; 1.2.8; 1.2.9; 1.4.5
8	Help information	3.3.5

To prioritize heuristics, we use the AHP method to organize and analyze complex decisions firstly developed in 1970s by Thomas Saaty. It is based on quantifying the weights of decision criteria and estimating the factors' relative magnitudes through pair-wise comparisons. The method has multiple applications such as: choice ranking, prioritization, resource allocation, benchmarking, quality management, conflict resolution, etc. [14]. The method is conducted in the following steps [7, 10, 19, 21–24, 27, 30, 34]:

- Modeling the problem as a hierarchy including the decision goal, the alternatives for reaching it, and the criteria for evaluating the alternatives;
- Clearing the criteria or factors that influence the goal. The structure of these factors into levels and sublevels are also formed;
- Setting of priorities for the hierarchy using paired comparisons of each factor. It is formed a comparison matrix with calculated weights, ranked eigen values, and consistency measures (index and ratio). The consistency index (CI) is calculated as:

$$CI = \frac{\gamma_{max} - n}{n - 1}$$

where γ_{max} is the maximum eigenvalue of the comparison matrix.

The consistency ratio (CR) is calculated as:

$$CR = \frac{100\% * CI}{RI}$$

where RI is a random consistency index.

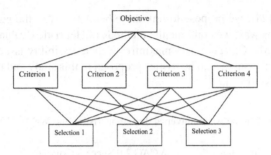

Fig. 1. AHP hierarchy

- Forming the ranks of alternatives until the final choice is made (Fig. 1).

In this study, we use the method to select the heuristics that are most important from the perspective of visually impaired people. To achieve this, we use the AHP Priority Calculator [16], which forms pairs of these heuristics. For each pair, we choose the priority of each criterion. Based on the priorities, the calculator generates a solution matrix (Table 3) and assigns weights to each of the heuristics (Table 4).

Table 3. The principal eigenvector of the decision matrix

	1	2	3	4	5	6	7	8
1	1	2.00	0.50	0.50	2.00	2.00	0.33	2.00
2	0.50	1	0.50	0.50	0.50	0.50	0.33	0.50
3	2.00	2.00	1	0.50	2.00	2.00	0.33	2.00
4	2.00	2.00	2.00	1	2.00	2.00	0.33	2.00
5	0.50	2.00	0.50	0.50	1	2.00	0.33	2.00
6	0.50	2.00	0.50	0.50	0.50	1	0.33	2.00
7	3.00	3.00	3.00	3.00	3.00	3.00	1	3.00
8	0.50	2.00	0.50	0.50	0.50	0.50	0.33	1

The number of comparisons is 28. The following values were generated: consistency ratio CR = 4.4% and principal eigenvalue = 8.428. Based on the table, it can be concluded that the provision of alternative content is essential for web accessibility from the point of view of the visually impaired and then ranked Perceptible information and Comfort in use.

5   Results

To achieve the goal of the current study, we selected academic sites. We used the rankings made through the U-Multirank web tool which compares universities "in the five dimensions of university activity: teaching and learning, research, knowledge transfer, international orientation and regional engagement" [35]. We selected Bulgarian and Polish universities, ranked according to Graduating on time (bachelors)[3]. The universities

---
[3] The ranking of universities is up to date 11.07.2020.

Table 4. The resulting weights for the universal design heuristics based on pairwise comparisons

	Universal design heuristics	Priority	Weight	Rank	(+)	(−)
1	Flexibility in use	11.4%	0.114	4	3.9%	3.9%
2	Aesthetic design	5.7%	0.057	8	2.0%	2.0%
3	Comfort in use	13.6%	0.136	3	4.7%	4.7%
4	Perceptible information	16.1%	0.161	2	5.6%	5.6%
5	Tolerance for error	9.5%	0.095	5	3.3%	3.3%
6	Cognitive resources	8.1%	0.081	6	2.8%	2.8%
7	Alternatives	28.8%	0.288	1	9.9%	9.9%
8	Help information	6.8%	0.068	7	2.3%	2.3%

from Bulgaria are 13 but we would like to take into account the top 6. They are the following ones: Nikola Vaptsarov Naval Academy (NVNA), University of Economics - Varna (UEV), D. A. Tsenov Academy of Economics (DAT), Medical University of Plovdiv (MUP), Technical University of Varna (TUV) and Sofia University St. Kliment Ohridski (SU). There are 37 universities in Poland, but we choose the top 6 in the ranking: Adam Mickiewicz University Poznań (AMUP), Medical University of Gdańsk (MUG), Academy of Fine Arts in Wroclaw (AFAW), Uniwersytet Ekonomiczny w Katowicach (UEK), Medical University of Bialystok (MUB) and Uniwersytet Szczeciński (USZ).

Code-based and image-based assessment tools can be used to assist in the evaluation process of websites [5, 6]. In this paper we use the WebAIM tool Wave, which performs automated testing of page code and outputs errors and recommendations for correcting them [38]. It will make it for us to check whether alternatives to the multimedia content of the aforementioned academic sites have been provided.

Table 5 summarizes the results of the site's analysis of the Bulgarian universities, and Table 6 - the sites of the Polish universities[4].

Table 5. Errors discovered on Bulgarian universities' websites

	Academic website	Errors	Contrast Errors	Alerts
1	NVNA (naval-acad.bg)	3	7	14
2	UEV (ue-varna.bg)	11	1	8
3	DAT (uni-svishtov.bg)	4	27	58
4	MUP (mu-plovdiv.bg)	19	42	22
5	TUV (tu-varna.bg)	35	0	41
6	SU (uni-sofia.bg)	3	56	100

---

[4] The accessibility testing results are up to date 11.07.2020.

Table 6. Errors discovered on Polish universities' websites

	Academic website	Errors	Contrast Errors	Alerts
1	AMUP (amu.edu.pl)	5	17	28
2	MUG (mug.edu.pl)	25	24	2
3	AFAW (asp.wroc.pl)	23	101	77
4	UEK (ue.katowice.pl)	9	2	271
5	MUB (umb.edu.pl)	0	24	16
6	USZ (usz.edu.pl)	2	11	45

From the analysis of Bulgarian universities websites with Wave we found that UEV and NVNA have the least problems with web accessibility, while the TUV site has the highest number of errors. The main problems found on all sites are missing alternative texts of images and links, blank links, missing form labels, empty buttons and empty table headers.

From the analysis of Polish academic websites with Wave we found that MUB has the least problems with web accessibility, while the AFAW site has the highest number of contrast errors. The main problems found on all sites are also missing alternative texts of images and links, blank links, empty buttons and missing form labels.

Polish academic websites (except AFAW) are characterized by better web accessibility than those of Bulgarian universities. In the context of accessibility for people with visual impairments, errors found on websites can initiate problems for users who access them through screen readers and speech synthesizers. Using such software, people with visual impairments read the content of web pages and interact with them. These problems correspond to our proposed universal design heuristics and more specially to Comfort in use, Perceptible information and Alternatives. The most of the websites do not cover success criteria 1.4.5 Images of Text, 1.4.6 Contrast (Enhanced) and 1.4.11 Non-text Contrast of WCAG 2.1.

Considering our approach to web accessibility heuristic evaluation we applied AHP method for comparing the universities' websites according to the weights and ranks in Table 4. We used a gradation scale for comparison of alternatives from 1 to 3. One is related to equal, 2 is marginally strong and 3 is strong. The results are summarized in Table 7 and Table 8.

Generally, we took into account the number of discovered errors summarized in Table 5. According to our calculations the UEV mostly follows the proposed universal design heuristics. The second place is for NVNA and the last – for MUP.

The Polish academic websites provide better support tools for visually impaired such as text resizing, contrast change, disable flashes and better contrast. USZ mostly follow the proposed heuristics. The second in the ranking list is MUB and the last one is AFAW.

Bulgarian academic websites have to add more accessibility tools for bettering the interactions of users with special needs.

Table 7. Local priorities for all the heuristics (Bulgarian websites)

University	1	2	3	4	5	6	7	8	SUM	Rank
	0.288	0.161	0.136	0.114	0.095	0.081	0.068	0.057	1	
NVNA	0,076	0,0314	0,0364	0,019	0,0203	0,0104	0,0114	0,0074	0,2123	2
UEV	0,04	0,0396	0,0422	0,019	0,0203	0,0289	0,0114	0,0203	0,2217	1
DAT	0,051	0,0166	0,0116	0,019	0,0203	0,0164	0,0114	0,0116	0,1579	4
MUP	0,026	0,0132	0,0214	0,019	0,0067	0,0066	0,0114	0,0046	0,1089	6
TUV	0,019	0,0497	0,016	0,019	0,0203	0,0138	0,0114	0,0097	0,1589	3
SU	0,076	0,0105	0,0084	0,019	0,0067	0,0049	0,0114	0,0034	0,1403	5

Table 8. Local priorities for all the heuristics (Polish websites)

University	1	2	3	4	5	6	7	8	SUM	Rank
	0.288	0.161	0.136	0.114	0.095	0.081	0.068	0.057	1	
AMUP	0,0533	0,0256	0,0222	0,0143	0,0178	0,0116	0,0114	0,008	0,1642	5
MUG	0,0179	0,0179	0,0483	0,0143	0,0178	0,0298	0,0114	0,021	0,1784	3
AFAW	0,0225	0,0095	0,0118	0,0143	0,0059	0,0049	0,0114	0,004	0,0843	6
UEK	0,0423	0,0581	0,0079	0,0143	0,0178	0,0116	0,0114	0,008	0,1714	4
MUB	0,0847	0,0179	0,0305	0,0143	0,0178	0,0116	0,0114	0,008	0,1962	2
USZ	0,0674	0,032	0,0155	0,0428	0,0178	0,0116	0,0114	0,008	0,2065	1

6 Conclusion

The access to information by people with disabilities is a logically interconnected system that must be observed and respected. In general, properly provided access must purposefully ensure that public benefit is maximized. Access for people with disabilities is an explicit prerequisite that is based on the principle of universal design in every area of public expression. Versatility is the observation and implementation of accepted and approved international standards that are tailored to individual needs, the type and extent of disability.

The access to web contents is increasingly important, but there is a real risk of excluding people with disabilities and disadvantaged groups due to technical barriers to using the Internet. Most of these barriers can easily be overcome if some simple rules regarding content, structure, and coding are followed when designing websites. The W3C develops interoperability technologies (specifications, recommendations, software, tools) in order to make the Web site the best forum for information, marketing, and communication.

In the present study, taking into account these prerequisites, the authors proposed an approach to web accessibility heuristic evaluation. We suggested eight web accessibility heuristics: Flexibility in use; Aesthetic design; Comfort in use; Perceptible information; Tolerance for error; Cognitive resources; Alternatives; Help information. They are paired with WCAG 2.1. Success criteria. We ranked them using AHP method. Our approach is approbated through testing Bulgarian and Polish academic websites. As a result, the Polish websites are characterized by better web accessibility than Bulgarian. They provide better tools for visually impaired users and number of errors are less than Bulgarian websites.

References

1. Acosta-Vargas, P., et al.: A heuristic method to evaluate web accessibility for users with low vision. IEEE Access **7**, 125634–125648 (2019)
2. Alexa Internet, Inc.: The top 500 sites on the web (2019). https://www.alexa.com/topsites. Accessed 14 May 2020
3. Armstrong, M.: How Many Websites Are There? (2019). https://www.statista.com/chart/19058/how-many-websites-are-there/. Accessed 14 May 2020
4. Bakaev, M., et al.: Analysis and prediction of university websites perceptions by different user groups. In: Proceedings of IEEE 14th Actual Problems of Electronic Instrument Engineering, pp. 381–385 (2018)
5. Bakaev, M., et al.: Auto-extraction and integration of metrics for web user interfaces. J. Web Eng. **17**(6 & 7), 561–590 (2018)
6. Bakaev, M., Heil, S., Perminov, N., Gaedke, M.: Integration platform for metric-based analysis of web user interfaces. In: Bakaev, M., Frasincar, F., Ko, IY. (eds.) ICWE 2019. LNCS, vol. 11496, pp. 525–529 Springer, Cham (2019). https://doi.org/10.1007/978-3-030-19274-7_39
7. Beiragh, R., et al.: An integrated multi-criteria decision-making model for sustainability performance assessment for insurance companies. Sustainability **12**, 789 (2020). https://doi.org/10.3390/su12030789
8. Center for Inclusive Design and Environmental Access: The Goals of Universal Design (2012). http://www.universaldesign.com/what-is-ud/. Accessed 14 May 2020
9. Czaplewski, M.: State of development of the information society in Slovenia, Croatia and Poland in comparison with the EU average. Econ. Soc. Changes Facts Trends Forecast **11**(4), 185–201 (2018)
10. Czekster, R., et al.: Decisor: a software tool to drive complex decisions with analytic hierarchy process. Int. J. Inf. Technol. Decis. Mak. **18**(1), 65–86 (2019)
11. Design for All Foundation: Design for All is design tailored to human diversity (2019). http://designforall.org/design.php. Accessed 14 May 2020
12. Dimitrov, G., et al.: The possibility of using 'video board' in the classroom. In: 58th Annual International Scientific Conference on Power and Electrical Engineering of Riga Technical University, RTUCON 2017 - Proceedings, 2017 November, pp. 1–5 (2017)
13. Eurostat: Internet use by individuals (2018). https://ec.europa.eu/eurostat/databrowser/view/tin00028/default/table?lang=en. Accessed 14 May 2020
14. Forman, E., Gass, S.: The analytic hierarchy process – an exposition. Oper. Res. **49**(4), 469–487 (2001)
15. Gaftandzhieva, S., Doneva, R., Pashev, G.: Learning analytics from the teacher's perspective: a mobile app. In: INTED2019 Proceedings, pp. 2340–1079 (2019)
16. Goepel, K.: AHP Priority Calculator (2019). https://bpmsg.com/ahp/ahp-calc.php. Accessed 14 May 2020
17. Hootsuite: Digital 2019 Global Digital Overview (2019). https://www.slideshare.net/DataReportal/digital-2019-global-digital-overview-january-2019-v01. Accessed 14 May 2020
18. Iliev, I., Dimitrov, G.: Front end optimization methods and their effect. In: 37th International Convention on Information and Communication Technology, Electronics and Microelectronics, MIPRO 2014 - Proceedings 6859613, pp. 467–473 (2014)

19. Ilunga, M.: Analytic hierarchy process (AHP) in ranking non-parametric stochastic rainfall and streamflow models. Syst. Cybern. Inform. **13**(4), 74–81 (2015)
20. ITU: Statistics (2019). https://www.itu.int/en/ITU-D/Statistics/Pages/stat/default.aspx. Accessed 27 Sep 2023
21. Kardaras, D., Barbounaki, S.: A website selection model in programmatic advertising using fuzzy analytic hierarchy process and similarity methods. In: Data Analytics 2019: The Eighth International Conference on Data Analytics, pp. 20–25 (2019)
22. Kie, C., et al.: An analytic hierarchy process approach in decision-making for material selection in an automotive company: a case study. In: FGIC 2nd Conference on Governance and Integrity 2019, KnE Social Sciences, pp. 472–484 (2019)
23. Kohli, R., Sehra, S.: Fuzzy multi criteria approach for selecting software quality model. Int. J. Comput. Appl. **98**(11), 11–15 (2014)
24. Moreno, L., Martínez, P., Ruiz-Mezcua, B.: A bridge to web accessibility from the usability heuristics. In: Holzinger, A., Miesenberger, K. (eds.) USAB 2009. LNCS, vol. 5889, pp. 290–300. Springer, Heidelberg (2009). https://doi.org/10.1007/978-3-642-10308-7_20
25. Muhammad, A., et al.: A hierarchical model to evaluate the quality of web-based e-learning systems. Sustainability **12**, 4071 (2020). https://doi.org/10.3390/su12104071
26. Nielsen, J.: Usability Engineering. Morgan Kaufmann, Burlington (1994)
27. Nurda, N., et al.: Change detection and land suitability analysis for extension of potential forest areas in Indonesia using satellite remote sensing and GIS. Forests **11**, 398 (2020). https://doi.org/10.3390/f11040398
28. Panayotova, G., Dimitrov, G.: Design of web-based information system for optimization of portfolio. In: Proceedings of the 13th International Symposium on Operational Research, SOR 2015, pp. 193–198 (2015)
29. Pashev, G., et al.: Personalized educational paths through self-modifying learning objects. In: ACM Proceedings of the 17th International Conference on Computer Systems and Technologies 2016, pp. 437–444 (2016)
30. Saaty, T.: Decision Making for Leaders: The Analytic Hierarchy Process for Decisions in a Complex World. RWS Publications, Pittsburgh (2008)
31. Statista.com: Global digital population as of October 2019 (in millions) (2020). https://www.statista.com/statistics/617136/digital-population-worldwide/. Accessed 27 Sep 2023
32. Steinfeld, E., Maisel, J.: Universal Design: Creating Inclusive Environments. Wiley, New Jersey (2012)
33. The Center for Universal Design, North Carolina State University: The Principles of Universal Design (1997). https://projects.ncsu.edu/ncsu/design/cud/about_ud/udprinciplestext.htm. Accessed 14 May 2020
34. Tran, T.: An empirical study by applying multi-criteria expertise analytic hierarchy process model in evaluation. Adv. Manag. Appl. Econ. **9**(2), 51–68 (2019)
35. U-Multirank: U-Multirank Project (2019). https://www.umultirank.org/about/u-multirank/the-project/. Accessed 14 May 2020
36. W3C: Web Content Accessibility Guidelines (WCAG) 2.1 (2018). https://www.w3.org/TR/WCAG21/. Accessed 14 May 2020
37. W3C: Internet Live Stats (2019). https://www.internetlivestats.com/. Accessed 14 May 2020
38. WebAIM: WAVE Web Accessibility Evaluation Tool (2019). http://wave.webaim.org/. Accessed 14 May 2020
39. World Bank: Individuals using the Internet (% of population) (2020). https://data.worldbank.org/indicator/IT.NET.USER.ZS. Accessed 14 May 2020
40. Kemp, S.: Digital 2023: Global Overview Report (2023). https://datareportal.com/reports/digital-2023-global-overview-report. Accessed 27 Sep 2023

ICT Governance and Management
for Digital Transformation

Improving Cybersecurity Capabilities at Nikola Vaptsarov Naval Academy by Building and Developing a Security Operations and Training Center

Borislav M. Nikolov(✉)

Nikola Vaptsarov Naval Academy, Varna 9002, Bulgaria
nikolov@naval-acad.bg

Abstract. Cybersecurity is becoming increasingly important in our daily lives. For the end-user of IT devices, this is a personal responsibility. In a corporate network, however, the responsibilities for implementing a certain level of cybersecurity are not individual or of a certain team, but of each of the employees. The development of capabilities to counter cyber threats is associated with certain organizational and technical measures. End-user training is undoubtedly one of the leading organizational measures. Conducting training in an environment as close as possible to the real one helps the trainees to better understanding the existing threats and the result of them. At the same time, the use of a real IT infrastructure for conducting trainings hides many challenges and leads to the need for specific planning and organizing the usage of the available information resources. The specificity of the main activity of Nikola Vaptsarov Naval Academy (NVNA) presupposes the building of specific capabilities for cyber defense and conducting training in the field of cybersecurity for users with different knowledge and skills. Particular challenges in this activity area are involved with the IMO requirements for cybersecurity at sea. This paper presents the adopted concept in NVNA for building and developing a Security Operations and Training Center (SOTC). Major design and organizations steps are described. A part of this concept was presented on "Digilience 2020" conference.

Keywords: Cybersecurity · Security Operations and Training Center · IT infrastructure · Cyber range · Virtualization · Exercise team

1 Introduction

In our days, the cyber threats increase their number because of the digitalization of human life. The hackers conduct targeted cyber-attacks that are vaster in terms of the damage caused, but also in terms of used resources. The inflicted damage has a significant financial impact.

In a corporate computer network, the cybersecurity is a responsibility of all employees, not only the IT staff. A good level of cybersecurity awareness of the employees

T. Tagarev and N. Stoianov (Eds.): DIGILIENCE 2020, CCIS 1790, pp. 219–242, 2024.
https://doi.org/10.1007/978-3-031-44440-1_30

and high level of qualification of the IT staff are inseparably connected and are required for achieving a certain level of cybersecurity for the corporate computer network. To achieve that is required a specific training. In addition, to implement the cybersecurity measures it is necessary to provide specific technical devices.

The business organizations and governments build and maintain Security Operations Centers (SOCs). On the other hand, training and qualification are in the field of activity of educational institutions and qualification centers. By decision of the Academic Board of Nikola Vaptsarov Naval Academy, reflected in the protocol № 105/29.07.2019, a roadmap has been adopted, which will be the basis for the successful training of officers in the specialty "Organization and management of military units on tactical level" with specialization "Cyber operations". One of the steps outlined in this roadmap is related to the building of a Security Operations and Training Centre (SOTC), which will have the functions of both an SOC for the academy's computer network and a training center for IT and cyber specialists. The "Concept for Establishing a Security Operations and Training Centre at the Bulgarian Naval Academy" was presented on the "Digilience 2020" conference [1].

There are many specialized in a certain field cybersecurity training center in the world. Some of them enable their clients to build and use SOC. The world trends must be taken into account in order to define the tasks, goals and functionalities for designing and building training and operational cybersecurity center.

The Persistent Cyber Training Environment (PCTE) is one of the popular cybersecurity training centers. It provides cyber simulations that will allow cyber mission forces from all military branches, especially from the U.S. armed force, to train together in a realistic environment. It will support individual instruction and certification to allow cyber operators to practice and rehearse missions simultaneously from locations around the world, meeting the needs of all four services and the U.S. Cyber Command [2].

Raytheon Intelligence & Space's solution for the new PCTE offers an open-architecture approach that will allow the Defense Department to connect cyber ranges, training environments and tool libraries seamlessly.

The environment provides U.S. cyber forces, across all military branches, a dedicated space to conduct individual and group training. PCTE becomes a place to practice and hone skills repeatedly, similar to marksmanship ranges used every day.

The Cyber Training, Readiness, Integration, Delivery and Enterprise Technology, or Cyber TRIDENT, contract scales the PCTE platform to support cyber training across the military. The result will deliver training from a single environment for forces to remotely conduct exercises, mission rehearsals and certifications [2].

Raytheon Intelligence & Space leverages its experience with large and complex training environments to connect PCTE locations around the world. Training is made more effective through artificial intelligence and software development best practices that will speed the development and delivery of new capabilities.

A request for proposals for Cyber TRIDENT is to be released in 2020 [2].

Authorized users of the U.S. DoD information systems must complete every year the Cyber Awareness Challenge to maintain awareness of, and stay up-to-date on new cybersecurity threats. The training also reinforces best practices to keep the DoD and personal information and information systems secure, and stay abreast of changes in DoD cybersecurity policies. Other agencies use the course to satisfy their requirements as well. There is also a Knowledge Check option available within the course for individuals who have successfully completed the previous version of the course. The course [3] provides an overview of cybersecurity threats and best practices to keep information and information systems secure.

The Defense Information Systems Agency developed the Cyber Awareness Challenge for the DoD Chief Information Officer [4]. Content of this challenge is based on input from the Workforce Improvement Program Advisory Council. DoD and other agencies use this course to satisfy mandatory training. The course addresses the DoD 8570.01-M Information Assurance Workforce Improvement Program (WIP), 10 November 2015, incorporating Change 4, Office of Management and Budget Circular NO. A-130, and the Federal Information Security Modernization Act (FISMA) 2014.

The Cyber Awareness Challenge begins with a message from the future describing serious vulnerabilities that were the result of certain decisions made in the present [4]. The student is asked to help prevent these incidents by making proper cybersecurity decisions about events from the evidence provided. Through this process, the student learns proper cybersecurity practices. Students are given the opportunity to take the knowledge check track. This knowledge check option allows users to answer questions related to subtopics in each area. If these questions are answered correctly, students are given credit and are able to move to other subtopics [4].

A similar course is the Cybersecurity Awareness course, which is conducted by the Security Awareness Hub [5]. The course introduces the automated information systems (AIS) environment and the threats and vulnerabilities faced when working within the government or defense industrial systems. It provides a working knowledge of cyber intrusion methods and cybersecurity countermeasures to assist employees in preventing cyberattacks and protecting their systems and information. The user experience centers on a single, large-scale, disastrous event. Several contributing scenarios are presented to show different vantage points related to the large event. Through the large event and associated contributing scenarios, students learn about different cyber threats and methods of operation, targeted information, countermeasures, and reporting requirements. This approach demonstrates for users that even small events can contribute and lead to immeasurable consequences.

The Cyber Center of Excellence (CCoE) of the U.S. Army is responsible for developing doctrine, organizational, training, materiel, leadership/education, personnel, and facility solutions related to the Cyberspace Operations, Signal/Communications Networks and Information Services, and Electronic Warfare (EW). A major aspect of the CCoE's mission is the training, education, and development of world-class, highly skilled Signal, Cyber, and EW professionals supporting operations at the strategic, operational, and tactical level [6]. The CCoE must enable commanders and leaders to seize, retain, and exploit freedom of action in both the land and cyberspace domains, while simultaneously denying and degrading the adversary use of the same.

Since 2008, DIATEAM has been developing Cyber Range Solutions designed for learning and training by practice, testing and experimentation [7]. Their solutions meet the needs of key players such as Computer Emergency Response Team, Operations Center, Forensics, judicial investigation, Pentesters, computer network defense, SOC, SIEM

Operators. This solution can conduct different cyber security tests and "benchmark" in a fully mastered and controlled environment (sandboxing, pentest, malware analysis, honeypots, solutions comparisons, realistic scenarios, legitimate and malicious traffic and behaviors simulation, etc.).

The Cybint Certified Cyber Center is an educational facility that provides accelerated career training to prospective cybersecurity professionals [8]. Their partners are located worldwide, expanding opportunities for high-paying technical positions locally. Cyber Center partners receive access to the Cybint Bootcamp. Cybint is a global cyber education company with a commitment to reskilling the workforce and upskilling the industry in cybersecurity. With innovative and leading edge education and training solutions, Cybint tackles cybersecurity's two greatest threats: the talent shortage and the skills gap.

The National Counterintelligence and Security Center (NCSC) provide courses in the Cyber Training Series [9]. That includes courses as followed:

- Cyber Explore – Fundamentals of Cyber. This learning experience is designed for professionals new to the cyber realm. It introduces users to the computer's component layers and associated functions, virtualization concepts, and security methods [9].
- Cyber Aware – Anatomy of a Hack. This learning experience is designed to increase awareness of the protocols that defend information systems and data. It demonstrates to users where network and system vulnerabilities may be while also helping them to understand common hacking methods [9].
- Cyber Exploits – Understand the Threat. This learning experience is designed to increase understanding of the broader categories of cyber-attacks. It introduces specific terminology and real-world applications so users can recognize the threat when they see it [9].

The Pinckney Cyber Training Institute (PCTI) is adding to the current Michigan Cyber Range Hub with a Security Operations Center (SOC) to provide better public entity cybersecurity defense [10]. This SOC will promote cybersecurity education within any public institution while building a technical workforce talent pipeline, and at the same time serve to strengthen the public and private sector's security posture. This initiative is all inclusive, offering network monitoring for hospitals, schools, municipalities, townships and even small businesses. Several free online courses are available on PCTI web site [10].

"Knowledge is power" and "Education is the last piece of the puzzle, and the most important" – these are some of the slogans of the Cyber Training Center (CTC) [11]. The courses in CTC are designed to provide participants maximum information with a dash of humor all in a short time. Each course is one hour with interaction and time for questions and there are 12 courses. These courses can be used as annual refresher training for client organization or take them on your own to help protect you and your family. If you complete all 12 courses, you will become "Cyber Certified" and receive a certificate [11].

PricewaterhouseCoopers (PwC) operates a Cyber Center that is a part of their Academy in Romania [12]. In today's business world, a cyberattack or breach is not a matter of "if" but "when". With their training sessions, they aim to help clients to anticipate, to properly evaluate the impact and to be prepared for when it does happen [12].

Cyber Arena is a software developed by PwC, which simulates behavior of a specific IT infrastructure. It offers a unique opportunity to experience and react to cyber-attacks affecting the company. It will help you and your company to check the efficiency of your digitalization strategy and modern technology development. This all accomplished with a safe tool authentically simulating your company's settings and processes [12]. The simulation in Cyber Arena is targeted primarily at top management, IT/Security management, production control and other key roles within the company. Certified tutors hosting the simulation observe the progress and methods of all client team members and in the end together assess the decisions they made during the simulation. Experiencing the simulation in Cyber Arena will enable client's employees to fully understand the importance and impact of each decision from various points of view. Clients will gain unique Experience of fighting together against a cyber-attacker, which will strengthen the efficiency of communication and understanding specific needs within the team [12].

At the National Cyber Training Center [13] is working on training security operators and security innovators for positions in cybersecurity and ICT, and there are also conducted research and development in these fields. In the training of security operators they targeting their efforts at information system managers and other cyber-security professionals by implementing two types of exercise—CYDER (Cyber Defense Exercise with Recurrence) and Cyber Colosseo. These are practical cyber defense exercises using real systems for the purpose of equipping people with incident response skills so they can respond promptly to emergencies where affiliated organizations are subjected to severe cyberattacks [13].

The most known cybersecurity training centers, as pointed out so far, provide only training environment for their clients to prepare them how to deal with cyber-attacks and response to cyber incidents. Extremely rare is integrated usage of an SOC with a cybersecurity training center. Because of this, the building of SOTC at NVNA is an innovative idea with a practical focus.

2 Security Operations and Training Center (SOTC) Purpose and Requirements

There are significant challenges when you build and commission a center with both training and operational purposes. What will be the main function of this center is the main question to be answered. After answering to this question, it will be possible to move to the design stage so that the implemented project is as functional and operational in terms of its tasks.

A serious challenge at the design stage is the variety of learning tasks that have to be covered in such type of training center. The wide range of possible simulation scenarios, both for beginners and advanced, implies a wide range of functional capabilities of the training center, so that you can quickly move from one task to another. This in turn leads to the need for the technical parameters of the individual structural components of the training center to cover a wide range of requirements, both in terms of performance and in terms of their functional capabilities.

The SOC has a clearly defined functional purpose that is to provide cyber protection of the corporate computer network. In this way, the range of tasks can be clearly defined, as well as the technical requirements for the structural components can be determined.

2.1 SOTC Purposes

The SOTC at NVNA will have two main purposes – a training center and a SOC for the academy's computer network. These two purposes are both complementary and mutually exclusive. It should be noted that the use of a productive environment to provide learning goals carries many risks related to compromising the functioning not only of the center itself, but also of the computer network of the academy.

Although the main reason for the realization of the project for building SOTC is the training at all levels of competence, the leading functionality in the design stage is that of SOC for the academy's computer network. It is more accurate to say that at the heart of SOTC, the SOTC Datacenter should be implemented all necessary measures to ensure a certain level of cybersecurity for the computer network not only of SOTC, but also of the academy.

The mission of each SOC can be compared to providing physical security at the sites of the organization. Nathans [14] defines the purpose of SOC as "to provide a real-time view into a network or an organization's security status, assuring that systems are not being negatively affected and has the ability to execute agreed upon protocols and processes in a consistent manner when issues arise as well as someone keeping an eye on the facilities at all times". In terms of cybersecurity, the focus of the SOC is network security. It can be said that SOC is an upgraded version of the functions of the Network Operations Center (NOC), which is used to monitor the operation of the computer network and maintaining this operation based on defined parameters. To the purpose of NOC are added the responsibilities for securing the data in the computer network, it is safely used and policies to respond to incidents with cybersecurity. In short, it can be said that the main purpose of SOC is to maintain the continuous in the business processes in the organization, realizing all aspects of the security of the used systems. Achieving this mission is unthinkable without utilizing up-to-date information technology.

When determining the purpose of an SOC for an organization, the operating mode of the center should also be determined. Whether this will be 24/7 mode, only during the working hours of the organization or with another time duration, depends on the specifics of the business processes in the organization. For example, in the case of production processes managed through IT services, even the slightest disruption in the operation of systems can lead to huge economic losses and in some situations even be detrimental to the organization. According to the Allianz Global Corporate & Specialty (AGCS) report "Allianz Risk Barometer" for 2020, the top threat to business organizations is the occurrence of cyber incidents. That means that business organizations must invest in their cybersecurity, and one approach for this is to build and properly operate their own SOC [15]. For such organizations, it is mandatory the SOC to operate in 24/7 mode. Ensuring such a mode of operation inevitably requires the presence of on-duty staff of administrators and analysts (Fig. 1).

On the other hand, NVNA is an educational institution with interrupted normal work schedule - from 8 a.m. to 5 p.m. on Monday to Friday. Of course, there are some deviations in this mode of operation. In certain periods, classes are planned on weekends, and if necessary after 5 p.m. on weekdays. For NVNA more appropriate is the mode of operation of the SOC, coinciding with the working hours of the academy. This will also

Fig. 1. The most important business risks for 2020 (source AGSC)

minimize the required staff to ensure the proper functioning of the SOC. Ensuring 24/7 duty means appointing three times as many administrators and analysts.

NVNA has a long tradition in conducting training of personnel for maritime business and officers for the Navy. In recent years, the training of IT specialists, including specialists in cybersecurity and conducting operations in cyberspace, has been successfully developed. Despite the long tradition as an internationally recognized educational institution, the educational material base of the academy is closely profiled and mainly focused on the sea staff, including the most modern simulation training complexes. In terms of IT specialists, there is still a lack of a functional simulation complex. The training of these specialists is provided by a sufficient number of hardware devices and computer workstations with the help of various technological solutions for computer virtualization. The lack of simulations with prepared scenarios for different cyber situations, including and attacks and incidents, is compensated by the lecturers in the Department of Information Technology, using various software products to simulate certain aspects of the processes in an IT infrastructure. This leads to many problems related to the integration of the work of individual software products, which are often from different vendors.

Building of a specialized simulation complex for training of IT and cybersecurity specialists will inevitably increase the quality of the conducted training. The possibility to use pre-defined scenarios and the modelling of these scenarios according to the curricula will enable the training of specialists in the IT sector to be raised to a global level, as well as the training of specialists in the maritime industry.

The integration of NVNA's SOC and the training simulation complex for IT specialists in one and its development as SOTC aims to create as close as possible to the real conditions for training. Trainees will have the opportunity to conduct their practical classes with an environment close to the real one in traditional SOCs. At the same time, SOTC staff involved in the security of academy's systems will be able to use a simulation environment to improve their skills, as well as to test new technical solutions, especially their security, before they are implemented in productive environment. Last but not least, there will be an environment in which to analyze cybersecurity incidents, in a "safe" and "isolated" environment, using simulation models. The latter, can be used as a business model for external organizations.

Building of SOTC at NVNA can be considered as a natural continuation of the strategy for successful training of IT specialists in the academy. After its completion and commissioning, students will be given the opportunity to access all elements related to their professional qualification on the territory of the academy, namely admission, training, qualification, certification. It should be noted that one of the previous steps in building the SOTC is the establishment of a Pearson Vue Test Center (PVTC) in the area of the Department of Information Technology. Building of SOTC will complete a properly planned strategy for training and qualification of IT specialists.

As the next step in the development of the simulation complexes at NVNA should be sought the integration of SOTC or rather its simulation models and available scenarios with other simulation complexes in the academy, providing training for seafarers. According to a 2019 survey by insurance broker Marsh on the impact of individual factors on the maritime industry [16], cyberattacks and data theft are ranked 5th with a score of 3.52 out of a maximum of 4 (for comparison, the 1st place factor is with score 3.69). According to the same study, the probability of a cyber-attack or data theft is ranked third with 0.04 behind the most likely factor. At the same time, the preparedness of maritime industry companies for this type of incident is extremely low. With its 2016 and 2017 recommendations [17, 18], the IMO draws attention to the need to increase the knowledge of all those involved in the maritime industry about cyber threats and risks. From January 2021, these recommendations will become mandatory. This will require a wide range of specialized training courses for seafarers at all levels, and the use of SOTC in conjunction with simulation complexes of Engine Room and Navigation Bridge would help to better interpret the problem for trainees.

2.2 SOTC Requirements

Based on the above functional purposes of SOTC can be defined and the requirements for its individual structural components. The key resources needed for the successful development of any business project can be categorized into four categories [19] – physical resources, intellectual resources, human resources and financial resources. The specifics of the implementation of SOTC at NVNA excludes the independent assessment of the required financial resource, as SOTC will not function independently. This does not exclude the creation of a business plan for the use of SOTC in its second main function - education and training. The purpose of this plan should be to ensure a return on investment and financial resources for maintenance of the Center operation, including its development.

The requirements for the structural components of the SOTC can be divided into two main groups depending on the function provided namely the training center and the SOC for the academy's computer network. In each of these two groups, three separate categories of key resources can be defined, for which separate requirements for availability and functionality can be imposed. The correlation between the same types of key resource categories from the two groups, without giving any priority to either group, will be used to determine the recommended requirements for the building and operation of the SOTC.

The three categories of key resources from each group are:

- Hardware – physical resources;
- Software – intellectual resources;
- Staff – human resources.

The "hardware" resource category includes all those physical IT components that will be used to build the SOTC. These components include communication lines, including wireless, computer workstations, physical servers and storage systems, communication devices of any types, peripherals, multimedia and presentation devices. These components will build the IT infrastructure of SOTC.

The "software" resource category includes all those software products that will be used to give essence of SOTC's IT infrastructure. Such are the software products for realization of computer virtualization in the Datacenter of SOTC, software for simulation of computer incidents and attacks, operating systems, office applications, software for video conferencing, e-learning and data sharing, etc.

In contrast to the above two categories, the resource category "staff" is somewhat abstract and difficult to assess. It refers to the availability of a sufficient number of qualified staff (employees) to use the other resources of the SOTC to perform its main functions. Staff is needed for administration, analysis, development of scenarios for conducting simulations, management of simulations, conducting training activities. The investments for the first two categories of resources are mainly during the building of SOTC and less during its operation, but the investment in the resource "staff" must be continuous from the design stage of the SOTC to its building as a functioning IT infrastructure, its maintenance and its development (upgrading).

Hardware. In the SOTC's design stage in terms of the "hardware" resource must be set the requirements for the basic structural elements of the IT infrastructure. Many of the hardware components can be specified later depending of technological developments in the specific IT segment. These are peripherals, multimedia and presentation devices. On the other hand, for the basic elements of the structure of the IT infrastructure should be set requirements at the design stage, and for some of them should be taken into account the specifics of the software intended for use in the SOTC.

To achieve a higher level of reliability of communication lines the use of cables is recommended. This physical resource does not differ in requirements for the two main functions of the SOTC. As the distances between the endpoints in the planned area for the building of the Center are not large, standard FTP cables are the most suitable for use. At the same time, in order to ensure communication connectivity between the Center and the academy's computer network with high speed (up to 10 Gbps), it is necessary to provide optical fiber communications, for which the leading factor is compatibility with the currently available devices. This involves the use of single-mode optical fiber cables. To ensure internet connectivity of trainees and employees in the SOTC, it is appropriate to use wireless communication according to the WiFi standard in all possible variants. It is desirable to be used wireless access points that can provide a maximum speed connectivity for the respective version of the standard, as well as compatibility with all currently applicable communication standards, including those that are in the process of widespread implementation. The security of wireless communications should not be neglected, which implies the use of the highest levels of network traffic encryption and WPA3 implementation.

The computer workstations must ensure the normal performance of the duties of each employee in the Center, including the trainees for the time of the training. For this physical resource, there are minimal differences in system requirements for the two main functions of the SOTC. The workstations should provide the necessary communication and visualization interfaces, as well as ensure the normal operation of the application software installed on them. In view of the existing ambiguities regarding the specialized software related to the simulation of cyber-attacks and incidents, it is recommended that the hardware parameters of the computer configurations be increased regarding to their overall performance.

It can be expected that the requirements of the SOTC education function should have a higher priority in the selection of computer workstations. As was mentioned there are ambiguities regarding the software products to be used, and in at the same time, the specific learning tasks should be more complex and with bigger quantity than the tasks solved by the administrative and analytical staff under the SOC function.

The specification of the requirements for computer configurations in SOTC is based on the following parameters:

- Processor – last or pre-last generation;
- RAM memory – optimal for the selected processor;
- Motherboard – support of the required number of communication interfaces and expansion slots;
- Video controller – to control the required number of monitors in accordance with the purpose of the workstation;
- Displays – with the necessary size for visualization of the information from the software products depending on the purpose of the workstation with maximum resolution.

For some of the workstations there are additional requirements in accordance with Classified Information Protection Act (CIPA) [20].

One of the components with the most technical requirements in its specification is the computer network equipment. The reason for this is that the building of a functional SOTC requires a large number of different types of devices that provide all aspects of communication between the other physical components of the Center, including the security of the exchanged data. Different types of the necessary devices are routers, switches, wireless access points, firewalls, systems for detecting malicious network traffic, VoIP phones.

The requirements for the specific type of computer network devices depend on its purpose in the IT infrastructure of SOTC. Unlike workstations in communication devices, the requirements with higher priority are those related to the provision of the SOC function, as the leading criterion is the provision of a level of security with a certain number of network connections and bandwidth.

Some technical parameters by which the selection of computer network devices can be made are:

- Number of communication ports with a certain maximum speed – to provide connectivity of workstations, servers, storage systems, connectivity between network devices, connectivity to external networks, connectivity of other devices requiring network connectivity for their normal operation;
- Total network bandwidth of the device – depending to the maximum number of active network interfaces and their maximum data exchange rate;
- The amount of filtered network traffic to ensure the certain level of security;
- Management and monitoring methods of the device parameters;
- Supported network protocols and standards – required to ensure the functions of the Center;

Other parameters specific to the different types of computer network devices.

Physical servers and storage systems must ensure the functioning of the SOTC's Datacenter. These devices should be considered as the core of the SOTC. Physical servers should provide the necessary computing power and resources. Data storage systems must have a sufficient amount of disk space to store all the necessary data, as well as procedures for their backup and recovery if necessary. The implementation of the two main functions of SOTC requires a sufficient number of physical servers to ensure the learning process without compromising the productive work of the Center in terms of ensuring the security of the computer network of the academy.

In terms of technical parameters, the physical servers in the productive environment must be able to ensure the normal operation of all necessary IT services. The storage system of the productive environment must provide disk space for storing the data necessary for the provision of services. In addition, it must be possible to back up and recover data critical to the operation of the Center.

At the same time, servers and storage systems intended for conducting a learning process must have similar technical parameters, but with reduced values. The possibility that, under certain conditions, learning devices may support a productive environment should not be ruled out. It is therefore necessary to provide full interoperability between these devices.

Technical parameters by which the selection of applicable physical servers can be made are:

- The total amount of processors and cores per processor;
- The total amount of supported RAM;
- Number of network interfaces and their bandwidth – for connectivity to storage systems, for connectivity between servers, for connectivity to the computer network of the Center and the academy;
- Types of storage media that the server can operate with;

- Additional interfaces and expansion slots;
- Redundancy of main hardware components – processors, memory (RAM and storage), network interfaces, power supplies and fans;
- Remote management independent of installed operating system;
- Supported operating systems and computer virtualization software.

Some important parameters for evaluating storage systems are:

- Maximum usable storage volume for a given disk types;
- Number of controllers and network interfaces;
- Supported RAID levels and the number of defective disks preserves the system's operability;
- Redundancy of main hardware components – controllers, network interfaces, power supplies and fans;
- Integration with computer virtualization software;
- Automation of the processes of creating archives and snapshots of certain data;
- Supported network protocols for accessing logical volumes and data shares.

In addition to the physical devices discussed so far, other highly specialized devices will be needed to build the SOTC and ensure its operation. Such are, for example, devices for providing physical access control to certain areas, devices for providing video recording and presentation of the learning process, public information displays and kiosks, specialized devices for testing certain aspects of cybersecurity and for conducting cyber-attacks, and etc. Due to their specificity and dynamics in the development of the technologies providing them, such devices should be specified for delivery at the time of completion of the physical building of the SOTC.

Software. For the normal functioning of the SOTC several different types of software products are needed, specific both for the productive environment and for realization of learning goals. The choice of these software products should be made depending on their purpose. The different purposes of the SOTC required different software products for their realization.

The most attention should be paid to the software through which the simulations of cyber incidents and attacks will be performed. There are many such products, known collectively as Cyber ranges [21]. This software will mainly provide the training tasks conducted in the Center, but can also be used to diagnose accidents, as well as to predict the effect of certain configurations of IT services and computer networks. The aim of the latter would be to minimize the risk to the assessed systems and services by timely detection of security vulnerabilities.

A key parameter in evaluating cyber range platforms is the amount of pre-defined simulation scenarios available, as well as the ability to create custom scenarios. The customer in this case is NVNA or any other organization that would benefit from the services of the SOTC, according to a developed business plan for the operation of the Center.

For the physical servers, it is necessary to provide a software platform for computer virtualization. The implemented computer virtualization will support both the operational activities of the Center and the ongoing learning process. When choosing a virtualization system in most cases the leading criterion is the licensing method of the system, related to the number of managed processors, physical hosts and number of running virtual machines on them, available functionalities that support administration and ensure continuous operation of the system.

All workstations require client operating system, and each virtual server require server operating system. The choice of operating systems depends on the purpose of the station. The main factor in choosing the specific systems is again the method of licensing. The same is true for all office applications needed by end users. The reason for this is that standard operating systems and office applications offer the same types of functionality. The security criterion of the application or system itself should not be underestimated, and the availability of software support from the vendor should be taken into account here.

Administrators and analysts performing cybersecurity tasks at SOTC and the academy's computer network will need specialized software products - to configure and monitor hardware, to analyze traffic data sets, to access remotely IT infrastructure resources, etc. These software products should be targeted for the specific task, and it is possible to use more than one software product for processing the same type of data in order to control the results and eliminate their shortcomings.

The software products used to provide different IT services will be selected purposefully and after additional analysis of the applicability of the products.

Staff. The staff of an organization is among its most valuable assets. Qualified staff is highly valued and a prerequisite for the successful implementation of the business goals of the organization.

Specialists in several fields are needed to ensure the functioning of the SOTC. These areas can be defined as:

- Information and software systems (ISS);
- Communications and computer networks (CCN);
- End-users support (Help Desk).

Between separate functional fields, there are interconnections, guaranteeing the normal operation of all technical systems and services (Fig. 2), and overlapping of responsibilities of 10–30% is expected.

Among the main functions of the employees from the functional field ISS are:

- System administration of all physical and virtual servers and workstations in the SOTC and the academy's computer network;
- Development, deployment and maintenance of information services;
- Administration of databases related to the functioning of the services provided in the infrastructure, including the simulation models at the SOTC.

As duties of the employees from the functional field CCN can be defined:

- Management of the computer network devices and computer network as well;
- Management of security systems, including physical security and cybersecurity;
- Management of communication networks of any type.

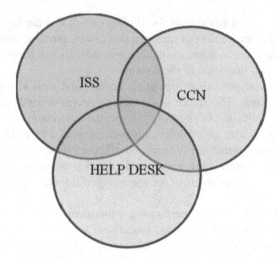

Fig. 2. Interrelationship between the functional responsibilities of the SOTC staff

The employees from the third functional field will have responsibilities to ensure the normal operation of workstations, including the installed on them software. In addition, they have to be responsible for technical support of any other devices that are necessary for the work of the end-users in the Center, as well on the computer network of the academy.

The responsibilities of the employees mentioned so far are related to the provision of one function of the SOTC - the security function of the computer network. In order to provide the other main function, conducting a specialized learning process, employees are needed to deal with the development of simulation scenarios, as well as their management. There is also a need for instructors to conduct practical classes with trainees.

The two main functions of the SOTC are so closely linked that employees engaged in one function should also have the necessary competence to perform tasks in the other function. In any case, creating a team of staff to handle all the expected tasks will be a complex process that requires understanding from the academy's management, especially in terms of investing in these staff and developing them as professionals. This in turn is related to the provision of periodic training of SOTC employees.

3   Utilized IT Technologies at Nikola Vaptsarov Naval Academy SOTC

The availability of hardware resources and trained staff are necessary conditions for building a functional IT infrastructure. However, without software usage the IT infrastructure cannot be exploited on the merits. Various software products are used to provide IT services. Various software products are also used to support the administration of the IT infrastructure. Conducting a learning process requires appropriate software products not only for the presentation of learning content, but also for tests, simulations, emulations and for more.

Each element of the IT infrastructure is associated with different IT technology solutions on which it is based. The individual elements of the IT infrastructure cannot work separately – the data from the servers operating in a virtual environment cannot reach the end-users devices without the presence of network connectivity between them. The last example shows the relationship between four separate categories of IT technologies, whose general purpose is end-users to receive certain information. These are network technologies, server virtualization technologies, technologies for providing a specific IT service and technologies related to the work of end-user's devices. Of course, it is possible to go into details and to describe these technologies through separate technological solutions, which are applicable depending on the specific implementation.

Regarding to the SOTC, used IT technologies must be considered according to the tasks. This, in turn, is related to the main purposes of the center. These are the tasks related to ensuring the security and functioning of the computer network of the academy, and the tasks related to the conduct of the learning process in the center. In view of the interoperability of the hardware resources intended to ensure the main purposes of the center, it can be expected that the same IT technology will ensure the implementation of tasks related to both network security and the learning process.

3.1 SOTC Datacenter

The main purpose of the SOTC datacenter is to ensure the functioning of all hardware components and software platforms related to the provision of IT services in the IT infrastructure, as well as the management of the infrastructure itself [22]. When setting the task for designing SOTC, the main goal of its datacenter is formulated. It is to provide the necessary computing resources and technical tools to ensure the operation and provision of services in the IT infrastructure of the center and the academy, as well as all necessary technical tools to achieve a certain level of cybersecurity for the entire IT infrastructure.

Because of the defined goal, all the necessary IT technologies are determined, through which to achieve it. The main IT technical solutions used in the SOTC datacenter are:

– Server virtualization;
– Storage systems;
– Different network technologies;
– Technologies for filtering and controlling network traffic.

Server virtualization is a technology that allows the creation of multiple virtual machines on a single physical machine (server) [23]. One of the main advantages of server virtualization is the isolation of running virtual machines – in virtual machines run different operating systems simultaneously, sharing the same hardware resources without sharing the data that is being processed.

Into the SOTC's datacenter server virtualization is the leading technology that ensures the provision of all necessary IT services for the operation of the center, by creating an infrastructure of virtual servers and desktops. Some of the main necessary IT services for normal operation of the SOTC are:

– Service for locating hosts (DNS);

- Service for dynamic configuration of workstations IP protocol parameters (DHCP);
- Service for users authentication and access control to IT infrastructure resources (Active Directory);
- Service for providing information through hyperlinks (Web service);
- Service for access to structured learning content (Learning Management System – LMS);
- Service for videoconferencing and chat;
- Service for starting cyber-attacks simulation models and simulations management (Cyber range);
- Service for access to virtual desktops (Virtual Desktop Infrastructure – VDI).

In addition to the mentioned above, it is possible to provide other IT services needed to perform a specific task. For deployment of this services when server virtualization is used, it is extremely convenient to use pre-configured virtual appliances.

There are many platforms for server virtualization. Previously was mentioned some of the main parameters by which such platform can be selected for implementation in the SOTC.

Creating and using multiple virtual machines requires sufficient disk space to store their files. In addition, disk space in a datacenter is needed to implement procedures for archiving critical data. Modern storage systems provide capabilities for automated creation of snapshots of stored data, as well as for copying data to new spare disks in case of failure of some of the active disks.

Storage systems use mainly two network communication protocols – FC and iSCSI. The choice of protocol used for the storage system must coincide with the choice of communication protocol in the physical servers as well as the switches for building the Storage Area Network (SAN). When choosing the storage system and the server virtualization platform, the way in which the virtual logical drives located on the storage system will be accessed must also be taken into account. Here again, there are two options – using NFS shares or using iSCSI LUNs. Both options have their advantages and disadvantages related to the used data exchange protocol [24]. The leading criterion in the choice of technology should be the compatibility with the selected server virtualization system.

One of the network technologies that must be implemented in the SOTC is the technology for building high-speed IP-based network connectivity between physical servers and storage system. The network built in this way is called SAN. For security and reliability reasons of the SAN, it is recommended that it be separate from the data network. Other network technologies, including wireless, are used to build the data network. It can be said that the greatest application has the technology for logical segmentation of the communication environment using virtual networks or VLANs. It is interesting that the physical servers are the intersection of the SAN and the data network, because they must be connected to the SAN to connect to the storage system, and at the same time, the virtual machines running in them must have a connectivity to the data network. Of course, physical servers must use different network controllers to connect to different types of networks. Otherwise, the principle of physical separation of the two types of networks is violated, which in turn can compromise the security of the SAN, as well as its operability.

Technological solutions for control of the exchanged traffic must be implemented in the communication environment for data transmission. The main goal is to provide the opportunity for timely detection of unwanted traffic caused by malware or actions of end-users. In addition, it is desirable to implement technological solutions that prevent the generation of such unwanted network traffic. To achieve these goals, modern computer networks use third-generation firewalls called Next Generation Firewalls (NGFWs). These devices combine the functions of a classic firewall with added functionalities for deep packet inspection (DPI) and detection and prevention of unwanted (not-compliant with the policy) network activity (Intrusion Detection and Prevention System - IDS/IPS). The use of NGFWs does not exclude the use of other techniques and technological solutions to reduce the possibilities for network security breaches such as anti-virus programs, network traffic encryption and integration with authentication and authorization systems.

At the design stage of the SOTC at NVNA the use of the above mentioned technologies is set. To implement server virtualization, it is planned to create a cluster of two identical physical servers integrated with a storage system. The communication network is intended to be built by ensuring the physical separation of the SAN from the local data network. To ensure a certain level of security at a given maximum data exchange rate, it is planned to implement a system of two NGFWs operating in fault tolerance mode. Because of the criticality of the services provided through the SOTC's datacenter to the IT infrastructures of the center and the academy, all hardware devices are planned to work in High Availability (HA) mode. To achieve this, the delivery of these devices is planned in sets of at least two devices of each type.

3.2 IT and Cybersecurity Software Relevant to Training at SOTC

SOTC will perform two main functions and one of them is related to the training process of IT specialists and cybersecurity specialists. Regarding this the technologies used in the creating of the SOTC's datacenter should be considered as technologies that are related to the ongoing learning process. It can be said that the learning process of IT specialists should be conducted using all IT technologies that are used into the real productive IT infrastructures, including their datacenters. In order to not compromise the SOC function of the center, productive devices should not be used for conducting a learning process. Similar devices should be used for this purpose. In other words, the mentioned above technologies also apply to SOTC training activities, but should be applied by separate devices. To increase performance for one of the two main functions if this is necessary, it is recommended that the hardware devices supported each of the functions should be interoperable.

If we need to assess the technologies discussed above from the point of view of the learning activity, then the server virtualization will be ranked first among the others. The reason for this is that using the server virtualization during the learning process it will be possible to simulate different situations in an IT infrastructure without affecting the performance of the real infrastructure. The functionalities of the server virtualization allow the rapid deployment of various IT services in a short time, their rapid recovery in its original state, as well as the isolation of the processes in the virtual environment from the real one.

Server virtualization is the basis for the operation of the platform for simulating cyber-attacks and incidents [21]. In turn, the Cyber range platform is the main IT technology for providing educational process and training related to cybersecurity at all levels.

In essence, most of the technologies needed to train IT professionals is provided by the SOTC's datacenter by supporting specific IT services or through similar to the technological solutions used to build the datacenter. Above is pointed out a list of services provided from the SOTC's datacenter and some of them are related to the learning process.

In addition to the described technological solutions in the training of cybersecurity specialists, the various tools for conducting cyber-attacks are used, as well as the tools for analyzing the processes in IT infrastructures. The range of available tools is innumerable, as they correspond to all possible points for conducting a cyber-attack and security breach in the IT infrastructure. Some of these possible points are:

– User account profiles and passwords for access to infrastructure resources;
– Authentication and authorization systems;
– Applications databases;
– Access points to the communication environment;
– User interfaces for access to various systems and services;
– User and server operating systems;
– And others…

There are various tools used by hackers to target any of these vulnerabilities, as well as the others possible vulnerabilities. These tools are either hardware or software, but usually specialized in attacking a particular vulnerability. A widely used complex tool is the Kali Linux system, which can be used both to conduct attacks and to test vulnerabilities.

The broad-based training of IT and cybersecurity professionals at the SOTC requires combining the usage of server virtualization, a Cyber range platform, and various vulnerability testing tools such as Kali Linux or similar, including standalone ones. The instructors from SOTC and the academic staff of the Department of Information Technologies will play a key role in the successful integration of all these technological solutions. At the same time, the principles for the integration of the mentioned software and hardware technological solutions are the basis for designing the physical layout of the area in the SOTC, as well as its datacenter.

4 Designing SOTC at NVNA

The design of the SOTC is conducted in accordance with the planned purposes of the center. The point of intersection between the two main purposes of the center is its datacenter, ensuring the functioning of the necessary computing resources. Conducting a learning process requires specific rooms related to the possibility of training in various aspects of both IT specialists and cybersecurity specialists.

If the design of the datacenter is aimed to provide the necessary computing resources with given parameters for availability and accessibility, the design of the rest of the SOTC is related to the learning function. It must be taken into account how the simulations of cyber-attacks and incidents will be conducted. In addition, it is necessary to take into account all aspects of IT technologies for which integrated training can be conducted. After the design, a construction phase must be undertaken, after which the SOTC will be able to fulfill its two main purposes.

The initial data required for the design stage are:

- Area for building the SOTC;
- Operation modes of the center for conducting trainings and exercises related to the used simulation models;
- Providing network connectivity of the center and the academy at certain levels of cybersecurity and integration of the center with other simulation complexes at the academy.

The last of the specified initial parameters for the design of the SOTC is actually taken into account when defining the minimum requirements for the available communication equipment, discussed above. The other two initial parameters are important for the physical structure of the center. The location area is important as the SOTC at NVNA is not being built as a new building, but the basement of the main academy building will be used. This imposes certain limitations in determining the location of the rooms, as well as causes additional requirements for available equipment to ensure the basic functions of SOTC. The area in which the design and deployment of the center should be carried out is presented on Fig. 3, highlighted in red. On the other hand, the possible operation modes of the center as an SOC and as a training center place additional requirements related to the location of the workrooms and the equipment located in them.

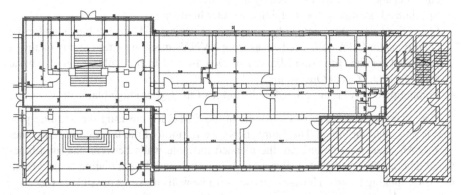

Fig. 3. Available workspace (highlighted in red) for building a SOTC at the basement of NVNA main building

4.1   Rooms Layout at SOTC

As already mentioned, the integration of SOC and a training center into one poses many challenges. One of them is related to the location of the workrooms. This is even more important when you have a certain pre-built space.

It is known what a modern operations center looks like visually, regardless of its purpose. The mention of the term "operations center" usually evokes the idea of a large hall in which one wall is equipped with devices for visualizing information from various sources related to the main function of the center. The hall is filled with many operators. Each of them has its own workplace, equipped with the necessary technical tools. The workstations are located so that all operators have direct visibility to the wall for information visualization. Operators are usually divided into teams of several people and each team have specific tasks.

In essence, the construction of the SOC is based on the same principles for placement of the workplaces of analysts, divided into teams to analyze specific data. At the same time, the datacenter ensuring the functioning of the SOC remains isolated and with limited access to it.

From a constructive point of view, it is not possible to create a similar operating room in the planned area for building of the SOTC at NVNA. A design approach is adopted, in which the function of the center for ensuring the training of IT specialists and cybersecurity specialists proves to be leading.

The design of the classrooms takes into account the peculiarity of the use of SOTC as an SOC, as well as a center for conducting exercises using simulation models of the Cyber range platform. The need for the following types of classrooms is defined:

– Lecture hall with a sufficient number of seats in accordance with the number of students;
– Computer laboratories with a certain number of places for conducting practical classes on certain topics in the field of IT technologies and cybersecurity, according to the curricula and programs approved by the academy;
– Specialized laboratory for studying computer hardware;
– Specialized laboratory for study, analysis and testing of IT technologies under the conditions for CIPA – the need arises from NVNA's mission to train highly qualified personnel for the Bulgarian Ministry of Defense and in particular cadets from the specialization "Cyber Operations";
– Simulation control room related to the usage of the Cyber range platform.

The planned workspace of the rooms in the SOTC for ensuring the learning process is presented on Fig. 4. The figure shows the location of the laboratories and other rooms. An interesting feature are the planned movable walls between the multifunctional laboratories, as well as between the lecture hall and the simulation control room (decision-making room). The use of these movable walls makes it possible to reconfigure the workspace to perform specific tasks. For example, if it is necessary to increase the area of the lecture hall, the wall to the decision-making room can be removed. The training laboratories are designed with 12 workplaces, which is the maximum number of students in a group for conducting practical classes. If it is necessary to conduct practical classes with a larger group of students, partition walls between the laboratories can be removed. In this way, a laboratory with up to 48 student workplaces can be obtained. This, in turn, allows interdisciplinary practical classes to be conducted in a laboratory that is "virtually" separated.

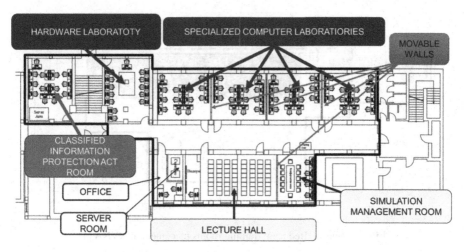

Fig. 4. Day-to-day IT training rooms placement at SOTC

4.2 Usage Scenarios

In addition to the described location of workplaces, providing a standard learning process, the SOTC should be able to conduct specialized practical classes for conducting cyber operations and implementation of cybersecurity measures. In most cases, this requires trainees to be divided into teams [21]. The names of teams may correspond to the generally accepted notions of the types of hackers - white and black hackers. Another approach is to name the teams in accordance with the accepted notions in the armed forces for denoting their own and enemy's forces - blue and red. Of course, it is possible use another principle of naming teams depending on the current scenario.

Because the military nature of the NVNA, the division of a blue and a red team is considered the main naming of teams in cybersecurity exercises. An exemplary division of the workrooms to provide these teams is shown on Fig. 5. The location of the two teams is principle and their places can be exchanged. This division of teams assumes that each of them will include up to 24 participants. To achieve a common workspace for each of the teams, two of the movable walls are removed. This scenario also requires workplaces to be reconfigured as is shown on Fig. 5.

The presence of three movable walls between the laboratories allows the teams to be in other configurations. For example, one team may consist of up to 36 participants using three of the standard rooms for its formation, and the other team may consist of only 12 participants. Of course, there is also the possibility in each of the rooms to work a separate team, consisting of up to 12 participants from different student groups, competing each other. Because of the movable walls question for the distribution of the workrooms between the participants in the cybersecurity exercises depending on the topic of the exercise itself remains open.

In addition to the participants in the exercises, an additional team is needed. This team will be responsible for the scenario of the exercise, setting tasks for the participants and last but not least to evaluate their actions. In current concept, this is the white team (Fig. 5).

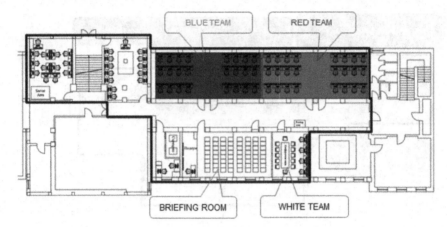

Fig. 5. Blue vs. Red team training rooms placement at NVNA [1]

At the beginning of each exercise (on each phase of the exercise) it is typical to be conducted a briefing to explain the situation and set the tasks to the participants. Accordingly, a debriefing should be conducted at the end of the exercise to analyze the actions of all participants and to assess the achieved results during the exercise. For this purpose, it is very convenient to use the available lecture hall on the territory of the SOTC. Regarding this, the presence of a movable wall between the lecture hall and the white team's hall is very important.

5 Further Work

Building the SOTC in the way discussed so far will create the conditions for conducting cybersecurity exercises. At the same time, the center will function as an SOC for the academy's computer network.

Assessing the cybersecurity of marine equipment or systems from other industries remain outsides the range of options for using the SOTC described so far [25]. The maritime industry is becoming increasingly dependent on information technology. In the near future, ships operated by a "crew" located in the ship-owners' office will be widely used. Now there are a significant number of cyberattacks target the ships at sea. This is the reason why the IMO pays more and more attention to these problems [17, 18].

NVNA owns and successfully operates several training complexes, used to train different marine specialists. A simulation complex to ensure the training of these marine specialists on the problems of cybersecurity of ship systems is still missing. Such a simulation complex would also be useful in preparing expert assessments of the cybersecurity of ship systems. At present, there are very few such complexes in the world [26].

The building of a separate simulation and research complex at NVNA, dealing only with the problems of cybersecurity of ship systems, would be an additional significant investment. It is cost-effective to integrate existing ship simulators with the SOTC. In this way, the capabilities of the SOTC will be expanded, and it will be possible to conduct research on the impact of various cyber threats to the ship systems without leading to a risk for real systems.

The integration of the simulation training complexes with different main purposes should be considered as a future step for their development. At the same time, this will further enhance the prestige of NVNA in the marine sphere.

Last but not least, the preparation of a business plan for public use of its analytical functions should be considered as a part of future work on the development of the SOTC. As a result, it is expected that the necessary funds should be generated for the maintenance of the center.

6 Conclusion

The building and development of the SOTC aims to solve several key tasks at NVNA. First, this is the achievement of a certain level of cybersecurity in the computer network of the academy. Next, an environment is expected to be created for cybersecurity training at all levels of competence. Last but not least, the possibility of integrating the SOTC with NVNA's maritime simulation complexes will allow the research in the field of cybersecurity of the maritime industry, in which the problems are many, but there are no real tools for their assessment and impact forecasting.

The proposed scenarios for the use of the SOTC are fully functional, and their successful implementation will depend on the staff of the center.

Because of the available area for the building of the center, the proposed location of workspaces is fully functional and operational, allowing the solving of a wide range of tasks assigned to this specialized simulation complex.

References

1. Nikolov, B.: A concept for establishing a security operations and training centre at the Bulgarian Naval academy. Inf. Secur. Int. J. **46**(1), 27–35 (2020). https://doi.org/10.11610/isij.4602
2. Persistent Cyber Training Environment. https://www.raytheonintelligenceandspace.com/capabilities/products/persistent-cyber-training-environment. Accessed 13 July 2020
3. Cyber Awareness Challenge. https://public.cyber.mil/training. Accessed 13 July 2020
4. Security education, training, and certification for DoD and Industry. https://www.cdse.edu/catalog/index.html. Accessed 13 July 2020
5. Security Awareness Hub. https://securityawareness.usalearning.gov/index.html. Accessed 14 July 2020
6. U.S. Army Cyber Center of Excellence – The official home page. https://cybercoe.army.mil/. Accessed 14 July 2020
7. HNS platform. https://www.hns-platform.com/. Accessed 14 July 2020
8. Cybint – A Cyber Education Company. https://www.cybintsolutions.com/. Accessed 15 July 2020
9. The National Counterintelligence and Security Center. https://www.dni.gov/index.php/ncsc-home. Accessed 16 July 2020
10. Pinckney Cyber Training Institute – The official home page. https://pinckneycti.org/. Accessed 16 July 2020

11. Cyber Training Center – The official home page. http://cybertrainingcenters.com/. Accessed 17 July 2020
12. PwC Cyber Training Center. https://www.pwc.ro/en/theacademy/cyber-training-center.html. Accessed 17 July 2020
13. National Institute of Information and Communications Technology (NICT) Report (2019). http://www.nict.go.jp/en/data/report/NICTREPORT2019_PDF/pdf/NICTReport_2019_14.pdf. Accessed 18 July 2020
14. Nathans, D.: Designing and Building a Security Operations Center. Syngress, USA (2014)
15. Allianz risk barometer – identifying the major business risks for 2020. https://www.agcs.allianz.com/news-and-insights/reports/allianz-risk-barometer.html. Accessed 31 May 2020
16. Marsh – Top Global Maritime Issues Facing the Shipping Industry. https://www.marsh.com/eg/en/insights/research-briefings/top-global-maritime-issues-facing-the-shipping-industry.html. Accessed 31 May 2020
17. IMO MSC.1/Circ.1526, 01 June 2016
18. IMO MSC-FAL.1/Circ.3, 05 July 2017
19. Osterwalder, Al., Pigneur, Y.: Business Model Generation: A Handbook for Visionaries, Game Changers, and Challengers. Wiley, Hoboken (2010)
20. Classified Information Protection Act, SG No. 17/23.02.2018
21. Yamin, M., Katt, B., Gkioulos, V.: Cyber ranges and security testbeds: Scenarios, functions, tools and architecture. Comput. Secur. **88**, 101636 (2020)
22. Geng, H.: Data Center Handbook. Wiley, Hoboken (2015)
23. Portnoy, M.: Virtualization Essentials. Wiley, Hoboken (2012)
24. Radkov, P., Yin, L., Goyal, P., Sarkar, Pr., Shenoy, Pr.: A performance comparison of NFS and iSCSI for IP-networked storage. In: Proceedings of the Third USENIX Conference on File and Storage Technologies, San Francisco, CA, USA (2004)
25. Dimov, D., Tsonev, Y.: Result oriented time correlation between security and risk assessments, and individual environment compliance framework. In: Rocha, Á., Serrhini, M. (eds.) EMENA-ISTL 2018. Smart Innovation, Systems and Technologies, vol. 111, pp. 373–383. Springer, Cham (2019). https://doi.org/10.1007/978-3-030-03577-8_42. Print ISBN 978-3-030-03576-1, Online ISBN 978-3-030-03577-8
26. Cyber-SHIP Lab. https://www.plymouth.ac.uk/about-us/university-structure/faculties/science-engineering/cyber-ship-lab. Accessed 25 May 2020

Showing Evidence of Safeguarding Networks in Cyber-Physical Domains by Societal Impact Assessment

Kirsi Aaltola[1]([⊠]) and Harri Ruoslahti[2]

[1] VTT Technical Research Centre Finland, Espoo, Finland and University of Jyväskylä, Jyväskylä, Finland
kirsi.aaltola@haus.fi, kirsi.aaltola@outlook.com
[2] Laurea University of Applied Sciences, Espoo, Finland

Abstract. Emerging technologies have increased the potential of cascading effects of technology-driven disruptions at the organizational and societal levels. The innovation funding of the European Commission aims to establish a European cybersecurity market (Aaltola and Ruoslahti 2020), increase European self-sufficiency and efforts to protect European citizens. While political priorities aim to strengthen ethics, trust, security (Malatras and Dede 2020) and fight against cybercrime (Prime Minister's Office 2016), the cybersecurity Research, Development and Innovation (RDI) establishments must show the evidence of increased capabilities, fostered markets and competences (Commission 2020). Even with the successful practices of sharing cybersecurity awareness, there is potential to fail to understanding how European cybersecurity RDI activities impact and effect society and its citizens (Bradshaw 2018). This research presents knowledge management framework and related toolkit of Key Performance Indicators (KPIs): Framework for Societal Impact Assessment for Network Projects. This paper includes a literature review of societal and knowledge management approaches relevant to analyze the societal effects of a network innovation projects. Moreover, we elaborate the elements for the framework presented earlier (Aaltola and Ruoslahti 2020) with a data analysis of selected network projects' KPIs to collect proof that demonstrates the impacts achieved by the selected activities at the societal level.

Keywords: Societal Impact · Societal Impact Assessment · Key Performance Indicators · Cybersecurity · Cyber-Physical Domain

1 Introduction

Funding programs for research and innovation by the European Union (EU) promote knowledge creation and innovation by engaging diverse organizations of academics, businesses and public organizations to form project consortia. Cyber-Physical Domain including cybersecurity has a lack of societal approaches, potentially due to threat and risk concerns over the Internet and attacks against critical infrastructures (Burton and

Lain 2020). Innovation projects have a strong focus in sharing insights and experiences, and yet participants may have conflicting interests for participation (Vos 2018) which have caused knowledge-transfer challenges and lack of trust within consortiums. Nevertheless, research and innovation network projects, increasingly face the challenge of mobilizing knowledge towards value creation in a manner that takes into account assessing its impact and effectiveness (North 2018). Societal expectations increasingly demand projects to review the criteria of the community and a comprehensive impact assessment processes that is capable of delivering outcomes, which address learning and sharing of knowledge (Sánchez and Mitchell 2017).

Whereas traditional social impact assessment about the processes of managing the social issues associated with planned interventions (Vanclay 2003), our approach to Societal Impact Assessment (SIA) is a multi-disciplinary method to show evidence of the interventions at different levels with use of the approaches of impact assessment, societal and organizational acquisition of knowledge, and knowledge management. Often SIA process is approached by using the cause-effect model with a variety of data collection tools, such as expert interviews or consultations (Takyi 1994), where as a multidimensional approach to the assessment has been argued to provide several benefits, including advancing the ability to communicate the value (Räikkönen et al. 2019). Commonly known information security risk management ISO 27005 standard (ISO/IEC 2018) recommends to conduct a risk assessment and take respective risk mitigation decisions in two or more iterations. For example, a high-level assessment to identify potentially high risks and then to conduct in-depth analysis with using a different method (Tagarev et al. 2020).

In this paper, we aim to provide additional elements of Key Performance Indicators (KPIs) to the multi-disciplinary nature of the body of knowledge framework that will cumulate in regards to assessment of societal impacts. Societal Impact Assessment (SIA) Framework (Aaltola and Ruoslahti 2020) presented the approaches to analyze the effectiveness and impacts of network innovation project at the societal level. The data of this study is collected from three network projects implemented between the years 2015 and 2023. Namely, the project ECHO (European Network of Cybersecurity Centers and Competence Hub for Innovation and Operations) (Tagarev et al. 2020) aims at organizing a networked approach through effective and efficient multi-sector collaboration that aims at strengthening proactive cyber security in the European Union; project GAP (Gaming for Peace) aimed to develop soft skills AR/VR innovation for peacebuilding (Hyttinen; Smith; & Timms, Soft Skills for Peacekeeping and Crisis Management Experts' Gaming for Peace Project 2017), and project IECEU (Improving the Effectiveness of Capabilities in EU conflict prevention) aimed to increase the effectiveness of European conflict prevention capabilities (Hyttinen, Human-centered Design Model in the Development of Online Learning Tools for International Security Training 2017) (Zupančič et al. 2018).

The SIA framework (Aaltola and Ruoslahti 2020) illustrates the building blocks that can be used to map the "logic" behind the actions taken and how these support the goals of the network project. This tool can be used to detect and summarize the relationship between the learning and co-creation approaches and dissemination evaluation to societal impact assessments. Inputs, throughputs and outputs elaborates the phases involved in the strategy. This article provides discusses performing Societal Impact Assessment, by elaborating the framework by Aaltola and Ruoslahti (2020) with a selection of identified SIA outcomes at different phases. Many innovation and research projects seem to fail in their ability to describe their impacts on society. This may be attributed to the lack of systematic collection of evidence, and measurement that their activities be in accordance to KPIs. This paper proceeds with the assumption that measurement of practices of organizational learning help boost the effects and provide evidence of impact. The research question of this study is "How to base Key Performance Indicators (KPIs) to Societal Impact Assessment (SIA) Framework in multi-sector project?".

2   Literature Review

In this literature we review the societal and knowledge management approaches by the scholars in relation to impact assessment perspectives in the Cyber-Physical Domains. Safeguarding critical Cyber-Physical Domains addresses human capacity and skills acquisition from individual to organizational levels, and to market spinoffs, innovation developments and policy level changes. Our multidisciplinary approach to impact assessment is based on the learning philosophy and psychology, economic and cultural knowledge management and communication theories.

2.1   Cyber-Physical Systems

Cyber-Physical Systems (CPS) integrate computation and physical processes by producing products that are intelligent, autonomous, and connected (Törngren and Grogan 2018). In situations of crises, the dimensions on all levels, from legislation to emergency procedures, influence the possibility of early detection, and rapid response within CPS. The use of cybersecurity dimension as a part of situational awareness can influence entire processes of continuity management (Simola and Lehto 2019). The protection of vital services such as energy, telecommunications, transport and finance by Critical Information Infrastructures (CIP) are essential for the well-being of nations. Unfortunately, during recent years, threats and attacks have increased in number. Increased automation and artificial intelligence (AI) open new vulnerabilities in many different sectors, such as aviation, maritime transport, and the automotive industry (Lehto, Cyber Security in Aviation, Maritime and Automotive 2020). The value of cybersecurity capabilities in both business and government are acknowledged (Lehto & Limnéll, Strategic leadership in cyber security, case Finland 2020), though we may often reluctant to analyze long-term effects of CPS.

The human-centered nature, when implementing innovation and development among networked consortiums, makes it important to take into account societal aspects, including values, concerns, interests and perceptions of implementation (Takyi 1994). In technology development, human-centered design and human-technology interaction (HTI) studies are widely known as some precise methods to study and perceive user involvement and user satisfaction (Kujala 2002) as well as how users interact with and anticipate technology. There is a raising interest towards values and ethics in technology design (Saariluoma and Leikas 2020), and assessment and evaluation framework perspectives can bring value also for ethical research agenda. As an example, the EU's seven requirements for achieving trustworthy are seen as extrinsic ethics since they are provided by the guidelines. In terms of ethics in design, the requirements by the EU are human agency and oversight; privacy and data governance; robustness and safety; diversity, non-discrimination and fairness, societal and environmental well-being transparency; and accountability. (Karvonen 2020).

The additional cognitive of socio-psychological effects of cyber activity, including cybersecurity of offending and defending the cyber domain from the threat or attack, is argued to be crucial to in moving away from militarized approach of cybersecurity (Burton and Lain 2020) but it may also be crucial in analyzing the societal impacts of cybersecurity activities. All information systems exchange knowledge, and therefore it is important to describe and organize domain-relevant information (Karvonen 2020). In this paper the focus is on the security in CPS were policies and RDI activities take place. Lately, the scholars have studied the societal influences on cybersecurity supplements. It has been identified that there is also cognitive influence of cyberattacks and the cognitive effects generated within target populations, such as in forms of opinions, decision-making, psychology and behavior of the people (Burton and Lain 2020). By understanding this, our approach to assess societal impacts of cybersecurity-related collaboration project, these dynamics in both cyber and physical domains are acknowledged.

2.2 Societal Approaches

When people are involved in working towards mutual common objectives, or a purpose that affects their communities, they become more responsible. This in turn reaffirms democracy. Webler et al. (1995) provide a basis for evaluating public participation processes through fairness, competence and social learning. On a societal level, this phenomenon can be described as social learning (Webler et al. 1995). Theory of cognitive development (Piaget 1950), theory of experience (Dewey 1938) and social constructivism (Miller 1991; Vygotsky 1978) were some of the key constructivist viewpoints, which have led to the societal education tradition. Studies have shown that individual learning processes are dependent of social interaction and external sources (Lewin 1997; Bandura 1971). It has been argued that also Piaget strongly built the basis for the constructive way of thinking (Rauste-von Wright and von Wright 1994). Constructivist learning theories believe in the role of social environmental contexts and interactions with others in molding individual development (Dewey 1938) and assert that learning becomes socially situated (Lave and Wenger 1991). Dewey (1938) addressed that humans are active learners and the nature of learning is based on problem solving. Network research and innovation projects are envisioned in line with the conceptual understanding of public participation where "*a community of people with diverse personal interests, but also common interests, who must come together to reach agreement on collective action to solve a mutual problem*" (Webler et al. 1995. p. 444).

Beyond the pedagogical or psychological tradition, social learning has been studied in the organizational and management studies (Argyris, Education for leading - learning 1993) with the use of concept organizational learning (Argyris & Schön, Organizational

Learning II: Theory, Method and Practice 1996). The German sociological critical theory by Habermas (1979) described social change as a process of social learning with cognitive and normative dimensions. Some knowledge is difficult to articulate with language and may exists in a form of experiences, and his understanding of tacit knowledge is in a relation with society and our personal interests and commitments (Polanyi 1967). Knowledge can be defined in relation to action and with commitment and beliefs on messages (Nonaka and Takeuchi 1995). Information is seen as a flow of meaningful messages, and communities of practice become central to learning, meaning and identity (Wenger 1998). Fact knowledge may include both forms of knowledge, tacit and explicit (Stenmark 2002), while paying attention to forgotten and avoided facts through stories and examples can promote organizational learning (Weick 2002).

Knowledge creation and learning theories strongly argue the relevance of understanding knowledge as a socially constructed process. In addition, experiential learning approaches and skill development highlight the role of experience, when the aim is to improve knowledge, skills and competences. The range of instructional and methodological design opportunities is quite broad, and the effective learning techniques support adaption of new competences in different contexts in a form of informal learning (Marsick and Watkins 2001). Organizational learning with ICT technology can have significant impacts in building innovative culture helping establish competitive advantages (Ruoslahti and Trent 2020) to economic effects and powers. Organizational learning approach can be treated purposefully as a method to raise the impact, which is facilitated through knowledge transfer-acquisition loops (Nonaka and Takeuchi 1995) and linked with best practices of stakeholder engagement (Sánchez and Mitchell 2017).

2.3 Knowledge Management Loops

Knowledge management has become complex in requiring, for example, comprehensive approaches to assessment. Some limitations of evaluation approaches that have can been recognized are their limited foci on degrees of influence, subjective satisfaction of results, or empowerment. Political theories have been used in the development of normative evaluation criteria, and to evaluate a wide variety of participation models (Fiorino 1990). The concept of public participation played a role in the impact assessment of public participation programs, and provided some added strength to earlier, more narrow, evaluation approaches, and has helped describe proper and improper conduct in public decision-making activities in democratic government (Laird 1993).

Good practices of traditional research dissemination and exploitation are needed (Henriksson; Ruoslahti; & Hyttinen, Opportunities for strategic public relations - evaluation of international research and innovation project dissemination 2018). A traditional documentation in evaluating research impacts with quality dimensions (clarity, environment orientations, consistency, responsiveness and effectiveness) (Palttala & Vos, Quality indicators for crisis communication to support emergency management by public authorities 2012) and systematic documentation activities (quarterly dissemination and progress evaluation, relevant exposures across targeted media sectors, successful two-way information transfer, committed project partners, and adoption of project processes (Henriksson; Ruoslahti; & Hyttinen, Opportunities for strategic public relations

- evaluation of international research and innovation project dissemination 2018). Organizational learning is a continuous process that requires dedication to innovation and collaborative activities from the entire organization, and dependent on the organizational culture in establishing support to the process that executives advocate the need for learning and that personnel are receptive to change in the company (Ruoslahti and Trent 2020). In our SIA Framework (Aaltola and Ruoslahti 2020), the outcomes were categorized into three different categories of acquisition of knowledge and skills, developing new behaviors and developing sustainability-oriented norms and values. In order to achieve in collaboration such outcomes, the methods and means include technology design, co-creation, innovation, experiential learning, learning through participation and learning organization practices with knowledge transfer and acquisition loops.

Beyond relevant evaluation and assessment processes, complex network reality requires people who are committed on both organizational and individual levels to learn and adopt the knowledge, skills and competences required by the network co-creation and communities that there are involved in. Development of professional expertise comply with networks, complexity and technological innovations at the same time. Complexity of research and innovation projects, raise the need of positioning variety of relevant approaches to impact assessment and evaluations. Network co-creation and learning approaches provide new systematic ways to analyze the impacts on a societal level of network projects funded by the public funding (Aaltola and Ruoslahti 2020).

Social indicators are defined with data collected in certain timeframe and allow comparison over time to show evidence from long-term changes, trends and changes (Mitchell and Parkins 2011). As we (Aaltola and Ruoslahti 2020) noted that positioning academic approaches can provide improvement for the design of SIA framework phases. Combining these academic societal level perspectives promote understanding of how structures foster information sharing, interpretation and enhance organizational memory. Learning Outcomes (LOs) have to go beyond instrumental learning to reach new behaviors, norms and values (Sánchez and Mitchell 2017) to enable an increasingly practical approach to SIA.

3   Methods

This study uses the Societal Impact Assessment framework by Aaltola and Ruoslahti (2020), where the societal phases were identified as Learning Outcomes (LOs) and as SIA-outcomes, visualized as a matrix of quality dimensions (Palttala and Vos 2012; Henriksson et al. 2018) to evaluate impacts of the innovation project. In order to assess impact, there are few measures identifying actual impact. To provide direct proof or evidence of multi-sector project impact we comprise the following methods:

a) performance measure with identification Key Performance Indicators (KPIs)
b) statistical counts based on the data collection
c) user satisfaction surveys

Table 1. Learning and SIA-outcomes Matrix (Aaltola and Ruoslahti 2020)

Level					
Learning outcome	Learning outcome 1:	Learning outcome 2:	Learning outcome 3:	Learning outcome 4:	Learning outcome 5:
Description	Development of Behaviours and Attitudes	Acquisition of skills and knowledge	Community norms and values	Dissemination Quality	Systematic documentation
Communication	Input	Input	Throughput	Output	Output
SIA-outcome	Action with commitment	Knowledge transfer loop	Collaboration objectives	Clarity	Dissemination progress
SIA-outcome	Stakeholder engagement	Social and informal learning	Collaboration arenas	Environment linkages	Targeted media sectors
SIA-outcome	Experiential learning	Cognitive development	Collaborators	Consistency	Two-way information transfer
SIA-outcome	Meaningful messages	Joint problem solving	Collaboration tools	Responsiveness	Committed project partners
SIA-outcome	Social change	Interactions in joint environments	Collaboration processes, contracts	Efficiency	Project processes

The colored areas in the above, Table 1 represent the linkages; blue areas to learning approaches to Societal Impact Assessment; yellow areas to co-creation for innovation activities to SIA; and grey to dissemination and exploitation evaluation activities in Societal Impact Assessment. The normal yearly dissemination statistics of activities, such as projects, show the quantity of input and output. Key Performance Indicators (KPIs) assess the also the quality dimensions of the services and the cost-effectiveness of service delivery. Both statistical data and the results of KPIs can be used for detecting developments that point to societal impact.

Data was collected from Grant Agreement of three different projects, ECHO, IECEU and GAP. Elements (n = 100) from the Impact section of the Grant Agreements were placed in this framework matrix as indicators to collect data and finally assess the impact.

4   Results

The results of this study are based on elements of expected impacts of the projects ECHO, IECEU and GAP. These elements were placed in the framework of analysis as Learning Outcomes (LOs) and Societal Impact Outcomes (SIOs), while also seen as input, throughput and output. Figure 1 (below) provides an overview of the Matrix with elements of impact/KPIs from the Impact section for the project ECHO GA (ECHO 2019).

4.1 Placing KPIs as Learning and Societal Impact Outcomes (LO/SIO)

As input and on a level of Learning Outcomes to assessment the development of behaviors and attitudes may enable to overcome the fragmentation of EU research capacities, and to not only raise knowledge and awareness of cybersecurity issues among a wide circle of professionals, but in cooperation with both EU and national efforts to develop and adopt cyber security skills and certification. The highest level in terms of the combination of LOs and SIOs is the adoption of project innovations by the external audience and end-users and therefore effect with an action of commitment.

Acquisition of skills and knowledge may demonstrate effective governance to provide collaborative solutions to enhance the cybersecurity capacities of the network and to develop needed cyber skills. This may include alignment of cybersecurity curricula on different levels of higher education, and of cybersecurity certification programs, with classification of skills and work roles. To create these impacts project ECHO develops a cyber-skills framework, with specific strategy and policy oriented and technology oriented trainings accompanied by either a self- or instructor-administered training assessment. The KPIs guide the data collection and evidence of the influence of knowledge transfer loop and organizational learning to the societal level impacts.

As throughput of LOs the project community work toward the setup, testing, validating and exploiting a cybersecurity competence network and central competence hub. Collective development and implementation of a Cybersecurity Roadmap may help addressing and improving multiple and complementary cybersecurity disciplines (e.g. cryptography, network security, application security, IoT/cloud security, data integrity and privacy, secure digital identities, security/crisis management, forensic technologies, security investigation, cyber psychology, bio-security, data mining for threat intelligence). Community performance can be analysed by the collaboration activities. For example in the project ECHO, the KPI "the signed partner relationship" was placed to the matrix as community and collaboration outcome.

KPI "establishment of cybersecurity certification" was placed as clarity and progress and systematic documentation outcome. The societal effect of quality dissemination and exploitation, engagement support certification authorities with testing and validation to strengthen cybersecurity capacities to close cyber skills gap. Systematic documentation, quality, progress and clarity KPIs are influencing on an output level.

4.2 KPIs for Societal Impact Outcomes

On an input level and action with commitment includes equipping stakeholders with some of the latest technologies and develop their skills to promote innovative security products and services for protection of vital assets against cyberattacks. KPI of stakeholder engagement includes network collaboration among 30 existing partners across 16 countries, and engagement of other cyber network projects, and increasing the network by at least fifteen (15) new partners before closing the project. Experiential

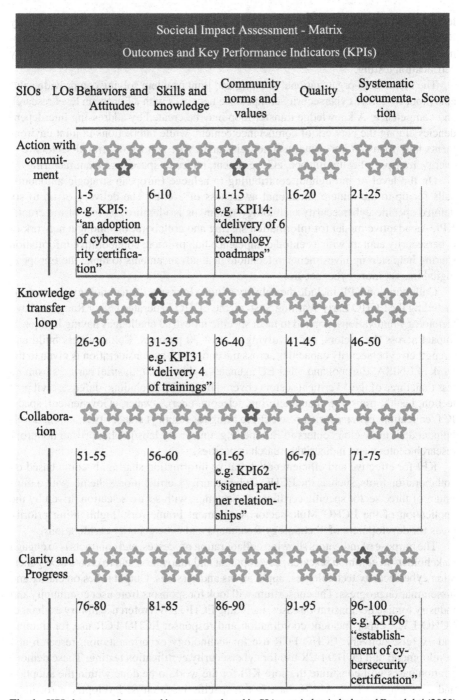

SIOs	LOs	Behaviors and Attitudes	Skills and knowledge	Community norms and values	Quality	Systematic documenta-tion	Score
Action with commit-ment		1-5 e.g. KPI5: "an adoption of cybersecu-rity certifica-tion"	6-10	11-15 e.g. KPI14: "delivery of 6 technology roadmaps"	16-20	21-25	
Knowledge transfer loop		26-30	31-35 e.g. KPI31 "delivery 4 of trainings"	36-40	41-45	46-50	
Collabora-tion		51-55	56-60	61-65 e.g. KPI62 "signed part-ner relation-ships"	66-70	71-75	
Clarity and Progress		76-80	81-85	86-90	91-95	96-100 e.g. KPI96 "establish-ment of cy-bersecurity certification"	

Fig. 1. KPI elements of expected impacts as placed in SIA matrix by Aaltola and Ruoslahti (2020)

learning and meaningful messages become promoted by the KPIs on the Technology Roadmaps and supported by Demonstration Cases of (i) training and exercises; (ii) technology roadmap research and development; and (iii) technology roadmap cybersecurity certification testing.

The methods of organizational learning and joint problem solving can provide valuable input for future cybersecurity competence networks with a European level research and competence. A knowledge transfer loop may be created by addressing interdependencies among the network of competence centers, while interactions in joint environments may focus on horizontal technologies and cybersecurity of critical sectors (e.g. energy, transport, health, finance, eGovernment, telecom, space, and manufacturing).

On the level of throughput contributing to achieve European strategic autonomy, calls for up-to-the-minute situational awareness of events. The delivery of up to six defined specific cybersecurity technology roadmaps is identified as one of the crucial KPI. An adaptive model for information sharing and collaboration among a network of cybersecurity centers with a central competence hub promote collaborative information sharing help step up investments in technological advancements to make the European digital market more cyber secure.

Collaboration KPIs include the delivery of up to four specific technology innovations including the ECHO Early Warning System, the ECHO Federated Cyber Range and two technology innovations targeted to meet specific industrial challenges having horizontal impact across the sectors, and involving at least 20 partners. Collaborators build and strengthen cybersecurity capacities across the entire EU, as consideration is given to the work of ENISA, Europol and other EU agencies and bodies. Industrial partners from no less than three of the 13 critical sectors covered by ECHO (including: defense, civil protection, health, transport, manufacturing, telecom, energy, water, eGovrnement, space, ICT, education, cybersecurity, research) to bring together cybersecurity research, development and innovation centers in Europe (e.g. university labs/public, private nonprofit research centers, and industrial research capacities).

KPI for effective and efficient collaborative information sharing, become based on collaboration tools, such as the ECHO Cybersecurity Certification Scheme, with a minimum of three sector specific certification schemes, with sector selection driven by the application of the ECHO Multi-sector Assessment Framework, highlighting priority areas for development of Technology Roadmaps and cybersecurity certifications.

The purpose of indicators showing collaboration processes, and contracts is to engage stakeholders in common research, development and innovation and to create next generation cybersecurity technologies, applications and services. Output relies on clarity and dissemination progress. The consortium will look for sponsors from user community and industry for five demonstration cases, including ECHO EWS reference library exchange; ECHO EWS cyber incident coordination and response; ECHO FCR use for training and exercise delivery; ECHO FCR use for technology experimentation, research and development; and ECHO FCR use for cybersecurity certification testing. These demonstration cases will constitute the core KPI for the work to be done within the adoption and engagement. They will be based on a specific research & development roadmap to tackle selected industrial challenges, covering a range of activities, from research & innovation through testing, experimentation and validation to certification activities.

Environment linkages promote resources for clustering activities with other projects funded under this topic to identify synergies, best practices and involving the subnetworks by awarded projects into one network. Targeted media sectors involve distinct cybersecurity research, development and innovation excellence centers of Europe, and with complementary expertise, from at least nine Member States or Associated Countries, and including widespread European coverage and good geographical balance of activities as regards the scope of work.

Assessment of various organizational and legal solutions for the Cybersecurity Competence Network may contribute consistency and clarity KPIs. A functional network of centers of expertise with a coordinating competence center promote two-way information transfer, with support and involvement of relevant governmental bodies and authorities (e.g. to monitor and assess project results during its life cycle). The five ECHO demonstration cases promote responsiveness, while the governance structure, with business model, operational and decision-making procedures, technologies and people, when implemented, tested and validated in the demonstration ensure systematic documentation and project progress (e.g. multi-sector assessment framework).

5   Discussion and Conclusions

Project consortiums aim to simultaneously deliver better and more effective solutions to increase capabilities and capacities for improved decision-making, strategy or industry autonomy (Aaltola and Ruoslahti 2020) (Henriksson; Ruoslahti; & Hyttinen, Opportunities for strategic public relations - evaluation of international research and innovation project dissemination 2018) (Zupančič et al. 2018). Network projects offer comprehensive empirical research, thinking and actionable roadmaps with a strong cooperation with different communities-of-practices. Through their various elements of research and innovation, projects are expected to affect society. Results from comparing measures and indicators defined by three selected project agreements show progress in the European RDI agenda. Whereas projects IECEU and GAP aimed to effect research and skills agendas by providing empirical findings on the domain-specific knowledge area, project ECHO has ambitious KPI elements to foster networked innovation of cybersecurity capacities and capabilities towards higher European autonomy in cybersecurity. On a policy-level, actions are expected to inform policymakers with empirical or evidence-based findings or towards desired goal or advancement.

As the literature review and out previous findings on quality indicators (Palttala & Vos, Quality indicators for crisis communication to support emergency management by public authorities 2012) and dissemination measurement (Henriksson; Ruoslahti; & Hyttinen, Opportunities for strategic public relations - evaluation of international research and innovation project dissemination 2018) indicate, communication and dissemination strategies may scale up impact, and thus, are vital instruments in constructing and implementing all networked innovation projects. Network projects use objectives, outcomes and KPIs to demonstrate expected impacts. Project objectives, activities, and outputs (e.g. products and services) contribute with a long-term perspective to work programs under the topic. In the short term, expectations of project impacts are in relation to knowledge use and benefits by building the awareness, strategic approach, co-creative cultures, governance, and thematic areas among end-users, researchers, policy makers and stakeholders. In the medium-term outputs, the projects are expected to promote knowledge use and benefits by encouraging participation and commitment across all stakeholders in productive trainings, workshops or other forums around key challenges.

Measurement of impacts through this Societal Impact Assessment framework can improve the evidence-based data collection, quality of value creation, and provide an applicable element towards a more comprehensive SIA-toolkit for the project networks, and for other European innovation organizations. Identifying the specific indicators for data collection within this overall SIA Framework Matrix at different levels (Learning and SIA Outcomes) and different phases (input, output, and throughput) can show both quantitative and qualitative evidence of short-term, medium-term and long-term societal impacts.

Further study and development is recommended to develop and pilot a questionnaire that can gather relevant data on the societal impacts of cybersecurity decisions made by European projects, organizations, and networks. Further, it is recommended to select applicable quantitative analysis methods to make sense of the data collected with survey, and consider how to store data and visualize results. Third, investigating how the concepts, or assets, that are being developed in project ECHO impact society as products, knowledge use, and benefit to society should be analyzed by e.g. conducting qualitative workshop hackathons with relevant asset owners and experts of the ECHO project. The SIA-Matrix should also be examined further when involving a wider range of ECHO partners to collect data to produce a set of selected case studies.

Acknowledgements. This work was supported by and contributes to the ECHO project, which has received funding from the European Union's Horizon 2020 research and innovation programme under the grant agreement no. 830943. The European network of Cybersecurity centres and competence Hub for in-novation and Operations (ECHO), and other cyber pilot projects funded by European Commission, bring opportunities for researchers to conduct experiments and gather experimental data to study different perspectives of cybersecurity.

References

Aaltola, K., Ruoslahti, H.: Societal impact assessment of a cyber security network project. Int. J. **46**(1), 53–64 (2020)

Argyris, C.: Education for leading - learning. Organ. Dyn. **21**(3), 5–17 (1993)

Argyris, C., Schön, D.: Organizational Learning II: Theory, Method and Practice. Addison-Wesley, Reading (1996)

Bandura, A.: Vicarious and Self-Reinforcement Processes. The Nature of Reinforcement. Academic Press, Inc., New York and London (1971)

Bradshaw, D.J.: Technology disruption and blockchain: understanding level of awareness and the potential societal impact. National College of Ireland, Dublin (2018)

Burton, J., Lain, C.: Desecuritising cybersecurity: towards a societal approach. J. Cyber Policy (2020). https://doi.org/10.1080/23738871.2020.1856903

Commission, E.: EU grants nearly €49 million to boost innovation in cybersecurity and privacy systems (2020). https://ec.europa.eu/digital-single-market/en/news/eu-grants-nearly-eu49-mil lion-boost-innovation-cybersecurity-and-privacy-systems. Accessed 12 2020

Dewey, J.: Experience and Education. Collier MacMillan, London (1938)

ECHO: Grant Agreement number: 830943 — ECHO — H2020-SU-ICT-2018–2020/H2020-SU-ICT-2018–2, Associated with document Ref. Ares (2019)654649 - 05/02/2019 (2019). Unpublished

Fiorino, D.: Citizen participation and environmental risk: a survey of institutional mechanisms. Sci. Technol. Hum. Values **15**(2), 226–243 (1990)

Habermas, J.: Communication and the Evolution of Society. Beacon Press, Boston (1979)

Henriksson, K., Ruoslahti, H., Hyttinen, K.: Opportunities for strategic public relations - evaluation of international research and innovation project dissemination. In: Bowman, S. , Crookes, A., Romenti, S., Ihlen, Ø. (eds.) Public Relations and the Power of Creativity. Advances in Public Relations and Communication Management, Croydon, UK, vol. 3, pp. 197–214. Emerald Publishing Limited (2018)

Hyttinen, K.: Human-centered design model in the development of online learning tools for international security training. In: Proceedings of the 9th International Joint Conference on Knowledge Discovery, Knowledge Engineering and Knowledge Management, vol. 3, pp. 275–282. ISE (2017). https://doi.org/10.5220/0006559902750282

Hyttinen, K., Smith, R., Timms, R.: Soft skills for peacekeeping and crisis management experts' gaming for peace project. In: Seminar Publication on Contemporary Peace Operations–From Theory to Practice, Helsinki. Finnish Defence Forces International Centre (2017)

ISO/IEC, 2: ISO/IEC 27005:2018. c. a. ISO/IEC JTC 1/SC 27 Information security, Performer (2018)

Karvonen, A.: Cognitive mimetics for AI ethics: tacit knowledge, action ontologies and problem restructuring. In: Rauterberg, M. (eds) HCII 2020. LNCS, vol. 12215, pp. 95–104. Springer, Cham (2020). https://doi.org/10.1007/978-3-030-50267-6_8

Laird, F.: Participatory analysis, democracy, and technological decision making. Sci. Technol. Hum. Values **18**(3), 341–361 (1993)

Lave, J., Wenger, E.: Situated Learning: Legitimate Peripheral Participation. Cambridge University Press, Cambridge (1991)

Lehto, M.: Cyber security in aviation, maritime and automotive. Comput. Big Data Transp., 19–32 (2020)

Lehto, M., Limnéll, J.: Strategic leadership in cyber security, case Finland. Inf. Secur. J. Glob. Perspect. (2020). https://doi.org/10.1080/19393555.2020.1813851

Lewin, K.: Behavior and development as a function of the total situation. In: Cartwright, D. (ed.) Field Theory in Social Science: Selected Theoretical Papers, pp. 337–381. American Psychological Association, Washington, D.C. (1997)

Malatras, A., Dede, G.: AI Cybersecurity Challenges. The European Union Agency for Cybersecurity, ENISA (2020). https://doi.org/10.2824/238222

Marsick, V.J., Watkins, K.E.: Informal and incidental learning. New Dir. Adult Contin. Educ. **89**, 25–34 (2001)

Miller, A.: Personality Types: A Modern Synthesis. University of Calgary Press, Calgary (1991)

Mitchell, R.E., Parkins, J.R.: The challenge of developing social indicators for cumulative effects assessment and land use planning. Ecol. Soc. **16** (2011)

Nonaka, I., Takeuchi, H.: The Knowledge-Creating Company: How Japanese Companies Create the Dynamics of Innovation. Oxford University Press, New York (1995)

North, K.: Knowledge Management - Value Creation Through Organizational Learning. Springer, Cham (2018). https://doi.org/10.1007/978-3-319-59978-6

Palttala, P., Vos, M.: Quality indicators for crisis communication to support emergency management by public authorities. J. Contingencies Crisis Manag. **20**(1), 39–51 (2012)

Piaget, J.: The Psychology of Intelligence. Routledge, London (1950)

Polanyi, M.: The Tacit Dimension. Anchor Books, New York (1967)

Prime Minister's Office: Government Report on Finnish Foreign and Security Policy. Prime Minister's Office Publications 9/2016 (2016)

Rauste-von Wright, M., von Wright, J.: Oppiminen ja koulutus. WSOY, Juva, Finland (1994)

Ruoslahti, H., Trent, A.: Organizational learning in the academic literature – systematic literature review. Inf. Secur. Int. J. **46**(1), 65–78 (2020)

Räikkönen, M., Uusitalo, T., Molarius, R., Kortelainen, H., Di Noi, C.: Framework for assessing economic, environmental and social value of monitoring systems; case water balance management in mining sector. In: World Congress on Engineering Asset Management: 14th WCEAM Proceedings, pp. 214–226 (2019)

Saariluoma, P., Leikas, J.: Designing ethical AI in the shadow of hume's guillotine. In: Ahram, T., Karwowski, W., Vergnano, A., Leali, F., Taiar, R. (eds.) IHSI 2020. AISC, vol. 1131, pp. 594–599. Springer, Cham (2020). https://doi.org/10.1007/978-3-030-39512-4_92

Sánchez, L., Mitchell, R.: Conceptualizing impact assessment as a learning process. Environ. Impact Assess. Rev. **62**, 195–204 (2017). https://doi.org/10.1016/j.eiar.2016.06.001

Simola, J., Lehto, M.: Effects of cyber domain in crisis management. In: Cruz, T., Simoes, P. (eds.) ECCWS 2019: Proceedings of the 18th European Conference on Cyber Warfare and Security (2019)

Stenmark, D.: Information vs. knowledge: the role of intranets in knowledge management. In: Proceedings of the Thirty-Fifth Annual Hawaii International Conference on System Sciences, 7–10 January 2002, CD-ROM, pp. 1–10. IEEE Computer Society Press (2002)

Tagarev, T., Pappalardo, S., Stoianov, N.: A logical model for multi-sector cyber risk management. Inf. Secur. Int. J. **47**(1), pp. 13–26 (2020)

Takyi, S.: Review of social impacts assessment (SIA): approach, importance, challenges and policy implications. Int. J. Arts Sci. **07**(05), 217–234 (1994)

Törngren, M., Grogan, P.: How to deal with the complexity of future cyber-physical systems? In: Designs; Challenges and Directions Forward for Dealing with the Complexity of Future Smart Cyber–Physical Systems, vol. 2, no. 40 (2018)

Vanclay, F.: International principles for social impact assessment. Impact Assess. Proj. Apprais. **21**(1), 5–11 (2003)

Webler, T., Kastenholz, H., Renn, O.: Public participation in impact assessment: a social learning perspective. Environ. Impact Assess. Rev. **15**(5), 443–463 (1995). https://doi.org/10.1016/0195-9255(95)00043-E

Weick, K.E.: Puzzles in organizational learning: an exercise in disciplined imagination. Br. J. Manag. **13**(S2), S7–S15 (2002)

Wenger, E.: Communities of Practice: Learning, Meaning, Identity. Cambridge University Press, New York (1998)

Vos, M.: Issue arenas. In: Heath, R., Johansen, W.: The International Encyclopedia of Strategic Communication (IESC). Wiley, Malden (2018)

Vygotsky, L.: Mind in Society: The Development of Higher Psychological Processes. Harvard University Press, Cambridge (1978)

Zupančič, R., Pejič, N., Grilj, B., Peen Rodt, A.: The European union rule of law mission in Kosovo: an effective conflict prevention and peace-building mission? J. Balkan Near East Stud. **20**(6), 599–617 (2018). https://doi.org/10.1080/19448

Author Index

T. Tagarev and N. Stoianov (Eds.): DIGILIENCE 2020, CCIS 1790, pp. 257–258, 2024.
https://doi.org/10.1007/978-3-031-44440-1

Printed in the United States
by Baker & Taylor Publisher Services